**TIERGARTEN
LANDSCAPE OF TRANSGRESSION
(THIS OBSCURE OBJECT OF DESIRE)**

PARK BOOKS

**EDITED BY
SANDRA BARTOLI AND JÖRG STOLLMANN**

Sandra Bartoli, *Introduction* .... p. 6

TRANSGRESSING HERITAGE   p. 14

Alessandra Ponte, *Governing Climate* .... p. 28

Gunnar Klack, *Tiergarten Today: A Product
of the "Kollektivplan"?* .... p. 46

Luise Rellensmann, *Heritage Is Subject to Change!* .... p. 58

Elizabeth Felicella, *Dispatch #1* .... p. 66

TRANSGRESSING URBANISM   p. 96

Fahim Amir, *Termites of Transnaturality:
Bambule in Habitat Hamburg* .... p. 104

Sandra Parvu and Piero Zanini, *Landscape
as a Means of Questioning the Temporal Frames
of Urban Planning* .... p. 114

Michael Baers, *Tiergarten: A Crime Story* .... p. 122

Jörg Stollmann, *In Campo Aperto: Urban Encounters
in the Open Field* .... p. 134

TRANSGRESSING ECOLOGY p. 146

Karin Reisinger, *Park Encounters, In City Centers, or Transplanted to the Hinterlands* . . . . p. 152

Eva Hayward, *Radiance of Cardinals, Shiver of Sharks: Multiplicities, Aesthetics, and the Limits of Ethics* . . . . p. 164

Elizabeth Felicella, *Dispatch #2* . . . . p. 178

TRANSGRESSING HUMANISM p. 192

Stefano Mancuso, *Green Therefore Smart: Intelligence and Consciousness in Plants*. . . . . p. 202

Chris Wilbert, *More-than-Human Heritage Spaces: Animal-Human Stories from Hoo to Tiergarten* . . . . . . p. 210

Sandra Bartoli, *From Tiergarten's Plant Societies and Berlin's Biotope Map to a Map of Neglect* . . . . p. 220

Christopher Roth, *Toni's Tiergarten* . . . . p. 255

Image Index . . . . p. 272
Biographies. . . . . p. 275
Acknowledgments . . . . p. 279

SANDRA BARTOLI

INTRODUCTION

"If future norms of society will be dominated by the mantra of sustainability, convenience, and security as opposed to liberté, egalité, fraternité, the question is where remains the space for the creative process of transgression?" Asked by Rem Koolhaas during the opening of the Venice Architecture Biennale in June 2014, this question is a call not to give in to the cynicism, egoism, and indolence intrinsic in today's dominance of that mantra. For both the symposium "Tiergarten, Landscape of Transgression" in 2015 at Haus der Kulturen der Welt in Berlin and this eponymous book, Koolhaas's question became a framework to view Tiergarten as a unique and idiosyncratic landscape of transgression.

For many reasons, Tiergarten cannot be inscribed in the confines defined by known types of public parks. It not only offers a way to look at the city in a different way but also changes the city at a very physical level. Tiergarten is Berlin's oldest park and also an ancient forest in the core of the city: 210 hectares of wooded area where aspects of ecology, urbanism, heritage, daily culture, and politics are present and visibly transgressed. Over time, Tiergarten has become an island of anomalies that can be read as the radical expression of what is most urban and public in the city. This urban intensity is not only registered in the conditions of a place where both human and nonhuman coexist in a fragile and somehow strangely stable form but that is, in Tiergarten, where human history and natural history are manifestly constructed together. This represents the core of Tiergarten's transgression, which can become a key to shift established ways to think of the built environment.

EVERYTHING THAT HAPPENS HAPPENS IN TIERGARTEN

The entire history of the city is here included: present before the foundations of the city were built, Tiergarten was a marsh forest grown on the floodplain and high ground along the Spree river and a deeply set area of the ancient glacial valley flowing from Warsaw to Berlin. In the fifteenth century, Tiergarten was fenced off to turn it into a royal hunting ground in the proximity of the walls of the city. A map of 1698 (*p. 18*) shows the dense forest of Tiergarten surrounded by a fence with an indication of the Großer Stern, the road of Unter den Linden, and Museum Island. In the eighteenth century, once Tiergarten was made accessible to the public, the forest was transformed and carved out by the landscape architect Wenzeslau von Knobelsdorf in a Baroque fashion to make space for allées, geometric green rooms, and salons, which are all visible in a 1765 plan (*p. 27*). In the first half of the nineteenth century, the work of the landscape architect Peter Joseph Lenné carried out a more radical thinning of the woods to make space for clearings and also introduced a system of water streams to create drainage in this largely alluvial forest. The painting *Gesellschaft im Tiergarten* of 1760 by Daniel Nikolaus Chodowiecki (*p. 101*) conveys an idea of the way people moved and lingered in Tiergarten, sitting in fine clothes on the forest's floor. Chodowiecki's painting shows a relaxed and voluptuous behavior in the visitors of Tiergarten compared to a later stage, visible in existing photos of the Sternallee from 1904, where a rigid posture is suggested by the Prussian self-celebratory craze that saw sponsored monuments erected all over Tiergarten. During the Third Reich, Tiergarten became a place for military parades when Strasse des 17. Juni and Großer Stern were dramatically widened. But it wasn't World War II that destroyed Tiergarten; instead, the cold winters of 1946–47 imposed their regime when more than 200,000 trees were cut for firewood.

REPLANTATION

Willy Alverdes, the park director appointed in the 1950s for the replantation of Tiergarten, worked from a condition of zero history and drew inspiration from natural history to replant a place that could be adequate for humans, animals, and plants all at once. Alverdes did so by planning interlacing layers of grasses, bushes, and trees to emulate the intricacy of diverse natural plant societies, implementing research from plant sociology and ecology. He foresaw the planting of six different plant communities typical of the Berlin region: as an example, the pine forest, the oak grove–hornbeam forests, and the white willow and poplar floodplain forest. The replantation of the Tiergarten forest followed pragmatic rules of reforestation where fast-growing pioneer trees such as poplars, birch, and ash trees were planted in-between the slower and more delicate beeches and oaks. The long-term plan in this scheme was to cut the pioneer trees down after thirty years to leave more space for the others.

THE WEST BERLIN BIOTOPE MAP

The growing ecological movement of the 1970s also increasingly influenced the understanding of German cities as they underwent paradigmatic changes. West Berlin, a city enclosed by a wall, was placed in a very peculiar psychological situation where all open green areas were viewed and cherished as a precious anomaly. The Berlin Senate commissioned the charting of all biotopes in West Berlin in an extensive map that interpreted the city as a habitat for nature, especially in relation to spontaneous plants growing in the urban environment. A frontier zone adjacent to the Wall, Tiergarten received new management directives from the Berlin House of Representatives with the political decision to considerably slow down, if not discontinue the tree-felling program planned in the 1950s by Alverdes that was to have the park naturally take on the quality of a primeval forest. As a result, Tiergarten developed exceptional biodiversity, containing dense groves not easily accessible to people and therefore becoming undisturbed havens for animals such as owls, falcons, and nightingales, and plants that would otherwise suffer from intense treading. What is essential to point out, however, is that the subtle diversity of Alverdes's plant societies, which still constitutes the foundation of the design of this park, can be easily read as the basis of the social diversity of this place—the prerequisite for a multiplicity of species and use.

FOUR QUESTIONS ABOUT TIERGARTEN

The example of Tiergarten is important in order to evaluate aspects of urban space that question and expand the discourse about sustainability in, for instance, the relationship between unbridled plant growth and the proximity of species, the unmaintained, the incommensurable, the extraterritorial, the outlawed, the forgotten, and the notion of ancient places containing contradicting simultaneous histories, to mention a few. To approach the conceptual transgression offered by Tiergarten, four sections were developed for the symposium of 2015; the same categories now structure this book in four chapters: "Transgressing Heritage," "Transgressing Urbanism," "Transgressing Ecology," and "Transgressing Humanism." Each section formulates a question:

TRANSGRESSING HERITAGE: It is a known fact that Tiergarten is ancient, perhaps the only constant in the city, and this is set deep in everybody's imagination; it is its true "authenticity." At the same time, it is known that having been completely replanted in the 1950s, Tiergarten is only sixty-eight years old. Is it possible that Tiergarten's true heritage lies in the fact that it allows multiple histories to be projected onto it?

TRANSGRESSING URBANISM: Tiergarten is possibly the most public space in Berlin. This almost utopian urban quality that developed in Tiergarten is the idea of the maximum dimension of tolerance, coexistence, and personal freedom but within a sense of community. It is planned and yet not divided into functional areas. It is not zoning but contingency that becomes the only rule, and the program is unforeseen use. This space, constantly open to interpretation, is comparable to the significance of the fallow land of West Berlin, when "the value of the city was in direct proportion to the possibility of gaps in the planning systems."[1] And yet, far from being a *terrain vague*, a space of emptiness, Tiergarten is richly constructed and also beautifully wild. Somehow, Tiergarten fulfills the most extreme dream of urban life because its conditions allow for a hundred-year-old gay-cruising area to exist in the proximity of a naturist meadow ("Fleischwiese"), and it does not only accommodate the homeless bag lady, the picnicker, the jogger, the nudist jogger, and the weekend SM fetishist, but also the falcon, the hawk, the night owl, the badger, and the newly arrived beaver as well as common and rare spontaneous plants in their adaptive intelligence. In terms of the vast transgression it fosters, is Tiergarten the only place where true urban life is possible?

TRANSGRESSING ECOLOGY: Tiergarten raises the challenge of juxtaposing high biodiversity, intense use, and heritage all in the same place. The intensity of coexistence is nearly at the level of science-fiction. Biodiversity is much higher than in Central Park in New York and Hyde Park in London. Can Tiergarten "offer an account of the city in which the human and the non human and the social sphere are created together and are mutually dependent"?[2] Is Tiergarten the embodiment of an expanded notion of ecology that can become a model for the city's future?

TRANSGRESSING HUMANISM: That Tiergarten stands on its own rules is not a surprise. Its considerable size and critical mass affect the climate of the city, and it is also large enough to be perceived as "incommensurable." The scale of biomass and the density of vegetation establish a level of autonomy that makes this place powerful. Tiergarten does not only dissolve the alleged antagonism between city and nature but also offers an alternate response to the Anthropocene, a model that conceives of human and nonhuman creatures as equal and mutually dependent. Tiergarten is ultimately post-human; the question is when does a human-constructed place go beyond the human, and how necessary is this transgression?

---

1   Wim Wenders and Hans Kollhoff, "The City. A Conversation between Wim Wenders and Hans Kollhoff," in "New Narration," special issue, *Quaderns*, no. 177 (April–June 1988): 70.
2   Irénée Scalbert, "London After the Green Belt," *AA Files*, no. 66 (Spring 2013): 4.

The title of the book, *Tiergarten, Landscape of Transgression (This Obscure Object of Desire)*, does not only mean that anything can happen in Tiergarten, but also that the very physical, historical, and future understanding of this place is at stake: Tiergarten as a generator of transgression is in fact locked in a fragile balance. Current park management policies are at work to "tame" Tiergarten, as an example, by making it spatially more accessible for the public. The degree of accessibility, however, is a key to its balance: in 2012 there were thirty-two nightingale couples; in 2015 only eight were left. Bushes and trees, the birds' breeding environment, have been cut down in order to discourage certain forms of social use. Plant control thus becomes social control.

Keeping in mind Koolhaas's question from the introduction, there is one more final question: Does a place that generates transgression through the allowance of an ambiguous degree of permeability and by areas that are not clearly defined allow for a more inclusive idea of liberté, egalité, and fraternité? The symposium was announced as a transdisciplinary exchange, and so is this book. It is not only the intention that the authors' contributions open different readings of Tiergarten's complex nature, but it is also that Tiergarten, itself a shapeshifter, is capable of provoking different critical reflections concerning the radical inclusion of the wild in the urban context. Most fundamentally, Tiergarten represents an effective example of the aesthetic, functional, and spatial dissolution of the dualism of nature and city.

Each of the four chapters of the book is introduced by an archive of selected images as a compendium to each theme of transgression:

HERITAGE: Starting this section is architect and historian Alessandra Ponte, who in "Governing Climate" writes about the genealogy of the meaning of environment and the preoccupations of environmental control in the deforested landscape of eighteenth-century France. Among the historical examples of Ponte's research, she recounts a refreshing plan to counteract climate catastrophe and air pollution where plants played a powerful central role. Gunnar Klack, an architect and history researcher, views the role of Tiergarten's postwar replantation during the time when Berlin was being reconstructed under the influence of the uncompromising Kollektivplan and its equation of city with landscape. Luise Rellensmann, a lecturer of architectural conservation, examines the recent reconstruction of Baroque elements in Tiergarten at the loss and expense of design elements from the 1950s. By critically viewing practices of heritage that tend to overwrite history, she introduces emergent approaches that counter this distortion by extending the understanding of heritage toward an intrinsic notion of change.

URBANISM: Philosopher and artist Fahim Amir, in "Termites of Transnaturality: Bambule in Habitat Hamburg," draws on Haraway's notion of "natureculture" and focuses on the role of termites as long-time inhabitants of Hamburg's underground, brought over a century ago on ships from Africa. In discourses and practices of urbanism, Amir's questions of significant otherness are incendiary, transcultural, Marxist, and ecological. Architect and urbanist Jörg Stollmann's contribution, "In Campo Aperto: Urban Encounters in the Open Field," is a structural interpretation of Pier Paolo Pasolini's film *Mamma Roma* (1962) that looks toward social readings of different conditions of public space in the social housing projects of Rome's periphery during the postwar time. The open field, wild, devoid of programs, and characterized by ruins, arises as an urban prototype worthy of research, offering open-ended interpretations of space, and therefore dignity and freedom, to the people using it. The artist Michael Baers, in "Tiergarten: A Crime Story," explores the concept of the park as an ideal site for a murder. In a twinned genealogy of artistic production and reality that informs the general perception of urban space, his investigation takes place in Tiergarten and is mirrored by an excursion through aesthetic works such as the 1966 film *Blow-Up*, where the park, in which the murder of a man takes place but whose evidence gradually vanishes, is the central conceit, and the way the painting *A Sunday on La Grande Jatte—1884* (1884–86) by Georges Seurat speaks about invisible class boundaries in "the uninflected space of fabricated nature." "Landscape as a Means of Questioning the Temporal Frames of Urban Planning" by architect researcher Sandra Parvu and anthropologist Piero Zanini delves into the multilayered temporal dimension of landscape as a conceptual framework in deciphering the reality of urban situations, their transformation, and the importance of derailed control in planning processes introduced by French gardener, ecologist, and botanist Gilles Clément.

ECOLOGY: Eva Hayward, in "Radiance of Cardinals, Shiver of Sharks: Multiplicities, Aesthetics, and the Limits of Ethics," questions individuality as a precondition to understanding animals, addressing Jacques Derrida's criticism of "speciesism" together with the artist Charley Harper's ecotonal approach; Hayward's research combining aesthetics, environmental and science studies, and transgender studies can be positioned within the legacy of Donna J. Haraway's *A Cyborg Manifesto* (1984) and *When Species Meet* (2007). Also overlapping these themes is Karin Reisinger, architect and lecturer of critical studies at the intersection of architecture, ecology, and feminism, who explores in "Park Encounters, In City Centers, or Transplanted to the Hinterlands" the transgressions of borders, cultures, and nature in two places: Losiny Ostrov, a national park near the Moscow city center, and the Gorongosa nature reserve in Mozambique. Reisinger reports about the discrepancy between daily use, local cultural practices, and the different frameworks of nature preservation.

HUMANISM: In "More-than-Human Heritage Spaces: Animal-Human Stories from Hoo to Tiergarten," the geographer and member of editorial collective Radical Philosophy, Chris Wilbert, brings to attention converging histories of human and animal heritage, introducing a multispecies understanding of landscapes with the example of the Hoo peninsula near London and the breeding nightingales that inhabit this area during the summer. Botanist and author Stefano Mancuso, one of the founders of the International Laboratory of Plant Neurobiology, through his groundbreaking research with other botanists provoking paradigm shifts in the awareness of the vegetal realm, opens a revolutionary perspective on the extraordinary intelligence of plant life in "Green Therefore Smart: Intelligence and Consciousness in Plants." My own essay, "From Tiergarten's Plant Societies and Berlin's Biotope Map to a Map of Neglect," considers the relationship of Tiergarten and its plant communities as prerequisites for the park's spatial diversity, which fosters many different species and use. Along with the fundamentally important biotope map of West Berlin, where the city is documented as an ecological space, the concept of a plan of loving neglect and indifference for the present city emerges.

A number of photo-essays are placed between chapters as necessary moments that visually dive into the lushness of Tiergarten. With a clear, cool eye, photographer Elizabeth Felicella attempts to unfold this strange place, often losing the open trail to find herself in the midst of thick vegetation: she threads her way between two series of photographs, one from the side of plants and another from the side of the city. Filmmaker Christopher Roth and Toni, of canine descent, human and more than human respectively, give an account of figments and instances of wild animals in Tiergarten during a number of their routine joy-walks through the park; in their pockets, they carry a copy of John Berger's "Why Look at Animals."

SANDRA BARTOLI, BERLIN, AUGUST 9, 2018

16

TRANSGRESSING HERITAGE

2014: TIERGARTEN'S UNDERFOREST

TRANSGRESSING HERITAGE

1946: HEIN GORNY, *TIERGARTEN*

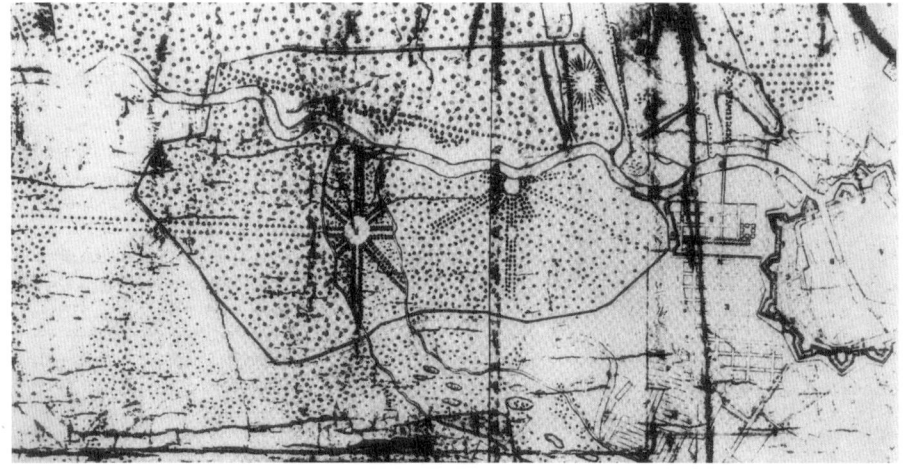

1698: A PLAN OF TIERGARTEN WHERE THE GROSSER STERN IS FIRST SHOWN

TRANSGRESSING HERITAGE

TRANSGRESSING HERITAGE

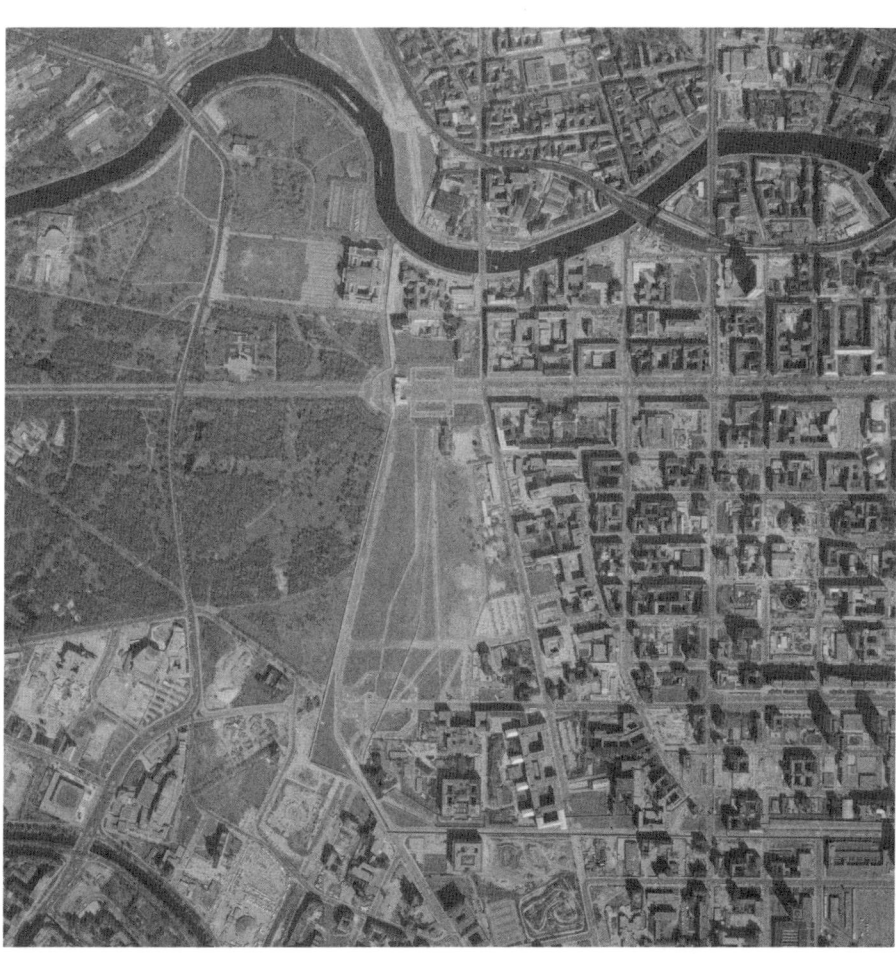

1984: TIERGARTEN NEAR THE DEATH STRIP

1946–48: FARMING IN TIERGARTEN

TRANSGRESSING HERITAGE

1954: *VERBASCUM THAPSUS* IN A REPLANTED TIERGARTEN

1860: JOHANN HEINRICH GUSTAV MEYER,
ILLUSTRATION FROM *LEHRBUCH DER SCHÖNEN GARTENKUNST*

2015: *ROBINIA PSEUDOACACIA* IN PFAUENINSEL

1947: TIERGARTEN'S COMMAND TOWER TURNING INTO AN ISLAND

2016: BIRD SANCTUARY ISLAND IN TIERGARTEN

2013: VENUS BASIN, TIERGARTEN

1765: PLAN OF TIERGARTEN WITH MULBERRY PLANTINGS ON BELLEVUE

ALESSANDRA PONTE
GOVERNING CLIMATE

[1]

A map of the zoo in Hamburg. Jakob von Uexküll and Georg Kriszat, *Streifzüge durch Umwelten von Tiere und Menschen (A Foray into the Worlds of Animals and Humans)* (1934).

The text I am presenting is part of two ongoing research projects that I've been conducting in parallel. The first is an inquiry into the relation between maps and territories; it became a chapter of a book I recently published, *The House of Light and Entropy* (2014), in which I address systems of representation, notions of space, the building of the territorial state, and the Deleuzian concept of territorialization and deterritorialization. The second is an investigation into the genealogy of the notion of environment in its many declinations. I began exploring this in a seminar taught at the ETH Zurich in 2012 and organized a colloquium held at the School of Architecture at the University of Montreal, which also took place in 2012. Both went under the title "Milieu, Environment, Umwelt."

I am beginning with a map (*fig. 1*), an image that perfectly conveys the coming together and intersection of questions of territory and environment. When I was invited to this project, I remembered a map published in *A Foray into the Worlds of Animals and Humans* (1934) by the Baltic biologist Jakob von Uexküll. Between the 1930s and '40s, Uexküll redefined the notion of environment through the introduction of the concept of *Umwelt*, which in fact in German means environment but which he understood as the discrete sphere created by humans and animals when they select only certain aspects or stimuli from their surroundings.

It is worth noting how Uexküll's thesis became very influential during his time. Mies van der Rohe and Martin Heidegger read him, for example. More recently, a number of scholars and thinkers have been revisiting the idea of *Umwelt* as defined by Uexküll, including Bruno Latour, Peter Sloterdijk, Giorgio Agamben, and Elizabeth Grosz. In *A Foray into Worlds of Animals and Humans*, a chapter is devoted to what in English is translated as "Home and Territory" but in the German is originally titled "Heim und Heimat."[1] The map I am showing is included in this chapter and represents the zoo of Hamburg and not, unfortunately, the one located in Berlin in Tiergarten as I had thought of initially—it would have been too much of a lucky coincidence. Uexküll, however, was familiar with Tiergarten and on friendly terms with the director of the zoo of Berlin with whom he exchanged information about animal life.

Here, Uexküll charts the paths followed by two male dogs that are taken to the zoo regularly for a walk. Dogs, as you know, mark their territory by urinating; what Uexküll is actually mapping is the pissing contest between the two male dogs walking in the zoo of Hamburg. I find this idea fascinating: it illustrates the case of domesticated animals—dogs—in the process of territorialization via a pissing contest that takes place in the recreated environments of wild animals. I consider it extremely significant to see how the animal subject appropriates and defines territory while inhabiting its own specific *Umwelt*. Here, I think, two major ideas or possibilities are suggested: the first is that interrogations concerning territory and the environment cannot be separated; the second is that both territory and environment can and should also be considered subjective productions.

Let me begin again with a different map or plan: the 1835 project for Tiergarten traced by Peter Joseph Lenné. I am employing on purpose three dissimilar terms—plan, map, and project—to denote Lenné's drawing and emphasize the multiple possible understandings encompassed by this image. Lenné studied at the Jardin des Plantes in Paris between 1811 and 1812. I will show the relevance of what was happening at the Jardin des Plantes

---

1   *Heimat* does not translate exactly as territory, but recalls connotations of "fatherland" or "motherland."

before, during, and after the Revolution for the comprehension of the representational regime in which Lenné's plan of Tiergarten was conceived.

To explain, let's now address the topic of representation, the representation of territory, and the relationship between cartography and the state. What is a map, and is a map the territory it represents? Yes, it is, at least in the context of the so-called Classical Age in France when the modern French state took shape, an epoch memorably examined by Michel Foucault in *The Order of Things* (1966). To clarify the relation between words and things during this period, Foucault quotes the *Port-Royal Logic* (1662) by Antoine Arnauld and Pierre Nicole: "In relation to natural signs, there is no difficulty, since the visible connection there is between such signs and things indicates clearly that when we affirm of the sign the thing signified, we mean not that the sign is really this thing, but that it is so in signification, and figuratively. And thus we may say, without introduction, and without ceremony, of a portrait of Cesar, 'This is Cesar,' and of a map of Italy, 'This is Italy.'"

Published during the reign of Louis XIV, in a cultural milieu highly influenced by Descartes, the *Port-Royal Logic* was more or less contemporary to the foundation and building of the Observatoire de Paris. The first task assigned to the royal cartographers at the Observatoire was the accurate charting of France, an urgent and necessary action needed for the ruling of the novel, modern territorial state, prefigured by Louis XIV and his minister Jean-Baptiste Colbert at the beginning of his long reign.

Precision in cartography consents processes of territorialization that begin with the definition of borders and proceed with the construction of what today we call infrastructure: bridges, roads, canals, fortifications, harbors, but also cities, gardens, and the ordering and management of forests, cultivated fields, and spaces of production. This operational cartography became more and more accurate and sophisticated, as displayed in the spectacular plates of the map of France drafted by many generations of the Cassini family at work at the Observatoire. Also employed by the state in a monumental cartographic effort were the engineers trained at the Ecole nationale des ponts et chaussées (the Royal School of Bridges and Roads). They produced a magnificent atlas of France (the *Atlas de Trudaine*, 1745–80), which represented not only the existing situation of the territories but also the projected interventions. The maps thus realized were in turn called *cartes* which in French means maps, or *plan* which signifies plan as in English. Therefore, a map drafted by the royal engineers, precisely like a plan, was ultimately a project. Conceptually the operation was the same: a map is a project about the territory, and the territory becomes the map. As in the *Port-Royal Logic*, the map of Italy is Italy.

An exquisite manual compiled for military engineers by Louis-Nicolas de Lespinasse, the *Traité du lavis des plans, appliqué principalment aux reconnaissances militaires* (1801), confirms such understanding. While in fact a textbook on how to draft maps, the French title refers to the drawing of plans. The manual presents a subtle and ambiguous technique of representation situated in-between a bird's eye view, cartographic projection, and a topographical view of the landscape. The delicacy of the plates, meticulously representing forests and groves, various species of trees, or cultivated fields next to watercourses and painstakingly delineated geological features, manifest the aesthetic intention that always informs cartographic exercises of the epoch.

Yet, a clear comprehension of the status of cartography, as developed by the state engineers in the context of the progressive territorialization of France, is somewhat disrupted by the "utopic" maps realized by students for the *concours des cartes* toward the end of the eighteenth century. These fantastic maps, mainly realized in trompe l'oeil, can be understood as privileged fields of experimentation in a double sense. In the first place, their aim was to assess the ability of students to design and visualize the insertion of "projects" into the territory at different scales and for different audiences: the king and his ministers, technically informed figures like engineers and superintendents, the "educated" public at large, or people employed to supervise work on the site, etc. But again, at the same time, the meaning and role of the map as a representational and design tool was also tested. The trompe l'oeil technique was used consistently to overlay different forms of figuration: sketches of human forms, plates of the *Atlas de Trudaine*, sheets of paper with musical notation, elevations and plans of buildings, torn and ripped maps of fictional journeys, title pages from manuals and textbooks, and even playing cards or visiting cards (a visual pun on the multiple meanings of *carte* in French). Despite this babel of signs and figurations, almost all the imaginary maps of the *concours des cartes* managed to convey a coherent and even harmonious image of a territory virtually recomposed in the figure of a well-cultivated garden, maintaining therefore the open possibility of a "project" about the territory and its government, even if a utopic one. Nevertheless, they also lead to the reexamination of the stability of the theory of signs (the "order of things") put in place by the *Port Royal Logic*.

What was happening in late eighteenth-century France when we begin to find this sort of fascinating representation? Michel Foucault, in his lessons at the Collège de France (1977–78), quotes research on the French population that was published in 1778 by a certain Jean-Baptiste Moheau: "It is up to the government to change the air temperature and to improve the climate; a direction given to stagnant water, forests planted or burnt down, mountains destroyed by time or by the continual cultivation of their surface, create a new soil and a new climate. The effect of time, of occupation of the land, and of vicissitudes in the physical domain, is such that the most healthy districts become morbific." Foucault considers Moheau the first great theorist of biopolitics or biopower and employs his inquest on the French population to prove how at the end of the eighteenth century, the state is no longer invested in governing the territory but, rather, concerned about administering a *milieu*, an environment. But what is the meaning of milieu in the eighteenth century? And does the concept appear in the text of architects, administrators, or political thinkers of the time? Foucault addresses the first question, referring to "The Living and Its Milieu," a text published in 1952 by the philosopher of science Georges Canguilhem, his thesis advisor. Following this highly influential essay, Foucault retraces the modern origin of the concept in the physics of Newton, and specifically in the idea of "ether," a sort of fluid that served as an intermediary between bodies, thus explaining their actions at a distance. Biology, in Lamarck for example, imported this model from physics. However, Foucault is interested more precisely by the problems of circulation and causality already present in the notion as formulated in physics, because from his perspective they were quite similar to the predicaments confronting architects and planners in the middle of the eighteenth century. The term milieu was never used in the contemporary literature concerning cities, but, insists Foucault, administrators and architects were already developing tools to secure and govern environments. Milieu, if never pronounced, is suggested in this literature as an assemblage of natural components like rivers, marshes, hills, fields, etc., and artificial agglomerations of individuals and buildings. Artificial and natural elements act and react upon each other in a closed, circulatory movement of causes and effects. Milieus became fields of intervention that targeted a "population" conceived of as a multiplicity of individuals profoundly and biologically bonded to the materiality inside which they existed. Foucault considers this the moment of "irruption" of the problem of the insertion of the "naturality" of the human species (the population) into the artificial milieu of political relations of power.

An array of discourses about life's survival and governance inside an artificial milieu, together with the question of the design of the environment, were already intersecting during the second half of the eighteenth century. This was happening at the junctions of politics, economy, medicine, agronomy, botany, geography, and the first methodical attempts (through the labor of agriculturalists and physicians) to build a science of meteorology. Fascinatingly, such intense preoccupation with climatic conditions and their relation to the health of the population and wealth of the nation lead to the elaboration of actual schemes to be executed at a regional or even worldwide scale. Possibly, best known among such proposals were the plans for the systematic reforestation of France, which was to be effected through governmental intervention as described by François Antoine Rauch, engineer-geographer of the Ponts et chaussées, in an 1802 publication dedicated to Napoleon that appeared under the remarkable title *Harmonie hydro-végétale et météorologique: ou recherches sur les moyens de recréer avec nos forêts la force des températures et la régularité des saisons par des plantations raisonnées*. Reforestation, an urgent undertaking required to remediate the shortage of timber for construction and the scarcity of fuel for industry and heating, had already been for a long time a preoccupation of many European governments. However, worried by the dismemberment of the national forests of France during the revolutionary period, Rauch, further elaborating the objectives in the amelioration of forestry, vastly expanded its scope. Echoing the thesis of Moheau on the influence of climate on the population, he insisted that special care should be employed by governmental organizations in planting terrains insalubrious or impoverished by prolonged cultivation. The soil of France will thus not only recover its lost fertility but also increase the vigor and prosperity of future generations. Moreover, the reforestation of the peaks of mountains and elevated sites (with the trees acting as cloud-catchers) would help to reestablish the hydrographic equilibrium of the original French climates, restoring a sort of lost arcadia. Considered as one of the forefathers of ecological thinking in France, Rauch expanded his study to include the harm provoked by worldwide deforestation in his *Régénération de la nature végétale* (1818), and went on to edit (from 1821 to 1827) the *Annales européennes de physique végétale et d'économie publique*, a periodical devoted to climate studies. He even attempted to create a society "for the general fructification of the soils and waters," which was to be charged with the task of assuring, in the course of ten years, the multiplication of wildlife in the lakes, rivers, and forests of France.

Less familiar than Rauch's proposals, or at least never truly examined within the background of late eighteenth-century concerns about climates and their government, are the bodies of research and projects that surfaced in *Plans raisonnés de toutes les espèces de jardins* (fig. 2 and 3), a treatise published between 1819 and 1820 by landscape architect Gabriel Thouin. In the modest introduction to this fine collection of projects, a result of more than forty years of practice, the author explains that he did not feel the need to propose a "theory" of the art of landscape gardening

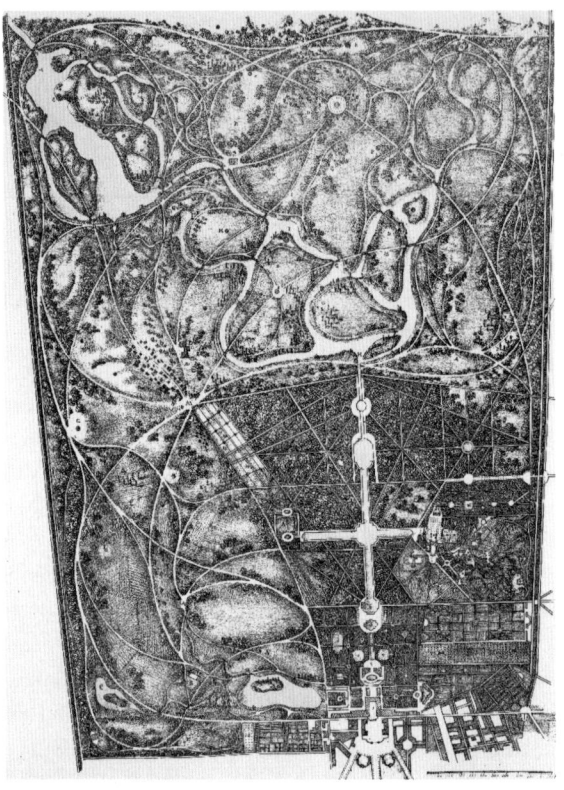

Gabriel Thouin, "Jardin Parcs ou Carrières," *Plans raisonnés de toutes les espèces de jardins* (Paris: Madame Huzard, 1828), plate no. 25.

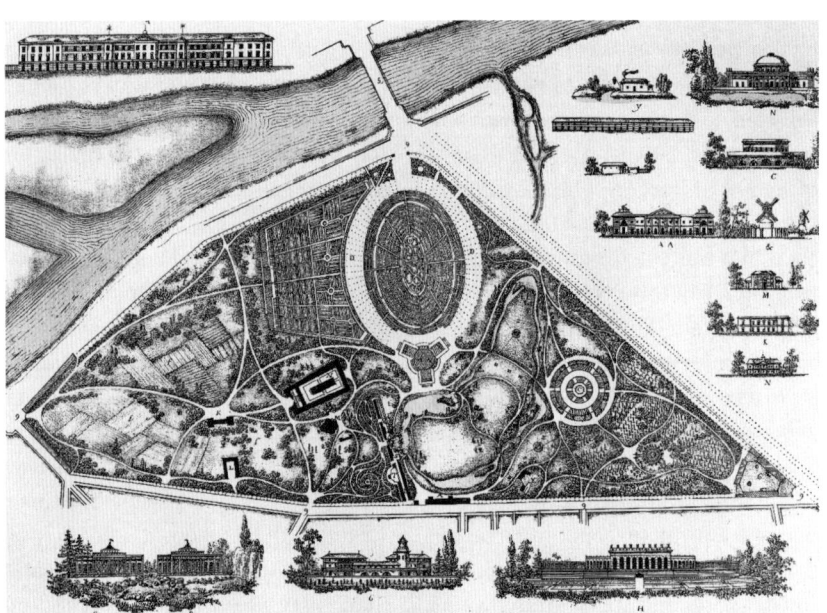

Gabriel Thouin, "Projet d'agrandissement du Jardin des Plantes de Paris," *Plans raisonnés de toutes les espèces de jardins* (Paris: Madame Huzard, 1828), plate no. 13.

and invited the reader to consult other more poetic works already existing. What Thouin proposed instead was a classification of "all the species of gardens" announced in the title. In a quite scientific-looking "Tableau des genres, des sections, et des sortes de jardins," Thouin identified four main types of gardens: *Économiques ou légumiers* (economic or vegetable gardens), *Fruitiers ou vergers* (orchards and fruit gardens), *Botaniques* (botanical gardens), and *Plaisance ou d'agrément* (recreational and pleasure gardens). In this classification, utility (and economy) vastly prevail over leisure and aesthetic contemplation. The drawings illustrating the plans reflect the same set of concerns and, among them, three striking schemes envisioned at a territorial scale suggest a novel, "revolutionary" conception of gardening. Represented with methods that closely approximate the one adopted by the engineers of the Ponts et chaussées in their cartographic exercises, the projects propose, respectively, a massive addition to the already huge gardens of Versailles (*fig. 2*); an equally colossal extension of the Jardin du Roi (the Royal botanical garden) in Paris (*fig. 3* and *4*); and an experimental farm for the tropics situated in a vast valley surrounded by a chain of mountains (*fig. 5*). At close examination the three schemes reveal how their conceptions were directly or indirectly inspired by the utopic visions of André Thouin, Gabriel Thouin's eminent brother, to which in fact the entire treatise was dedicated.

Head gardener of the Jardin du Roi in Paris, protégé of Buffon, collaborator of the *Encyclopédie methodique* (1787), superintendent of the collections of the museum of natural history, specialist in the culture and acclimatization of exotic plants, member of the Société d'agriculture, the Académie des sciences, and seventy more scientific societies, André Thouin enjoyed an illustrious and long career that comprised momentous episodes of engagement during the French Revolution. These last episodes include his crucial contribution to the epic struggle for the survival of the Jardin du Roi, later renamed and transformed into the Muséum national d'histoire naturelle (in 1793, it was the only scientific or academic institution of the old regime not abolished and replaced by revolutionary committees), and his role in compiling inventories and selecting and rehousing plants and specimens from private and public gardens, cabinets, museums, experimental farms, and arboretums expropriated during the Revolution in France or officially plundered during the triumphant Napoleonic wars in various European countries.

Strategically positioned within the administration of the Jardin du Roi, one of the foremost French scientific institutions (or "centers of calculation" in Bruno Latour's parlance), André Thouin was key to the implementation of a doctrine inspired by the French Physiocrats, the eighteenth-century school of "nature's economy." In his "Essai sur l'exposition et la division méthodique de l'économie rurale, sur la manière d'étudier: cette science par principes et sur les moyens de la perfectionner," the introductory analytical dissertation begins precisely with a chain of statements belonging to the philosophy of the Physiocrats: public economy should be founded on rural economy because land and human labor are the sources of the wealth of the nation. Consequently, the soils and climates in which plants, animals, and human beings thrive or fail should be objects of careful study and management or governance. In the synthetic tableau that follows, André Thouin adopts the classificatory methods employed in the contemporary "natural histories" and subdivides rural economy into five principal branches: agriculture, animal care, economic arts, rural architecture, and the commerce of agricultural products. Agriculture is in turn subdivided into four classes: cultivated fields (divided into plants for human food, plants for

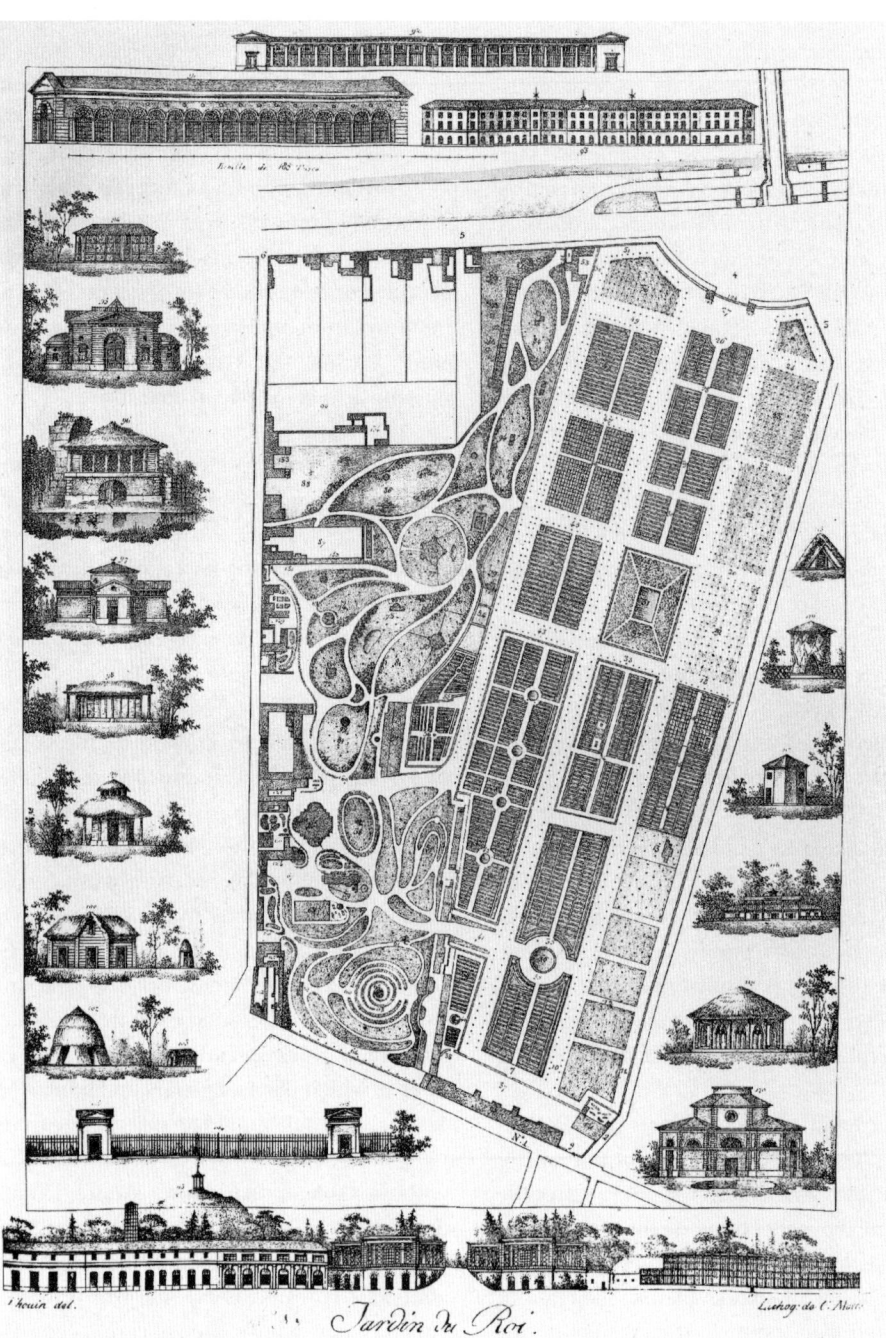

Gabriel Thouin, "Jardin du Roi," *Plans raisonnés de toutes les espèces de jardins* (Paris: Madame Huzard, 1828), plate no. 97.

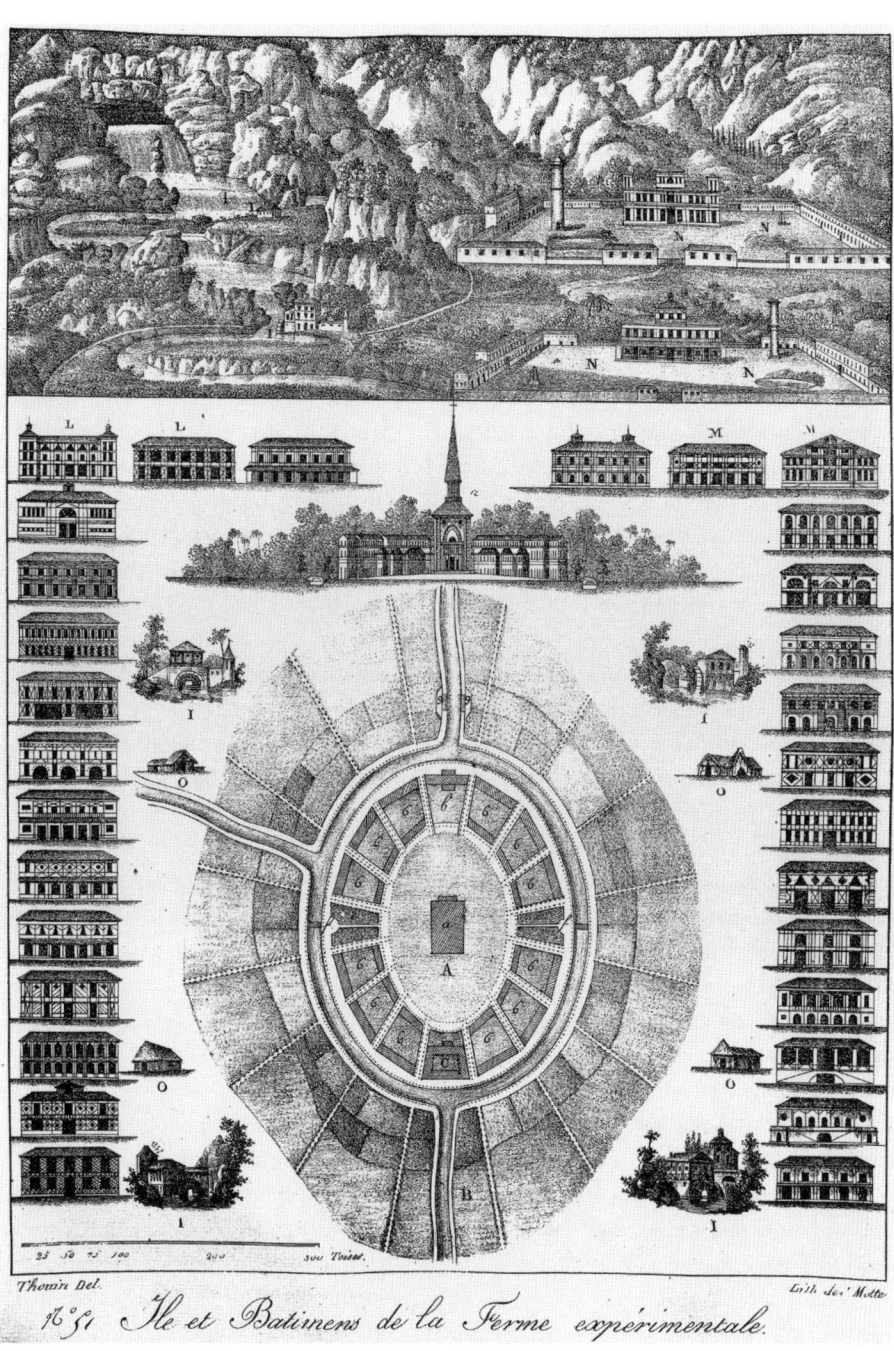

Gabriel Thouin, "Ile et Batimens de la Ferme expérimentale," *Plans raisonnés de toutes les espèces de jardins* (Paris: Madame Huzard, 1828), plate no. 51.

animal food, and plants for industry), culture on hills (orchards and vineyards), and forests and gardens. Gardens are subdivided into five sections: vegetable culture, flower gardens, tree culture, pleasure gardens, and botanical and pharmaceutical gardens. In this perspective, the classification of gardens proposed by his brother Gabriel, beyond being clearly inspired by the economic-scientific method of André Thouin, appears as a subdivision of an overall plan devised for the management of the "economy" of the entire country. To help the implementation of such a grandiose vision, André Thouin proposed to develop, again at a national scale, a systematic program of agricultural education that involved the creation of fourteen experimental farms, one for each of the natural basins of the French territory, or of at least four establishments corresponding to the "principal climates" of France. Moreover, a vast terrain in the south of France presenting a variety of soils and diverse exposures to the sun was to be preserved for the acclimatization of tropical plants, while high mountain grounds, close to perennial ice, were necessary for testing the acclimatization of plants and animals from the coldest climates and highest regions of the earth. André Thouin also finally proposed the creation of a central bureau, near or in Paris, for the coordination of the knowledge acquired through the experimental activities conducted in these laboratories and the data and expertise accumulated by expressly equipped and trained scientists during their journeys to the most remote regions of the earth. In fact, Thouin's visionary rural economy, reaching beyond French borders, included the administration and circulation of plants and knowledge about climates and environments at a worldwide scale.

To this task André Thouin was well trained by his prerevolutionary work at the Jardin du Roi, where he was at the center of a vast, international network of scientists (which included Carl Linnaeus, Joseph Banks, and, later, Alexander von Humboldt), gardeners, missionaries, engineers, administrators, and colonists that connected and operated in collaboration with the diplomatic corps, the French Navy, and other institutions associated with the government of the French colonies. He had a primary role in the accumulation of information related to botanic sciences and the development of techniques for the acclimatization of plants. Thouin contributed vastly, for example, to the organization of Jean-François de La Pérouse's expedition to the South Seas, and to a second one devoted to its rescue. Recommending the utmost care in the preservation of "local climate and native soil" during the shipping of plants from distant countries, Thouin furnished seeds for testing and exchange on foreign grounds, tools, sets of instructions, and expert gardeners to accomplish the delicate missions. Together with the minister of the Navy, Thouin also discussed the reorganization or creation of botanical gardens in the principal harbors of France and in the colonies in order to ameliorate production and stimulate the markets. After the Revolution, with the loss of virtually all French possessions overseas, he revisited the problems posed by such an economy of global exchange and acclimatization in his major opus published posthumously in 1828, the *Cours de culture et naturalisation de végétaux* (Course on the culture and naturalization of vegetables). *Cours de culture* progresses from general observations on the terrestrial globe and its climates to the description of useful exotic plants for naturalization and methods of acclimatization in France. At the very end, he introduces a final chapter presenting an experimental farm to be realized in the tropics or in a mountainous region in the south of France (*fig. 6*). In describing his proposal André Thouin affirms that, solicited by the government to present opinions about the means to improve rural and domestic agriculture in the French colonies (the *deux Indes*, India and the West Indies) and

Gabriel Thouin, "Projet d'une ferme expérimentale de la zone torride," *Plans raisonnés de toutes les espèces de jardins* (Paris: Madame Huzard, 1828), plate no. 52.

convinced that it was more effective to teach through examples than theories, he submitted to the minister a scheme for the settlement of about 1200 colonists. Conceived possibly before 1800, the project was drafted and published in the 1820 volume by his brother Gabriel Thouin, the landscape architect, and presented again in the atlas of the *Cours de culture et naturalisation de végétaux* (fig. 7 and 8). The experimental colony, meticulously described and illustrated by the Thouin brothers, was shaped in the form of a vast amphitheater and occupied a basin irrigated by a small river. Fed by a high-altitude lake (used by the settlers for bathing and as a breeding pond), the stream descended into the valley in a series of waterfalls that sustained flour mills and other agricultural machinery. Joining its waters to other brooks and rivulets, the river converged around a central island on which were situated a temple, dwellings, and attendant offices for the foremost administrators of the colony (directors, engineers, architects, priests, physicians, and veterinarians), and a hospice with gardens for the cultivation of medicinal plants. On the island, space was also reserved for military exercises while all around it were prairies for pasture and the cultivation of grains. A surrounding belt was subdivided into sixteen portions of land, each worked by a farmhouse responsible for the culture of a specific useful plant (from cotton and coffee to pepper and cinnamon). Heading up the slopes of the mountains, a large ring was reserved for the planting of valuable tree species. Here again, sixteen farms with annexes for the working of timber were charged with the task of toiling upon equal parcels of terrain. Finally, near the summit of the mountains, land was reserved for the cultivation of plants from glacial climates and for the pasture of llamas, alpacas, cashmere goats, and even the breeding of foxes and sables. Plans and elevation were provided for buildings described in the scheme, including huts designated as housing for the "workers."

Thouin's was not the only plan proposed to remediate the dramatic loss of the colonies through the naturalization of exotic plants in the most favorable climates of France. Yet, Thouin, in giving shape to his unique project, beautifully combined two emblematic diagrams: in his plan he replicated the figure of the paradigmatic disciplinary scheme proposed by Jeremy Bentham for the panopticon, while in elevation he followed Alexander von Humboldt's famous "Essay on the Geography of Plants," which charted the distribution of the vegetation from different climates at different altitudes as exemplified in the case of the equatorial Cordillera region of the Andes. The "Geography of Plants" appeared in the *Tableau physique des régions équatoriales* published in Paris by Humboldt in 1805, a work quoted at length in Thouin's *Cours de culture*. Thouin had firsthand knowledge of Humboldt's research and voyages, having introduced Aimé Bonpland (Humboldt's traveling companion) to the techniques of naturalization practiced at the Jardin des Plants and also through personal acquaintance with Humboldt himself. As for the panoptic diagram, Thouin quite possibly knew Bentham's work through the intermediary of Sir John Sinclair, the Scottish agriculturalist, politician, and author of the pioneering series of publications *Statistical Accounts of Scotland* (1791–99). Instrumental in the founding of the British Board of Agriculture, Sinclair supported the publication of important volumes on farming and rural architecture and advanced several schemes for the improvement of agronomy. As a member and correspondent of several European academic institutions (including the French Société d'agriculture to which André Thouin was also associated), most of Sinclair's initiatives were widely known, and some of the literature produced under his stimulus or supervision, including his own proposals, were promptly translated and published in several venues. This was the case of *The Plough, or Joint Stock Farming*

Society, for Ascertaining the Principles of Agricultural Improvement (1800), Sinclair's plan for the creation of experimental farms to test methods of improving and increasing the crops necessary for feeding the growing populations of the major cities of the kingdom and relieve the costs of pauperism without "depending on foreign industry and cultivation." The experimental farms of Sinclair, a response to the British loss of the American colonies, were conceived in the form of villages and organized according to a panoptical radial plan. In each, at the center of a circle of cottages, Sinclair situated a community kitchen, workshops, and symmetrically disposed schools for boys and girls. The central lawn was reserved for the play of children while the cottages (round in plan) were provided with individual kitchen gardens. Evidently informed by Bentham's theories, the scheme was instantly made accessible to an eager French audience of politicians, architects, engineers, and agronomists fervently adhering to the Revolutionary rhetoric of conjugating patriotism and economy with the virtuous farming of the soil of the nation.

Beyond ascertaining sources and influences, topical in scrutinizing the Thouin brothers' proposal is the intersection and strategic manipulation of the two diagrams. The geographic specificity of Humboldt's plants is employed to model (within the limit of the nineteenth-century *savoir*, or knowledge in Foucault's parlance) a technology of climate management that was implemented through Bentham's panopticon. This last, in turn, should be understood as a social technology or a mechanism that affects visible matter (prisons, schools, hospitals, barracks, places of productions) and passes through every articulable function. As Deleuze explains in his book on Foucault, "The abstract formula of Panopticism is no longer 'to see without being seen' but *to impose a particular conduct on a particular human multiplicity*." Foucault in his writings repeatedly evoked the figure of the diagram to illustrate apparatuses of power control or the unstable, fluctuating fields where forces of different intensities combine to give shape to systems in perpetual disequilibrium. Following Deleuze's interpretation of Foucault, a diagram "is a display of the relations between forces which constitute power" and "in so far as it exposes a set of relations between forces, is not a place but rather 'a non-place': it is the place only of mutation." The diagram, writes Deleuze in a chapter titled "A New Cartographer," for Foucault "is no longer an auditory or visual archive but a map, a cartography that is coextensive with the whole social field."

The aims and scope of such new cartography were clearly enunciated by Foucault in the famous lesson of *Security, Territory, Population: Lectures at the Collège de France, 1977–1978* (2004), where he first delineated the notion of governmentality. As seen before, at the end of the inaugural lecture, Foucault found in Moheau's *Recherches et considérations sur la population de la France* (1778) a program for climate change that signaled a pivotal shift in the "art of government." The seventeenth-century concerns over the government of territories (their acquisition, defense, description, inventory, and administration) had given way during the second half of the eighteenth century to the formation of novel (modern) security apparatuses aimed at the population and its milieu. To examine this conversion, Foucault relocated the focus of his analysis, shifting it to questions of power and "governmentality" which he defined as "the ensemble formed by the institutions, procedures, analyses and reflections, the calculations and tactics that allow the exercise of this very specific albeit complex form of power, which has as its target population, as its principal form of knowledge political economy, and as its essential technical means apparatuses of security." Declaring

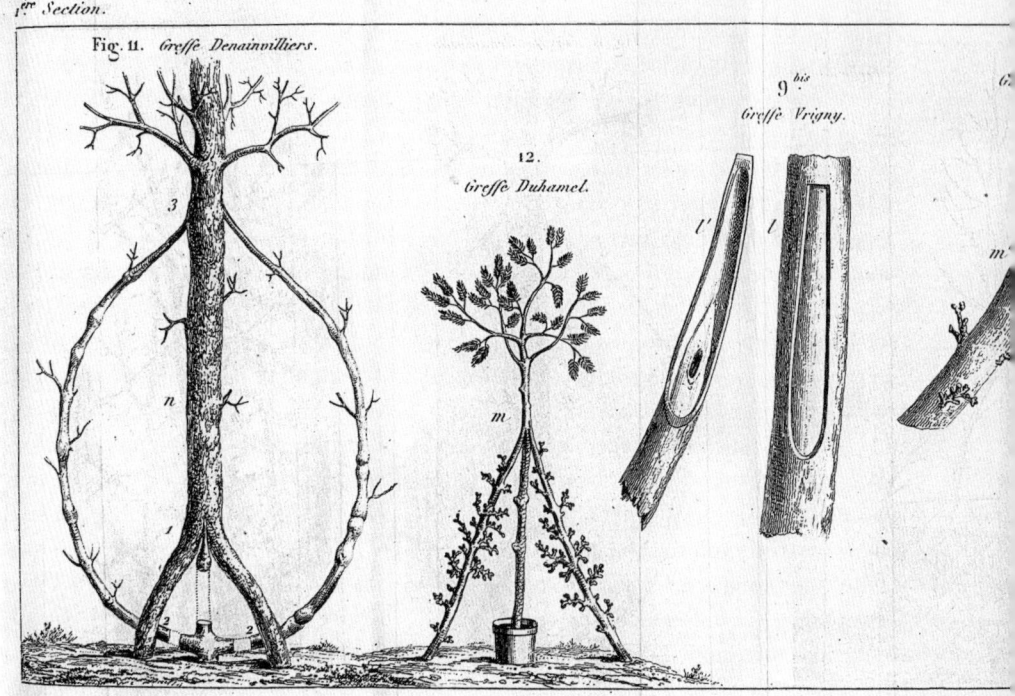

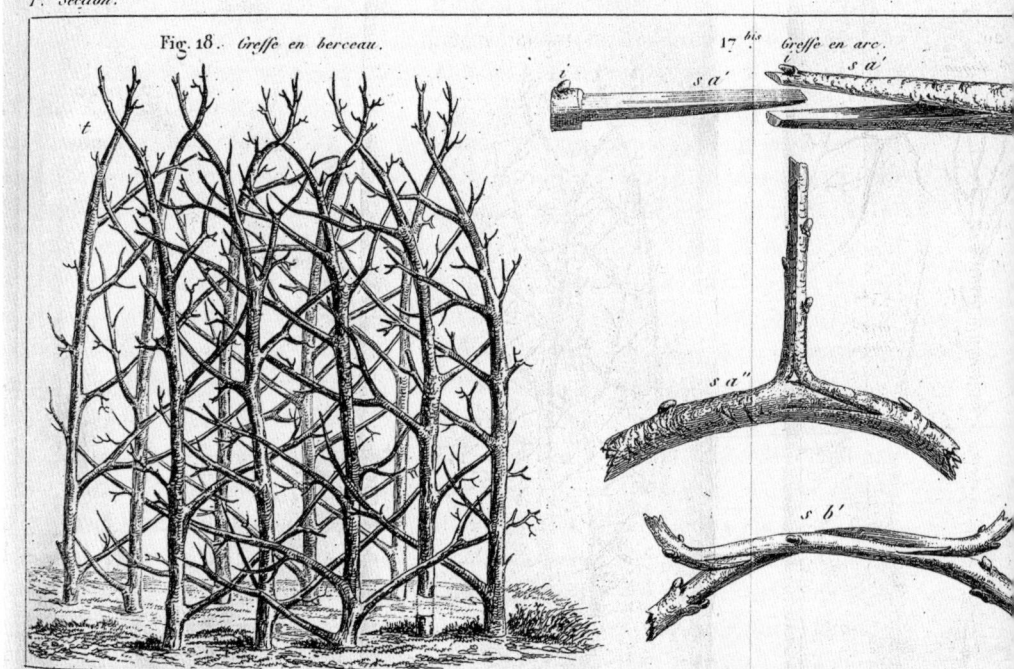

André Thouin, "Greffes," *Monographie des greffes, ou, description technique des diverses sortes de greffes employées pour la multiplication des végétaux* (Paris: Librairie encyclopédique de Roret, 1851), first section, plate no. 3 (*fig. 7*), plate no. 4 (*fig. 8*).

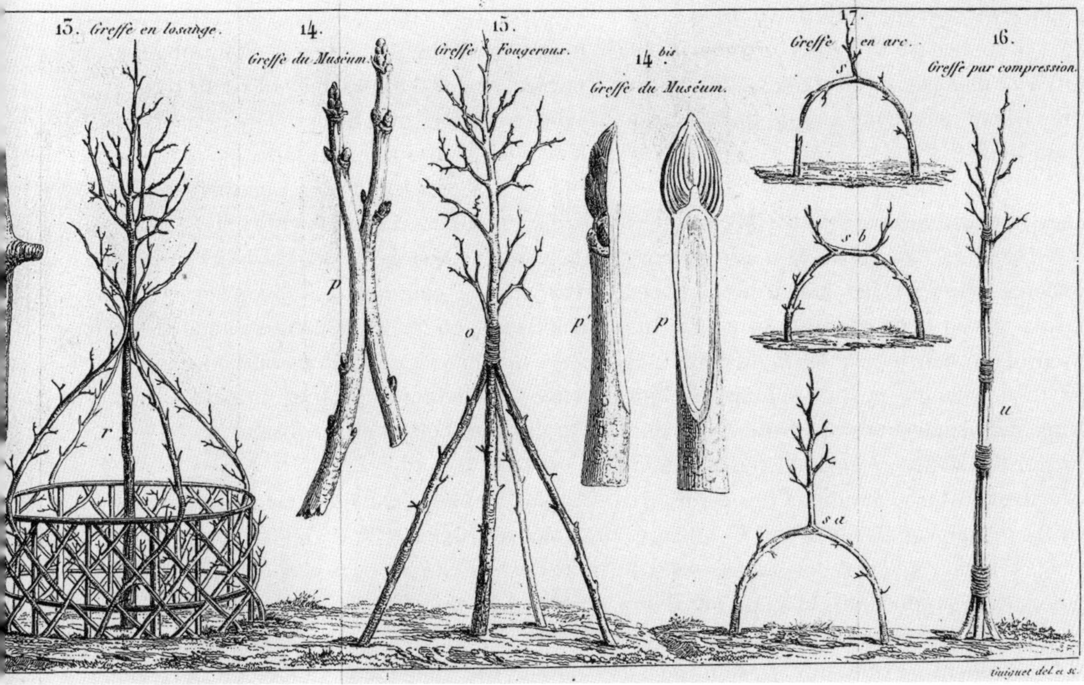

Greffes. Pl. 3.

13. Greffe en losange.
14. Greffe du Muséum.
15. Greffe Fougeroux.
14 bis. Greffe du Muséum.
17. Greffe en arc.
16. Greffe par compression.

Guiguet del. et sc.

Greffes. Pl. 4.

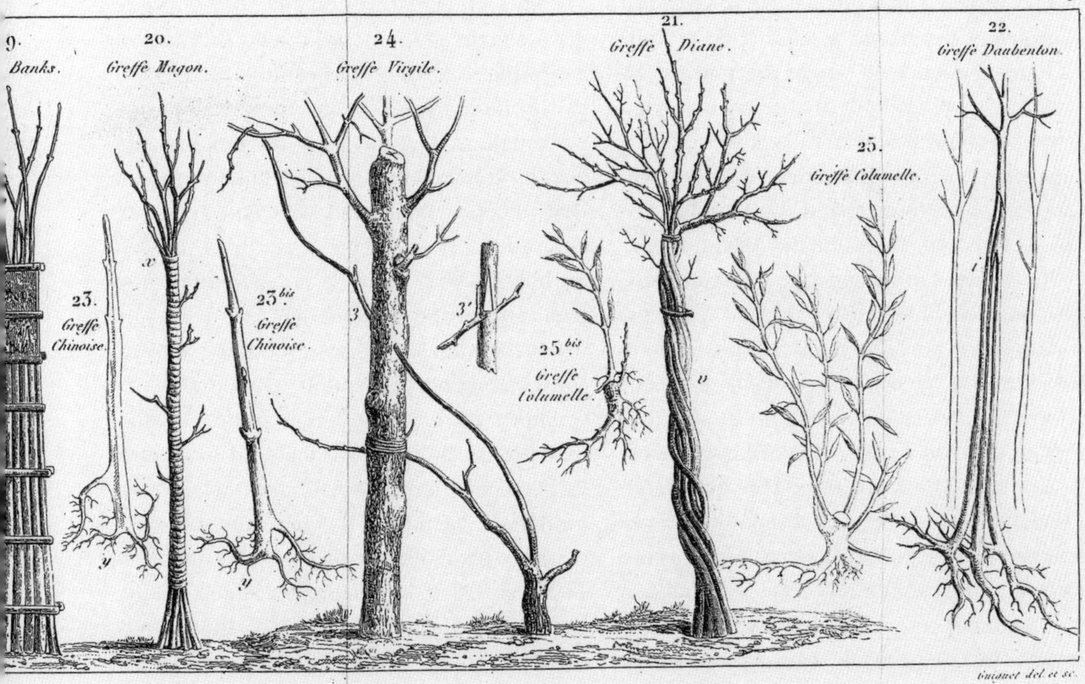

9. Banks.
20. Greffe Magon.
24. Greffe Virgile.
21. Greffe Diane.
22. Greffe Daubenton.
23. Greffe Chinoise.
23 bis. Greffe Chinoise.
25. Greffe Columelle.
25 bis. Greffe Columelle.

Guiguet del. et sc.

his intention to rename the entire course of lessons, Foucault announced that he was now going to undertake a history of governmentality and then set out to chart emerging diagrams of power, tracing a route that Deleuze would follow.

Gilles Deleuze, together with Félix Guattari in *A Thousand Plateaus* (1980), also explore the connections between milieu and territory, first as spatial constructions on which the power of the state (or capitalism) is exercised, and then, opening up possibilities of countering such impositions of power, as productions of the subject. Uexküll's theses, which I sketched at the beginning of this essay, are crucial in helping Deleuze and Guattari to think of milieu and territory as subjective and aesthetic productions. In fact, against life sciences' presumption of a possible "objective" apprehension of reality, Uexküll poses multiple subjective realities and an equally subjective production of territories. Toward the end of *Foray into the Worlds of Animals and Humans*, he writes: "Each and every subject lives in a world in which there are only subjective realities and that environments themselves represent only subjective realities. Whoever denies the existence of subjective realities has not recognized the foundations of his or her own environment." Uexküll then briefly attempts to explore the interrelations between individual environmental bubbles or, in his own words, to answer the question: "How does the subject exempt itself as an object in the different environments in which it plays an important role?" Uexküll introduces the example of an oak tree. The tree itself is understood as a subject responding to selected environmental marks or signs. But the oak tree also plays different roles as an object in a multitude of other individual environments: a forester considers how much wood can be obtained from its trunk; a little girl is scared by the dreadful face she sees inscribed on the bark; a fox inhabits the roots while an owl takes shelter in the branches; an ant uses the bark as hunting grounds whereas a bark beetle lays its eggs in it (*fig. 9*). Following the musical analogy proposed by Uexküll, to each subject the oak presents a different "tone": a use tone (for the forester), a magic tone (for the girl), a protection tone (for the fox and the owl), or a food tone (for the ant). Uexküll concludes avowing the impossibility of summarizing the multiple tonal characters of the oak tree as an object, while maintaining that such multiplicity represents only partially a subject "solidly put together in itself, which carries and shelters all environments."

Appropriating Uexküll's theory of nature as composer, Deleuze and Guattari state in *A Thousand Plateaus* in a chapter aptly titled "Of the Refrain": "Jakob von Uexküll has elaborated an admirable theory of transcoding. He sees the components as melodies in counterpoint, each of which serves as a motif for another: Nature as music. Whenever there is transcoding, we can be sure that there is not a simple addition, but the constitution of a new plane, as of a surplus value. A melodic or rhythmic plane, surplus value of passage or bridging." The territory, for Deleuze and Guattari (borrowing from Uexküll), is an "act that affects milieus and rhythms, that 'territorializes' them." The territory is marked by indexes that "may be components taken from any of the milieus: materials, organic products, skin or membrane states, energy sources, action-perception condensates." A territory materializes when milieu components cease to be directional and functional to become dimensional and expressive. Functions, maintain Deleuze and Guattari, do not explain the territory but presuppose it. The territorializing element resides "in the becoming expressive of rhythm and melody, in other words, in the emergence of proper qualities (colour, odour, sound, silhouette ...)." And they ask: "Can this becoming, this emergence, be called art?"

Bark beetle on an oak tree. Jakob von Uexküll and Georg Kriszat, *Streifzüge durch Umwelten von Tiere und Menschen (A Foray into the Worlds of Animals and Humans)* (1934).

GUNNAR KLACK

TIERGARTEN TODAY: A PRODUCT OF THE "KOLLEKTIVPLAN"?

What do we see when we look at Tiergarten today? Do we see artifacts from the eighteenth, nineteenth, or twentieth century? Tiergarten is one of Berlin's oldest structures. Its history spans over five centuries. Yet today's most significant artifacts of Tiergarten are much younger, most of them from the 1950s. This essay will examine one particular time in its history: the reconstruction after World War II. This era produced most of the present artifacts in Tiergarten. The first plans for reconstructing the park were drawn in 1947 according to the ruling planning paradigm of the day, the Stadtlandschaft (City-landscape), which called for the reconstruction of Berlin as a merging of landscape and city. The so-called Kollektivplan (Collective plan) was the first master plan for reconstructing Berlin after 1945. This essay explores the hypothesis that it might have had a substantial impact on the redesign of Tiergarten, to the extent that the artifacts of Tiergarten built in the 1950s are a materialization of the ephemeral and quasi-utopian Kollektivplan.

To understand today's material substance of Tiergarten, it is necessary to look specifically into the second part of the twentieth century. This essay is divided into three sections covering different moments of this time span: 1) an overview presenting Tiergarten's existing artifacts, 2) how the Kollektivplan shaped Tiergarten, 3) the origin, meaning, and context of the concept of the Stadtlandschaft, from which the draft of the Kollektivplan is based.

1. AN OVERVIEW OF TIERGARTEN'S EXISTING ARTIFACTS

World War II had a vastly destructive effect on Berlin. Tiergarten was no exception, yet most destructive was the general poverty and lack of resources immediately following the war. Thousands of trees that had survived the war were cut to provide firewood, and only a few hundred remained. Even more radically, the park served a largely agricultural purpose from 1945 until 1949,[1] subdivided in small garden plots where people grew vegetables. Beginning in late 1949, replanting Tiergarten became a project of national interest. The principal planner was the landscape architect Willy Alverdes who, taking office in 1950, used modern landscape architectural principles and dismissed the idea of rebuilding the most formal elements of the park's layout, which had existed before.[2] And yet Tiergarten is not purely an artifact of the 1950s. Some of its structures, like pathways, allées, buildings, and bodies of water, have existed since the nineteenth century and make up a number of present-day artifacts. In fact, the 1950s redesign included some of the allées that were originally built in the late seventeenth and the eighteenth century.[3] There are basically three different types of elements anchored to specific times in Tiergarten: a) sporadic artifacts from the nineteenth century, b) an overall redesign and new planting from the 1950s and c) the

---

1   Folkwin Wendland, "Der Große Tiergarten in Berlin: seine Geschichte und Entwicklung in fünf Jahrhunderten" (Berlin: Gebrüder Mann Verlag, 1993), 246.
2   Previous to the damage suffered through the war, the latest design of Tiergarten was made by the landscape architect Peter Joseph Lenné who, working on the park between 1818 and 1840, combined principles from the typical nineteenth-century landscape gardens and integrated more formal elements from the Baroque period.
3   A comprehensive program for reconstructing previously destroyed historical elements had been in place since the late 1980s. By the time Tiergarten was listed as a heritage site and historic garden in 1991, many alterations had already been made. The large roundabout, with the Siegessäule (Victory Column) at its center, dates back to the seventeenth century, and yet its current geometry and artifacts are much younger. Still, the roundabout has persisted continuously through the centuries; therefore it is technically an artifact of the seventeenth century, even if there isn't anything left from that period. What exactly needs to be preserved here—the overall layout, the built structures, the plants themselves? Some of Tiergarten's trees had been replanted in the 1980s according to the design of the nineteenth century. See also Wendland, 31, 266ff.

reconstruction of artifacts and replanting from the 1980s. Another aspect has to be considered as well: Tiergarten developed a degree of wilderness during the time of Berlin's division. The original 1950s design foresaw the incremental natural growth of plants. Alverdes paid particular attention to this projected natural development. This indicates that a certain wilderness was already anticipated within the original postwar design.

The reconstruction of Tiergarten began in 1950, but the planning process started five years earlier as the Berlin Senate had already made the decision to rebuild the park by July 2, 1945,[4] less than two months after the war's end.[5] The large-scale deforestation of 1946/47 happened even after this decision was made, and detailed plans for reconstruction were drawn immediately afterward. The design that Alverdes proposed—and later carried out—is that of a landscape park.[6] But Alverdes's design was not the first one: it was the final design in a series of proposals starting from 1946.

The plan by Alverdes essentially executed ideas that were first proposed in 1946 in the Kollektivplan, which was named after the group that created it, the Planungskollektiv (Collective of planners). One of its members was the landscape architect Reinhold Lingner, who drafted detailed plans for the open green areas in the reconstruction of Berlin (fig. 1). He also made a first design proposal for rebuilding Tiergarten in 1947 (fig. 2). By comparing Alverdes's plan from 1952 (fig. 3) and Lingner's design, the similarities outweigh the differences by far. It is safe to say that Alverdes's plan was committed to the same ideas as Lingner's. The following section will take a closer look at the Kollektivplan and specifically Lingner's design from 1947, as it represents the strongest link between the Kollektivplan and Alverdes's executed design.

2. HOW THE KOLLEKTIVPLAN SHAPED TIERGARTEN

The Kollektivplan, described and analyzed in numerous publications, represents an oddity in the history of Berlin since it was ultimately dismissed but, at the same time, remained highly influential. Surrounded by an air of mystery, it appeared at a time where the future of Berlin was very uncertain.

Immediately after the end of World War II, Berlin's administration, the Magistrate, was largely under the control of Soviet forces, who had fought the ground battle in the city during the final weeks of the war. The architect Hans Scharoun, who was not a popular choice with the socialist Magistrate,

---

4   Wendland, 248.
5   This is a remarkable fact given the context of Berlin's destruction and reconstruction. Even when there was no way of knowing how Berlin was going to develop, it was clear to politicians that reconstructing Tiergarten would be self-evident. Tiergarten was apparently given first priority, even before the Kollektivplan or any other plan for Berlin's reconstruction was made. This somewhat surprising priority was probably caused by the role that Tiergarten always played for the morale of Berlin's citizens, as it represented something like the spiritual heart of Berlin.
6   With only a few allées carried over from previous designs, Alverdes's Tiergarten is composed of a series of large open spaces surrounded by dense tree areas planted similarly to natural forests. This modern design contrasted and referenced the historic design at the same time. Alverdes had also referred to Lenne's plans as the main reference. The bodies of water, planned by Lenné, remained largely unchanged.
7   The Magistrate evolved from the Gruppe Ulbricht, a group of communist politicians around Walter Ulbricht, who would become the GDR's head of state in 1960. When the personnel for the Magistrate was publicly announced in May 1945, the list did not include Hans Scharoun. Not the first choice for the office of the Baustadtrat, his name only appeared in the second session of the Magistrate. The Magistrate also appointed a deputy to Scharoun, effectively serving as a political watchdog, since Scharoun was not a communist. Ural Kalender, *Die Geschichte der Verkehrsplanung Berlins* (Cologne: Forschungsgesellschaft für Straßen- und Verkehrswesen, 2012), 317.

A plan for green areas (part of the Kollektivplan) by Reinhold Lingner, 1946. Johann Friedrich Geist and Klaus Kürvers, *Das Berliner Mietshaus: 1945–1989*, vol. 3 (Munich: Prestel, 1989).

was appointed municipal building officer (Baustadtrat).[7] The first and most challenging task Scharoun had to complete was organizing an exhibition about Berlin's postwar development. This event was only created to showcase ideas for the reconstruction of Berlin, and it was scheduled to open as early as 1946. Within only a few months after the end of Nazi Germany, Scharoun managed to orchestrate this exhibition, which took place in the remaining halls of the Prussian Royal Palace. On August 22, 1946, the exhibition "Berlin plant/Erster Bericht" ("Berlin Is Planning/First Report") opened to the public, displaying Berlin's (and Germany's) commitment to the newfound freedom and democracy. The exhibition republished ideas from the 1920s to exemplify that any traces of Nazi architecture and urbanism were now discarded in favor of the ideas from that democratic time. The centerpiece of the show was a brand new master plan, the Kollektivplan, which envisioned Berlin similarly to a form combining a linear city and garden city. The radical nature of the Kollektivplan is remarkable: the design proposed an almost complete removal of all historical structures, by building Berlin completely anew as an ultramodern utopia. It suggested a type of urbanism that was a hybrid between city and landscape, not a city *in* the landscape, but a city *as* landscape itself. This concept was called Stadtlandschaft and was never adopted as a legally binding master plan for Berlin; in fact, it was discarded as quickly as it was produced.

The group of planners who produced the Kollektivplan included Wils Ebert, Peter Friedrich, Ludmilla Herzenstein, Luise Seitz, Selman Selmanagić, and Herbert Weinberger.[8] It is worth noting that the Planungskollektiv at first did not include Scharoun. Most of the members had close ties to the political left, and they were more popular with the Magistrate than Scharoun,[9] who was known for being more centrist.[10] Scharoun endorsed the Kollektivplan when it was made public although, behind the scenes, he opposed its radical design. It was mostly Ebert and Friedrich who did the design work on the Kollektivplan, and in their records, they point out that Scharoun was only a bystander in the whole process. They even explicitly thanked him for not interfering with their ideas.[11]

In the Kollektivplan the city's geographic conditions, which date from the last ice age, were conceived as the "natural" shape of Berlin and therefore used as the design's main feature (*fig. 4*). Berlin was to be rebuilt as a linear city corresponding to the natural topography, running east-west with a slight curve, following the river Spree (*fig. 5*). By making the Spree's own natural valley the defining feature, this plan attempted a return to a "natural" state, a symbolic move to a time before civilization. The inspiration for the immediate future laid in a distant, prehistoric past.[12] A large-scale model was also created to further exemplify the design's close connection to the natural conditions

---

8   Johann Friedrich Geist and Klaus Kürvers, *Das Berliner Mietshaus: 1945–1989*, vol. 3 (Munich: Prestel, 1989), 6.
9   Kalender, *Die Geschichte der Verkehrsplanung Berlins*, 318.
10 Gerd de Bruyn, *Fisch und Frosch, Oder die Selbstkritik der Moderne: ein architekturtheoretischer Essay*, Bauwelt Fundamente Band 124 (Berlin: Birkhäuser Architektur, 2001), 91ff.
11 The Kollektivplan was usually attributed to Scharoun. The majority of existing publications assume Scharouns's unrestrained identification with the Kollektivplan. The fact that he was internally opposed to the Planungskollektiv was only revealed recently by Ural Kalender's publication about the history of transport planning in Berlin (See Kalender, *Die Geschichte der Verkehrsplanung Berlins*). Scharoun never publicly criticized the Kollektivplan, and even spoke fondly of it, as for example, in his speech accompanying the opening of the exhibition "Berlin plant/Erster Bericht."
12 Gabi Dolff-Bonekämper, *Das Hansaviertel: Internationale Nachkriegsmoderne in Berlin* (Berlin: Huss-Medien, 1999), 303.

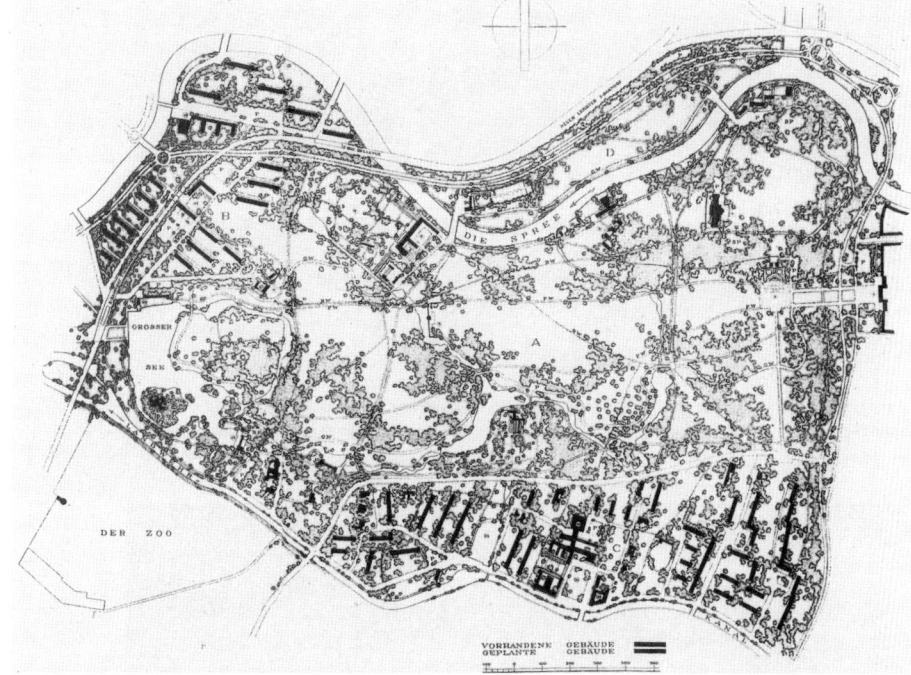

A design for Tiergarten by Reinhold Lingner, 1947; drawing by A. Waschneck. Folkwin Wendland, *Der Große Tiergarten in Berlin: Seine Geschichte und Entwicklung in fünf Jahrhunderten* (Berlin: Mann Verlag, 1993).

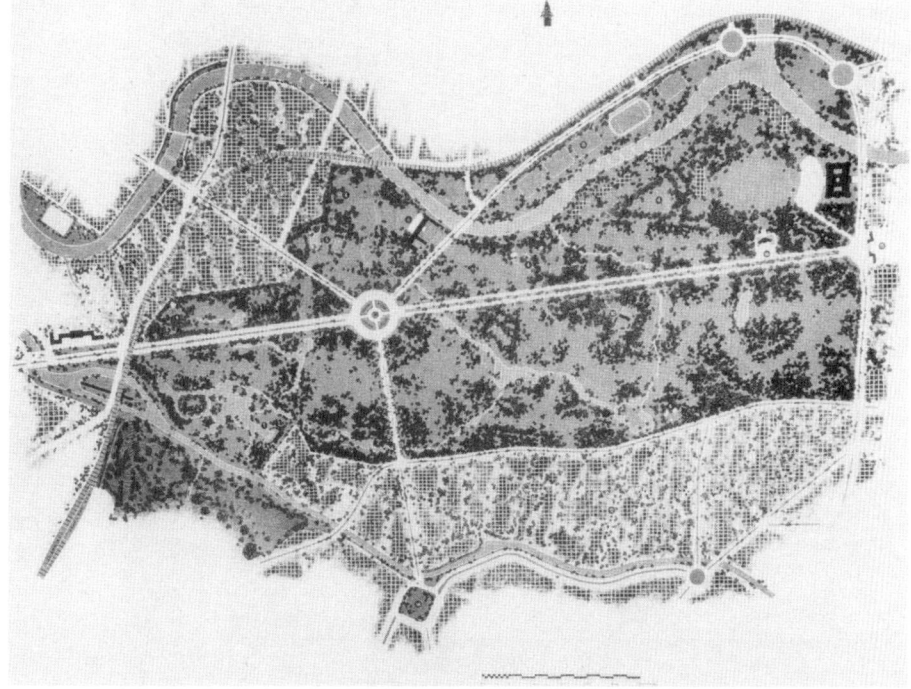

A design for Tiergarten by Willy Alverdes, 1952; drawing by A. Waschneck. Folkwin Wendland, *Der Große Tiergarten in Berlin: Seine Geschichte und Entwicklung in fünf Jahrhunderten* (Berlin: Mann Verlag, 1993).

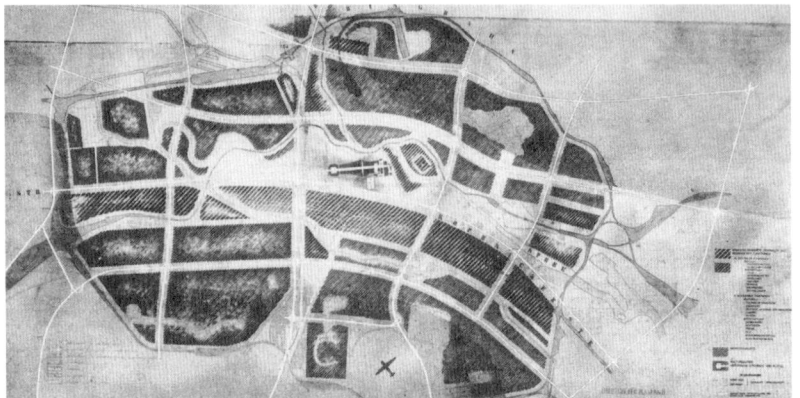

A section of the Kollektivplan showing the Berlin city center, 1946. Johann Friedrich Geist and Klaus Kürvers, *Das Berliner Mietshaus: 1945–1989*, vol. 3 (Munich: Prestel, 1989).

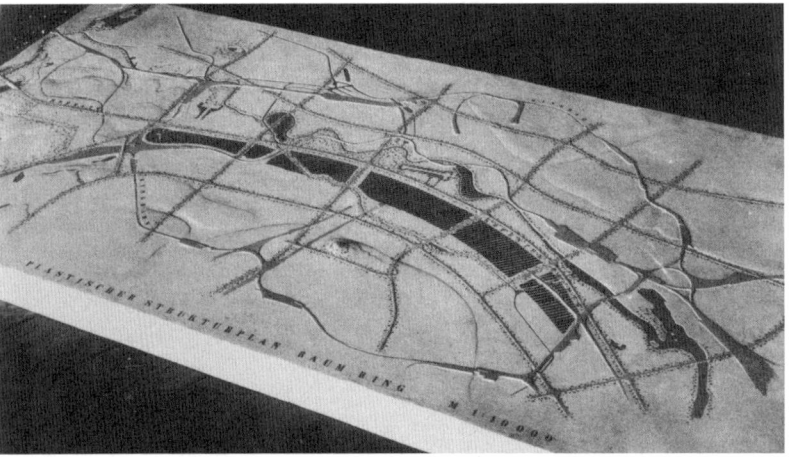

Three-dimensional model of the Kollektivplan, 1946. Johann Friedrich Geist and Klaus Kürvers, *Das Berliner Mietshaus: 1945–1989*, vol. 3 (Munich: Prestel, 1989).

An illustration of the Kollektivplan by Selman Selmanagić showing the view from a residential building onto the rebuilt city, 1946.[13]

of the territory: the topography, rendered three-dimensional, was clearly visible. Two other important features of the Kollektivplan were prominent in the model: the uniformly low building density and the regular traffic grid. A rectangular network of high-speed roads was only slightly warped to match the "natural" shape of the city. The plan had no center because the building density was the same all over the city's area. The drawing by Selman Selmanagić showing the view from a high-rise building onto the city is particularly impressive: housing blocks rise like rocks from a sea of vegetation, and apart from the highway roads, everything seems to be covered by plants, with the historical city vanishing without a trace. There are no visual clues that give hints about the city center or periphery (fig. 6). Explanatory captions accompanied the display, stating that a large portion of Berlin's future citizens would be homesteading self-sufficient farmers. The city would become in this way a landscape, not only metaphorically but also factually.

For the Kollektivplan to have only the slightest chance of implementation, real estate in Berlin would have had to be largely socialized. This premise fit the ideas of the socialist members of the Planungskollektiv, but it did not sit well with Scharoun, and it was even less popular with Western-allied military forces, who controlled the western part of Berlin. When a new Magistrate was elected in 1946, the Social Democrats emerged victorious. Scharoun was not confirmed in office as Baustadtrat, and he himself did not make a great effort at keeping this position. Instead, the conservative architect Karl Bonatz was appointed, a favorite of the United States Army Military Administration.[14] The Kollektivplan was discarded immediately after Bonatz took office, but nevertheless, it captured the imagination of numerous planners and, its ideas were incorporated into various other plans for Berlin.

Lingner, a key figure in the Kollektivplan but whose achievements extended far beyond, became the most influential landscape architect of the GDR. In the pressing issue of removing the detritus of World War II ruins, Lingner opposed the plan to use the bodies of water in Tiergarten as landfill locations. Instead, he suggested using the debris as landscaping material to accentuate and extrapolate the natural topography of Berlin.[15] In this way, not only did he save one of Tiergarten's main features, its streams and ponds, he also laid the groundwork for Berlin's remarkable rubble heaps, called *Trümmerberge* (rubble mountains), for which he is most famous.

Lingner, unlike Scharoun, remained part of the municipal administration. From 1947 to 1950, he was responsible for overseeing all landscape architecture projects in Berlin. From this position in 1947, he published his own plan for Tiergarten.[16] This

---

13 In Jörn Düwel, "Berlin: Planen im Kalten Krieg," in *1945: Krieg – Zerstörung – Aufbau. Architektur und Stadtplanung 1940–1960*, ed. Akademie der Künste Berlin (Berlin: Henschel, 1995).
14 Kalender, *Die Geschichte der Verkehrsplanung Berlins*, 333 ff.
15 Ulrike Forßbohm, *Kriegs-End-Moränen: Zum Denkmalwert der Trümmerberge in Berlin* (diploma thesis, Berlin 2011), http://dx.doi.org/10.14279/depositonce-2952.
16 It is worth noting that Lingner's design was not the only proposal for Tiergarten in 1947. Landscape architect Georg Béla Pniower drew plans that were radically opposed to Lingner's ideas. Pniower suggested building a university campus on one section of Tiergarten. He designed the rest of the park as a formal garden in an eccentric art nouveau style (fig. 7). Pniower and Lingner publicly criticized each other's designs. In the end, it was Lingner's plan, and consequently the Planungskollektiv's design, that had a lasting effect on Tiergarten, as later planners didn't pick up either Pniower's undulating formal creations or his usage scenarios. Geist and Kürvers, *Das Berliner Mietshaus*, 363.

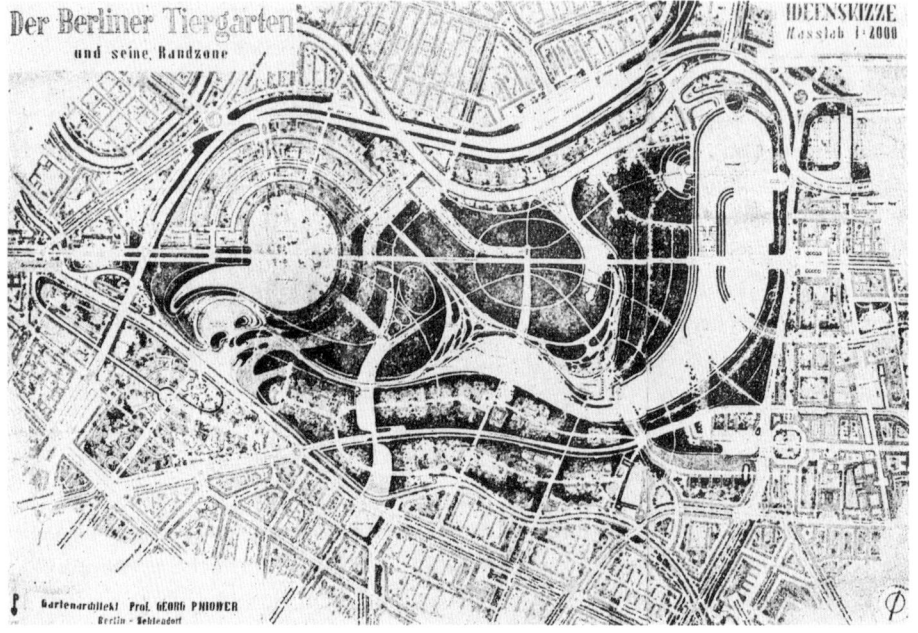

A design proposal for Tiergarten with a university campus by Georg Béla Pniower, 1947. Folkwin Wendland, *Der Große Tiergarten in Berlin: Seine Geschichte und Entwicklung in fünf Jahrhunderten* (Berlin: Mann Verlag, 1993).

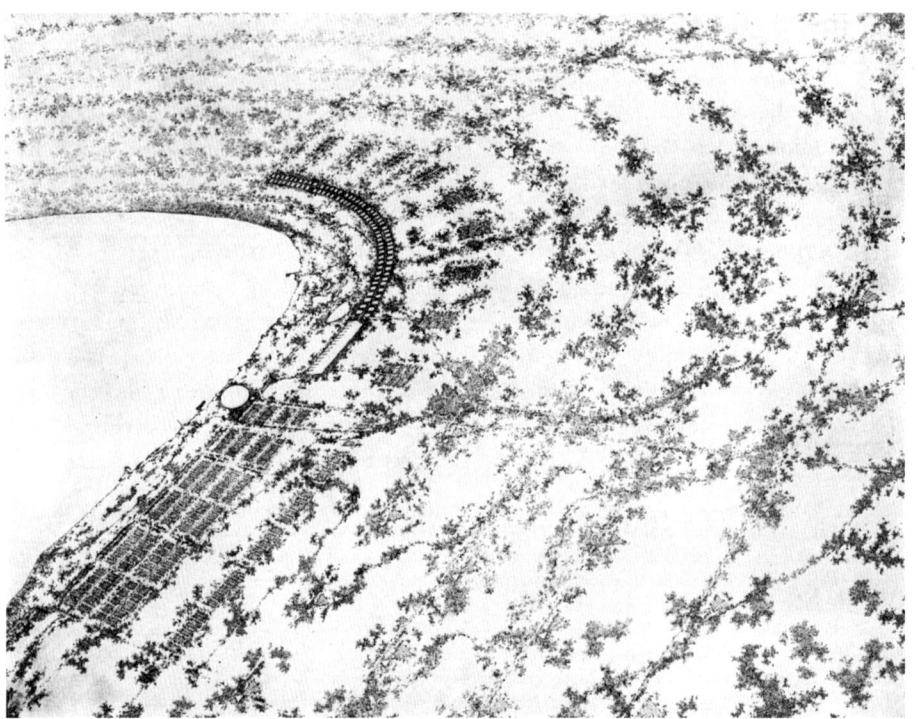

Aerial view of the replanned city of Chicago by Ludwig Hilberseimer, 1944. Ludwig Hilberseimer, *The New City: Principles of Planning* (Chicago: Theobald, 1944).

design was so committed to the ideals of the Stadtlandschaft that it looked as if it was directly cut out of the Kollektivplan. In a 1947 publication, Lingner explained his new design in great detail, explicitly linking it to the Kollektivplan.[17] Lingner's ideas for Tiergarten were based on how he designed all public green areas for the Kollektivplan. The radical Stadtlandschaft—which the Kollektivplan is known for—only covered a small portion of Berlin: its historic center and the area east of Tiergarten is shown in most of the images produced for the plan. The design for the rest of the city was treated with much less detail. Lingner's Grünflächenplan in the Kollektivplan, included in the 1946 exhibition, shows Tiergarten incorporated into a large band of green spaces along the river Spree. Lingner wanted to connect all existing green pockets and form a green city center that would stretch across the whole city from east to west along Berlin's glacial valley (*Urstromtal*) and natural topography (a main feature in the Kollektivplan). Tiergarten in the plan becomes the nucleus of this linear city (*fig. 1*).

Imagining Berlin as a linear city with a wide strip of public green at its center was one of the main design ideas for the *whole* Kollektivplan. Furthermore, this center would consist of two different types of green spaces: the ones that would also feature some buildings were called Parkbebauung (building development as park), and areas of public green without any buildings, which were called Städtische Grünanlagen (municipal green spaces). Tiergarten, was the core of this latter category, whereas most of the city's center would be Parkbebauung. The latter is the concept which Lingner further explored when he published his detailed design for Tiergarten, whose most striking feature is the elimination of almost all buildings—even the building of the Reichstag—and all existing roads inside of Tiergarten, in this way accomplishing an uninterrupted continuity of the park. This was also the biggest difference to Alverdes's design five years later. One area for which Alverdes and Lingner made almost the same proposal is the transitional zone between park and city, where low-density housing frames Tiergarten. In fact, the seamless blending of city to landscape is the key feature of any Stadtlandschaft, and Lingner's and Alverdes's plans show this very clearly (*figs. 2 and 3*).

The idea of gradually morphing park into city was eventually transposed into the design of the Hansaviertel estate, neighboring Tiergarten. The building exhibition "Interbau" from 1957 showcased the Hansaviertel estate as the materialization of the concept of Stadtlandschaft: high-rise and low-density housing seamlessly blending into the landscape park of Tiergarten.

The fact that planners and politicians could use the Stadtlandschaft concept to endorse contrary political positions does not suggest that it had no political content. The direct reference to "nature" made the concept ultimately versatile, having a significant effect on the development of Berlin to the point that many of the city's features owe their existence to it. Similarly to the Hansaviertel estate, ideas from the Kollektivplan materialized in Berlin over the years. Its ghost haunted planners in both East and West Berlin until the mid-1970s.[18]

17 Reinhold Lingner, "Aufgaben und Ziele der Grünplanung," in *Der Bauhelfer* 4, no. 2 (February 1947): 5ff.
18 Two examples for the long-lasting impact of the Kollektivplan are the Kulturforum and the Stadtautobahn. The autobahn highway system for Berlin was one key feature of the Kollektivplan. Undergoing several transformations, the Stadtautobahn is still being discussed today. Like the Kulturforum, the Stadtautobahn is an ongoing building project.

3. THE ORIGIN, MEANING, AND CONTEXT OF THE CONCEPT OF STADTLANDSCHAFT

When the Kollektivplan was unveiled, Scharoun delivered a speech in which he praised the Stadtlandschaft as an expression of freedom and democracy: its apparent contrast to the formal rigidity of Nazi neoclassicism made an ideal concept for rebuilding Berlin, but it was also inherently connected to specific political principles that made it flexible and well adaptable to contrary ideologies.

The term Stadtlandschaft had been used throughout the 1920s only to describe the unplanned suburbanization around cities in Germany. But by 1930, planners were beginning to use it to describe planning ideals.[19] Stadtlandschaft was suddenly perceived as a solution to a problem that had been troubling planners for a long time: the antagonism between city and landscape, nature and culture. Even Friedrich Engels, friend and publisher of Karl Marx, explicitly stated that society could overcome its own injustice only after the duality of city and landscape was resolved.[20] Planners in the Soviet Union were working on the concept of a city that would be tailor-made for socialism, the so-called Sotsgorod which was also intended to be a hybrid city-landscape.[21] It should be noted here that most of the proponents of the Stadtlandschaft belonged to the political left, and the fact that socializing real estate was necessary for this kind of large-scale development resonated well with their politics. Replacing historical Berlin with a Stadtlandschaft, like the Kollektivplan suggested in 1946, had a strong communist connotation, as historical Berlin was not only the city of Hitler's fascism but also of the Prussian Empire and its laissez-faire capitalism.

Many principles found in the Stadtlandschaft also played a central role in the planning strategies of the National Socialists. Konstanty Gutschow's designs for Hamburg made use of it, beginning in 1941. Other notable examples from the Nazi era include those produced by "the task force for planning the reconstruction of bombed cities," assembled by Albert Speer in 1943, the Arbeitsstab für den Wiederaufbau bombenzerstörter Städte. Furthermore, plans with an affinity to the Stadtlandschaft were drafted for the most efficient colonization of occupied territories.[22] Immediately following the invasion of Poland, German planners developed ideas about how to permanently secure German authority in Polish territory. Two main principles took form: low-density settlements would cover much more ground than concentrated cities, and the belief that a nature-like appearance could foster a stronger emotional bond between the new German settlers and the occupied land, as an example, in the plans for modern cities replacing historic Polish towns, drafted by Hans Bernhard Reichow and Wilhelm Wortmann.[23] After 1945, quite

---

19 Franziska Bollerey, Gerhard Fehl, and Kristina Hartmann, eds., *Im Grünen wohnen – im Blauen planen: Ein Lesebuch zur Gartenstadt* (Hamburg: Christians Verlag, 1990), 50ff.
20 Friedrich Engels, *"Zur Wohnungsfrage"* (Berlin: 1948), 13.
21 Elke Sohn, "Zum Begriff der Natur in Stadtkonzepten: Anhand der Beiträge von Hans Bernhard Reichow, Walter Schwagenscheidt und Hans Scharoun zum Wiederaufbau nach 1945" (Hamburg: LIT Verlag, 2008), 178.
22 Reichow and Rudolf Schwarz relabeled their Nazi-era designs as Stadtlandschaft after 1945 and removed all hints that they were originally wartime designs for occupied territories. Reichow had made plans for the Szczecin metro area in Poland and Schwarz for Thionville, France. In contrast, Walter Christaller's plans for occupied Poland were infrastructural schemes, and were labeled under the term *Siedlungslandschaft* (landscape-settlement).
23 Werner Durth, *Deutsche Architekten: Biographische Verflechtungen 1900–1970* (Stuttgart: Krämer, 2001), 168ff, 175ff.

a number of Nazi-collaborating planners just relabeled their designs from the fascist era and called them Stadtlandschaft. This metaphysical twist was possible because the term referred to "nature," a concept that was considered to be something lying beyond the political. Invoking "nature" became a popular tactic among former Nazi-planners to divert attention from their own political past.[24] On the other hand, the Stadtlandschaft and the concept of a "natural" city were highly ambivalent. The Kollektivplan showed strong similarities to plans that were made only five years before under the Nazi regime.[25]

If the Tiergarten redesign that Lingner proposed in 1947 was in essence a piece of Stadtlandschaft that inspired Alverdes's reconstruction work, then the Stadtlandschaft and all its complex historical connotations together with the haunting effects of the Kollektivplan ultimately become the spiritual ancestors of Tiergarten's existing 1950s artifacts.

---

24 Durth, *Deutsche Architekten*, 267.
25 Other notable examples similar to the Stadtlandschaft designs originated at the same time in Great Britain and the United States. The Kollektivplan held a strong resemblance to a design for a future London made in 1941 by the Modern Architectural Research Group (M.A.R.S.). This design also completely replaced the historical London with a new linear city. Niels Gutschow, "Europa: Verbrannte Erde und Zukunft," in *1945: Krieg – Zerstörung – Aufbau. Architektur und Stadtplanung 1940–1960*, ed. Akademie der Künste Berlin (Berlin: Henschel, 1995), 189f. However, the strongest point of reference for the Kollektivplan was probably the work the architect Ludwig Hilberseimer published in the United States. Hilberseimer had previously taught urban design at the famed Bauhaus School in Dessau. By 1929, he was working on design projects for replacing the city of Dessau with a Stadtlandschaft. Hilberseimer continued his studies in the United States and projected his ideas onto American cities like Chicago and Washington, D.C. (*fig. 8*). See Ludwig Hilberseimer, "The New City: Principles of Planning" (Chicago: Theobald, 1944) 196. Ebert, Friedrich, and Scharoun, all members of the Planungskollektiv, remained in close contact with Hilberseimer throughout World War II.

LUISE RELLENSMANN

HERITAGE IS SUBJECT TO CHANGE!

Every place is subject to change and transformation, and, in heritage preservation theory generally, the construction of meaning and cultural significance follows similar modalities everywhere. Tiergarten represents a heritage that goes beyond artistic and historic values, comprising layers and meanings that were created not only officially, for example in the design of the landscape architect Peter Joseph Lenné in the early nineteenth century, but also informally by various users and uses. The contemporary discourse on preservation, rooted in the history and philosophy of conservation, shows ideas that address the complexity and layers of Tiergarten, thus transgressing the preservation practice implemented in the park during the last twenty years.

Taking up Rem Koolhaas's statement projecting a society where *liberté*, *egalité*, and *fraternité* are supplanted by sustainability, convenience, and security,[1] preservation—a discipline only concerned with sustainability—appears to be a field that leaves little freedom for transgressing ideas. However, one could also argue that the "mantra of sustainability" and, respectively, preservation, is not a restriction but a challenge that stimulates creative thinking. In fact, Koolhaas had proven exactly this when he came up with a provocative concept in 2004 in a preservation study for Beijing.[2] This concept could be easily transferred to the landscape of Tiergarten. With the grid system, OMA introduced a different model of preservation that avoids focusing "on the center – as the oldest, the most beautiful and the most historic part"[3] but instead protects random square areas. These squares preserve a section of the urban landscape that is supposedly truly representative of Beijing's built heritage. While everything outside is available to be transformed freely, with these selected areas to be protected, the importance of the decision lies in *what* to preserve, not *how* to preserve it.

Should these areas be frozen in time? A common prejudice against preservation practice is that the preservationist is someone who prohibits others from making any changes to a protected building. If this were the aim, nature, and practice of preservation, every place would *turn into a museum*, which is easier than what preservation actually is. There is not such a thing as a general preservation practice, but certainly, different tendencies within the practice. In fact, there have always been—or at least since philosophers, art historians, or architects have been thinking about it—two different lines of preservation. The Austrian art historian Alois Riegl (1858–1905) described these lines as irreconcilable, namely the direction in favor of restoration in order to achieve a unity in style,[4]

1   This is a reference to the opening of the call for papers for the symposium "Tiergarten, Landscape of Transgression (This Obscure Object of Desire)": "'If future norms of society will be dominated by the mantra of sustainability, convenience and security as opposed to *liberté, egalité, fraternité*, the question is where remains the space for the creative process of transgression,' asked Rem Koolhaas during the opening of the Architecture Biennale in Venice in June 2014. Koolhaas's question is a call to reconsider the urban realm anew, and it is adopted here as a general thematic framework to view and explore Berlin's oldest park understood as a unique and idiosyncratic landscape of transgression. Tiergarten transgresses heritage, ecology, urbanism, and humanism, existing as a precious anomaly, a rogue model challenging questions of future environments in an ever-expanding sea of urbanization. This transgression can become a key for a shift in the established discourse about the city."
2   In 2004 Rem Koolhaas held a lecture titled "Recent Work" at Columbia University, presenting possible preservation strategies for Beijing; see Rem Koolhaas and Jorge Otero-Pailos, "Preservation is Overtaking Us" (transcript of a lecture at Columbia Graduate School of Architecture, Planning and Preservation, 2015), 9–17.
3   See OMA's Beijing Preservation Project, 2003, accessed May 25, 2015, http://www.oma.eu/projects/2003/beijing-preservation/.
4   The term "unity of style" refers in particular to Eugène Viollet-le-Duc (1814–1879) and his practice and writings about restoration. To Viollet-le-Duc, "restoring" meant perfecting given structures to a condition that might not even have existed at the time the structures were built, including new techniques and materials. He published his principles in the *Dictionnaire raisonné de l'architecture française du XIe au XVIe siècle* in 1868; see also: Leo Schmidt, "Architectural Conservation: An Introduction" (Berlin: Westkreuz Verlag, 2009), 27ff.

and the one recognizing the age value, protean, and dynamic character of a monument whose meaning is generated by the value it has acquired throughout time.[5] It seems that the Tiergarten's recent preservation practice follows the first line, as (former) authorities have decided to restore parts of it to an alleged "original state."

TIERGARTEN'S PRESERVATION — PHILOSOPHY AND PRACTICE

Tiergarten is formed by various histories, which existed partly simultaneously: the park was royal hunting grounds throughout the sixteenth century, a Baroque pleasure garden in the eighteenth century, it was used as a landscape park from the late eighteenth to the nineteenth century, and since the 1920s, it has became a popular gay cruising area—in particular, places such as Löwenbrücke and the former Goldfish Pond have been known as hot spots.[6] In its more recent history, streets and pathways were transformed to stage Nazi parades, and the park became a battlefield during World War II. In post-war years, almost all its timber was logged and used as firewood, while its grounds were used as farming and gaming land. Later in the 1950s, it was replanted and then grew wild in the 1970s and 1980s in the shadow of the Berlin Wall, and since the mid-1990s, it has hosted mass public events such as the Love Parade (1996–2003 and 2006) and the "Fan-" and "Festmeile,"[7] attracting hundreds of thousands of people on a single day.[8]

It was only in 1991 that Tiergarten became a historic monument. However, this wide range of histories, uses, and diverse social meanings don't seem to find consideration in the current era of preservation planning. In the years after the German reunification, and particularly in the years between 2006 and 2009, Baroque elements were reconstructed under the lead of Klaus-Henning von Krosigk, the horticulture director of the Berlin Preservation Office from 1978 until 2011. Among other things, "historic" pathways were recreated where the former bypass road was constructed as an underground roadway.[9] Critics have claimed that the rather wild and nature-like character of this part of the park has been lost through these measures.

These interventions in restoration are a testimony of von Krosigk's way of understanding Tiergarten, redesigning it according to plans by Peter Joseph Lenné.[10] The restoration of the Venusbecken (Venus Basin) serves as one example of his preservation measures, which are driven mainly by an aesthetic and "artistic" appreciation of the park, customary to traditional German preservation practice in which the park is interpreted as a mere *Gartenkünstlerisches Denkmal* (an "artistic garden-monument"). The long and narrow water basin situated in the east part of the park originated from the late Baroque garden design of Georg Wenzeslaus von Knobelsdorff. In the late 1830s, Lenné adapted the elongated basin to the fashions of the time—widening its middle part and both ends with rows of chestnut trees at its borders. This part was

---

5 Thordis Arrhenius, "The Fragile Monument: On Conservation and Modernity" (London: Artifice, 2012), 9ff.
6 Several online portals of the gay community quote these particular places as relevant within the scene.
7 From 2006 onward, the Straße des 17. Juni running through Tiergarten between Brandenburg Gate and Großer Stern has been used as a public viewing area for up to 750,000 viewers for large events such as football's World Cup.
8 Sandra Bartoli, "Tiergarten," *Architektur in Gebrauch* 4 (Berlin: Büro für Konstruktivismus, 2014), 30.
9 According to von Krosigk, the Parkpflegewerk by Gustav and Rose Wörner, which had been developed between 1983 and 1993, implemented measures that mainly took into account "park-aesthetic considerations." Klaus von Krosigk, "Der Berliner Tiergarten – Pflege und Entwicklung nach der Wiedervereinigung," in *Berlin im Wandel: 20 Jahre Denkmalpflege nach dem Mauerfall*, ed. Landesdenkmalamt Berlin (Petersberg: Michael Imhof Verlag, 2010), 344.
10 Peter Joseph Lenné (1789–1866) was the landscape architect under the service of the Prussian king Friedrich Willhelm III. Between 1833 and 1840, Lenné turned the Baroque forest of Tiergarten into a landscape park in the English style.

devastated during the battles of World War II. With the challenge of redesigning this former battlefield, Willy Alverdes, the garden director of Tiergarten from 1950 to 1961, integrated the bombed edges of the water basin, transforming it into a softer form,[11] which became known as the Goldfish Pond (fig. 1). The restoration measures directed by von Krosigk also lead to the erasure of the Goldfish Pond: the sludge was removed, the edges were transformed into a straight embankment, and red blossoming chestnut trees were planted as a direct reference to Lenné's design of the early nineteenth century.[12] Not only did von Krosigk sacrifice the work of Alverdes, he also erased a layer which belonged to a time of post-war Berlin (which had been present for more than fifty years at the time of the restoration work) in order to create his own historic interpretation of Tiergarten as a monument. While von Krosigk values the Englischer Garten as an important testimony of post-war garden design in the northwestern part of the park, he does not perceive it as a proper "historic" layer in the history of Tiergarten.[13] To him, the eastern part had lost its historical meaning because of its peripheral location in times of the divided city.[14]

On the occasion of the opening of the district administration of Berlin Mitte, von Krosigk justified this reconstruction in a press release, claiming that the east part of Tiergarten had not been able to live up to its true "historical significance"[15] but that now, the Goldfish Pond was "restored back to its rich and authentic historically developed design based on traditional garden history"[16] (fig. 2).

Back in the nineteenth century, there had been protests against Lenné's planning measures in Tiergarten in "making many clearings, opening meadows and trails."[17] Today, groups such as Steppengarten Berlin,[18] an initiative that takes care of and maintains the plants of the Steppengarten in the eastern part of Tiergarten (a garden also designed by Alverdes), perceive von Krosigk's restoration as a damage and disruption of the design carefully developed in the 1950s.[19]

ASSESSMENT IN THE CONTEXT OF CONTEMPORARY APPROACHES

From the perspective of contemporary heritage discourse and practice, the work of von Krosigk must be discussed critically. Modern approaches to heritage preservation are considering the transformative character of

---

11 Bartoli, "Tiergarten," 50.
12 "Presse-Einladung: Wiederherstellung des Venusbassins (Goldfischteich) im östlichen Tiergarten," berlin.de, press release, November 26, 2009, https://www.berlin.de/bamitte/aktuelles/pressemitteilungen/2009/pressemitteilung.237088.php.
13 The Berlin Preservation Office refers to the measures taken for the existing pool as a "restoration," while according to the definitions by the ICOMOS Australia Burra Charter the recreation of the Venus Basin should instead be categorized as a "reconstruction." (See Article 1.7: *Restoration* means returning a *place* to a known earlier state by removing accretions or by reassembling existing elements without the introduction of new material, and Article 1.8: *Reconstruction* means returning a *place* to a known earlier state and is distinguished from *restoration* by the introduction of new material.)
14 Von Krosigk differentiates between historical design and postwar design: "In all works of heritage preservation (in Tiergarten), it is not only historical elements that should be considered, but also the situations created during the postwar period."See von Krosigk, *"Der Berliner Tiergarten,"* 344. Editor's translation.
15 Von Krosigk, 348.
16 "With the restoration of the Composers Monument, recently completed, this part of Tiergarten, in close proximity to the Straße des 17. Juni, reacquires its rich and *authentic* image, accumulated over centuries of garden history [...] Due to its peripheral location in the urban structure of West Berlin during the postwar years, this Eastern section of Tiergarten had not been able to reconnect with its historical meaning." See "Wiederherstellung des Venusbassins," *berlin.de.* Editor's translation.
17 Bartoli, "Tiergarten," 46.
18 *Steppengarten*, accessed June, 23, 2015, http://steppengarten.de/de/english.html.
19 *Steppengarten*, http://steppengarten.de/de/garten/geschichte.html.

monuments and heritage places. A key document that addresses this issue is the ICOMOS Australia Burra Charter, first adopted in 1979. According to the Burra Charter, preservation aims at retaining the cultural significance of a place, and that is not limited to its aesthetic and historical values alone but embraces social and spiritual values as well. Instead of talking about objects or buildings, the document talks about "places of cultural significance." Their significance is "embodied in the place itself, its fabric, setting, use, associations, meanings, records, related places and related objects."[20]

With the implementation of these diverse dimensions, it becomes clear that the Burra Charter opens a new approach to a field that much too often talks about monuments, or *Denkmale* in German, in a way which automatically evokes images of pedestals and palaces, together with a genius creator or original maker. This latter discourse disregards the fact that most objects or places do not come into existence as monuments but become monuments through human perception and through what people attribute to them.

The Burra Charter therefore puts the people and their perception at the center, asking the fundamental question: For whom do we need to preserve what? From this perspective, the emphasis is on a more holistic understanding of place, which informs different ways of management, successional transformation, and change in the future.

Outside of Australia, the guidelines of the Charter have become increasingly influential in Africa, India, and other countries in Asia. However, they have not been recognized or applied as much in a European context. Looking at Germany, one of the reasons for this dismissal might be the guideline's emphasis on the involvement of the public: an approach that might challenge the authority of the Federal Preservation Office in the definition and interpretation of what is worth protecting and preserving.

Many scholars criticize the fact that the decision of what to protect and preserve is mainly drawn by governmental preservation authorities backed up by organizations such as ICOMOS or UNESCO. Laura Jane Smith, Australian professor in Cultural Heritage Studies, described this phenomenon as *authorized heritage discourse*, which is dominated by professional institutions. Under this sovereignty, only *experts* are allowed to continue to define what heritage is. She claims that this leads to a reduction of the true variety of cultural heritage[21] and criticizes that an authorized heritage discourse puts the public into the role of passive spectators witnessing the decisions of others (those who are entitled to "authority").

Contrary to current *authorized* practice (in Germany), preservation should be a process to be constantly negotiated afresh, conferring in order to retain the cultural significance of places, bypassing the dogma that a place has to be kept in a particular state.

Referring to Alois Riegl's irreconcilable lines in preservation practice, "modern" (second generation) preservation scholars such as Jorge Otero-Pailos from the Columbia University Graduate School of Architecture, Planning and Preservation (Columbia GSAPP) in New York are promoting and performing a practice that discloses and respects dimensions that were never intended to be monumental at all.[22]

In fact, these notions aren't new. The

---

20 The Burra Charter, Article 1.2, ICOMOS (adopted 2013).
21 Laura Jane Smith, *Uses of Heritage* (London: Routledge, 2006), 12f.
22 Jorge Otero-Pailos, "Creative Agents," *Future Anterior* 3, no. 1 (Summer 2006): iii.

architect and art historian Cornelius Gurlitt (1850–1938) already described the density of histories and meanings of places by claiming that a work of art consists of successive acts of creation. Therefore its historic qualities are not represented in a form "belonging to its oldest phase but in the existence and the recognizable sequence of witnesses from as many and as long phases as possible."[23]

What does this all mean for Tiergarten? The preservation work done here can be critically discussed in the light of current preservation ethics and academic discussions on value-based preservation. The approaches discussed suggest that preservation practice does not follow any rigid or strict system. In a value-based approach such as suggested by the Burra Charter, a place or an object is analyzed and interpreted. By understanding the significance of heritage as a social construct, it includes different perceptions of place and thus carries different conclusions on what to preserve and what to give up to change. It also helps us to understand preservation work and approaches to history: any act of preservation unavoidably leaves its own traces, inevitably reinterpreting a place; any action taken is a testimony of individual ideals and understandings of objects and places. Even doing nothing has consequences, leading to decay, or in the case of a park, to "untidy" wilderness, as it was in the case in the east part of Tiergarten bordering the Berlin Wall during the division of the city.

Von Krosigk's approach puts focus on formal and aesthetic aspects of places with the aim of reenacting a specific historical time layer. From a contemporary perspective, the reasons why traces of relevant time and use in the park were not considered worthy of preservation are questionable—as an example, the postwar condition in consideration of Alverdes's design, where the testimony of Tiergarten's apparent neglect and wilderness, in the shadow of the Berlin Wall, could have been respected in the recent management of the park.

Under this light of the Burra Charter, the decisions on how to manage and maintain the park should be taken with the responsibility of various values and stakeholders. The destruction of Alverdes's Goldfish Pond implies the disregard for a significant time span of fifty years. The reconstruction of Baroque axes and water basins follow a purely historicist and formal approach to the park's heritage. This practice disrespects the fact that places may have a range of values for different individuals or groups at different times. Meanings and uses are always manifold and changing, from firewood supplies to popular gay cruising, forming a living heritage of the park that goes far beyond a mere picture of a Baroque park.

Looking at Koolhaas's inspiring project, even though his preservation approach for Beijing did not offer a true solution on how to manage heritage places *into the future*, what he recognized was that throughout the course of preservation history, sociological substance increasingly gained in importance.[24] It is time that institutional preservation practitioners become aware of the creative potential of their own practice. Preservationists should embrace a heritage practice, acting beyond purely material and aesthetic manifestations, and to truly consider and implement the use, associations, and meanings of places.

---

23 Cornelius Gurlitt, *Über Baukunst* (1904), in Schmidt, *Architectural Conservation*, 43.
24 "We then looked at the history of preservation in terms of what was being preserved, and it started logically enough with ancient monuments, then religious buildings, etc. Later, structures with more and more (and also less and less) sacred substance and more and more sociological substance were preserved, to the point that we now preserve concentration camps, department stores, factories and amusement rides. In other words, everything we inhabit is potentially susceptible to preservation." Koolhaas, "Recent Work," in Koolhaas and Otero-Pailos, "Preservation is Overtaking Us," 15.

Goldfish Pond in the eastern section of Tiergarten, 1984.

Venus Basin (former Goldfish Pond) in the eastern section of Tiergarten, 2016.

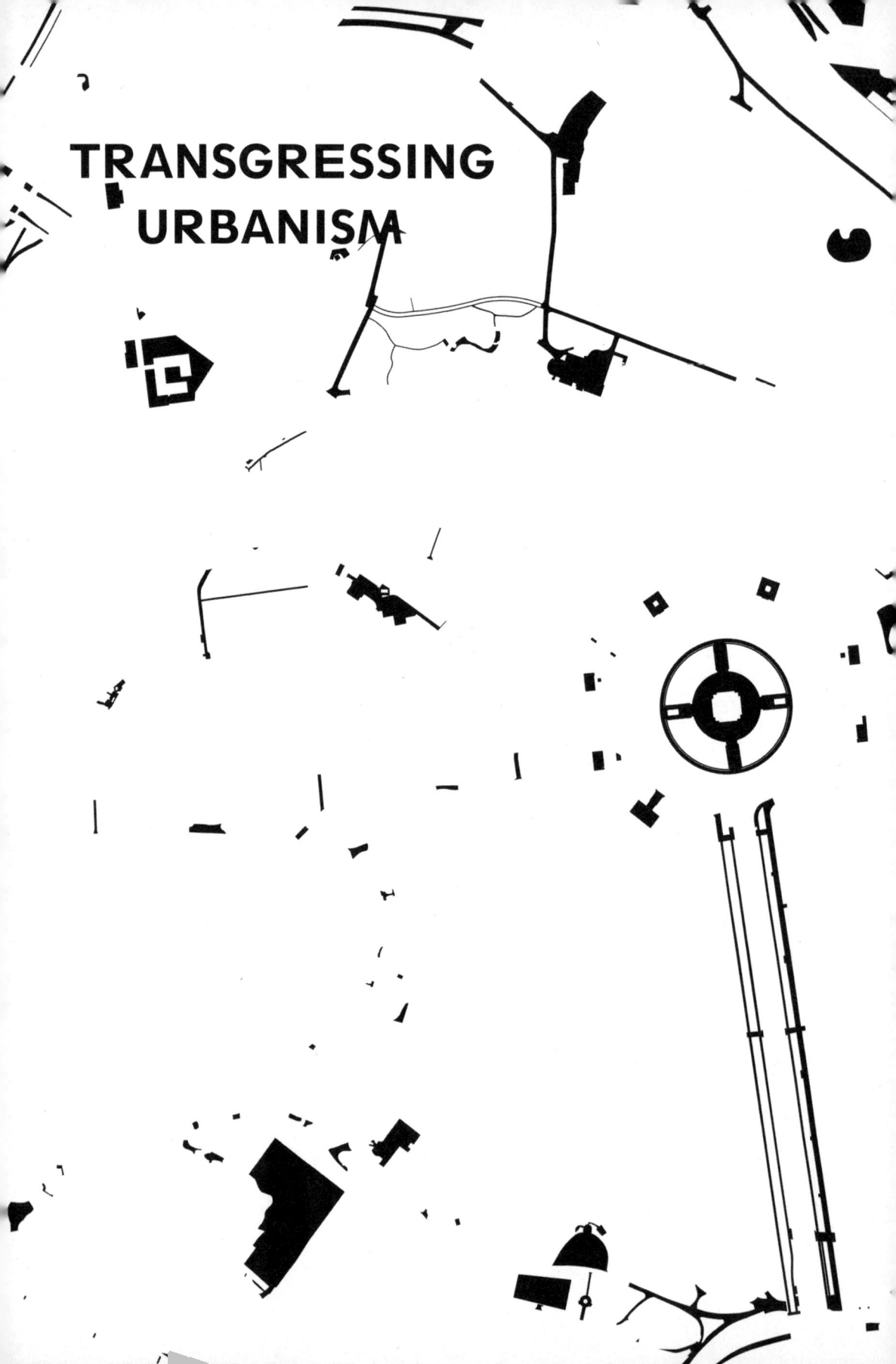
TRANSGRESSING URBANISM

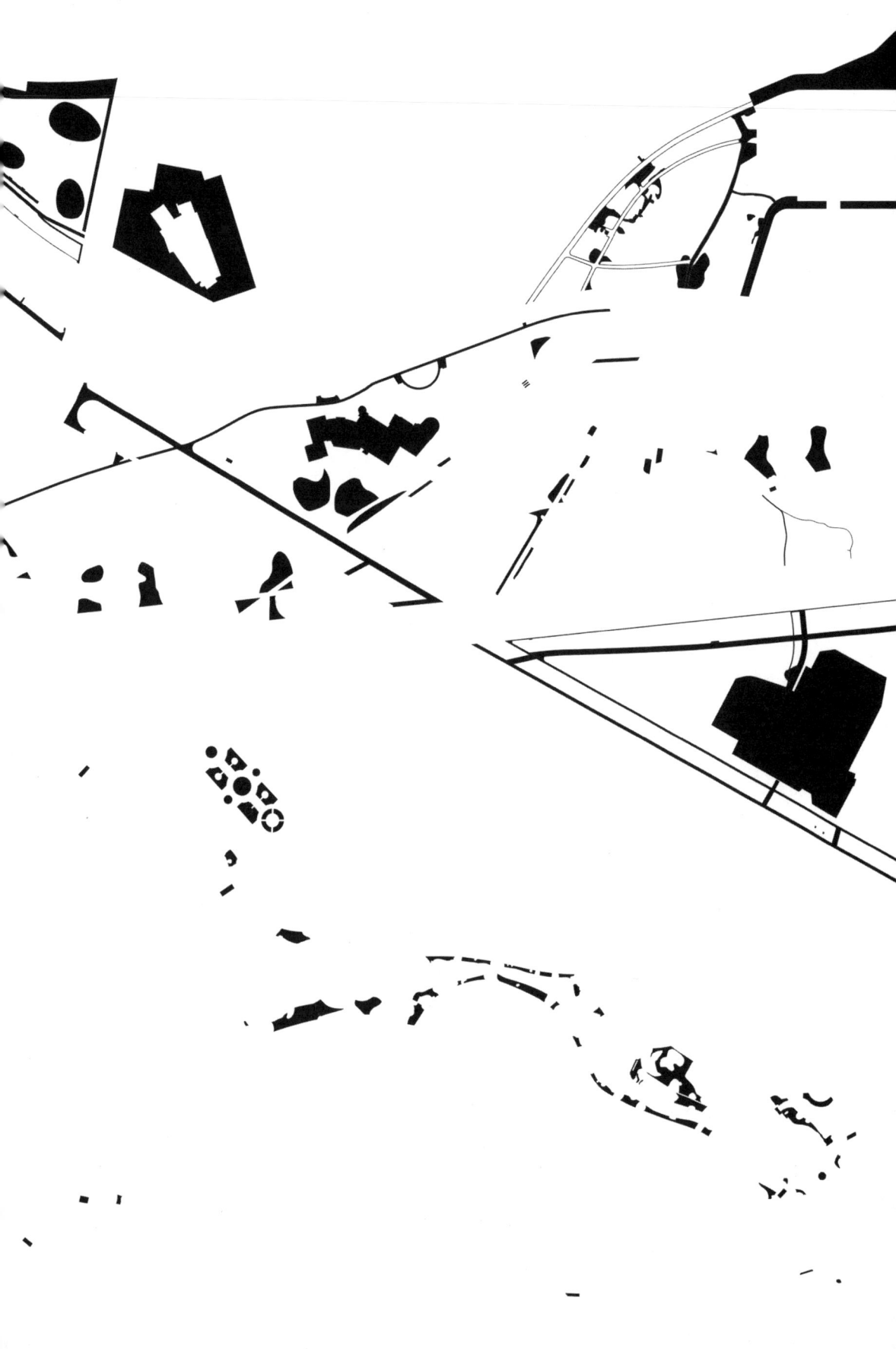

2013: HOMELESS CAMPSITE, TIERGARTEN

2014: FANMEILE WORLD CHAMPIONSHIP, TIERGARTEN

2015: RHODODENDRON GROVE, TIERGARTEN

TRANSGRESSING URBANISM

1760: DANIEL NIKOLAUS CHODOWIECKI, *GESELLSCHAFT IM TIERGARTEN*

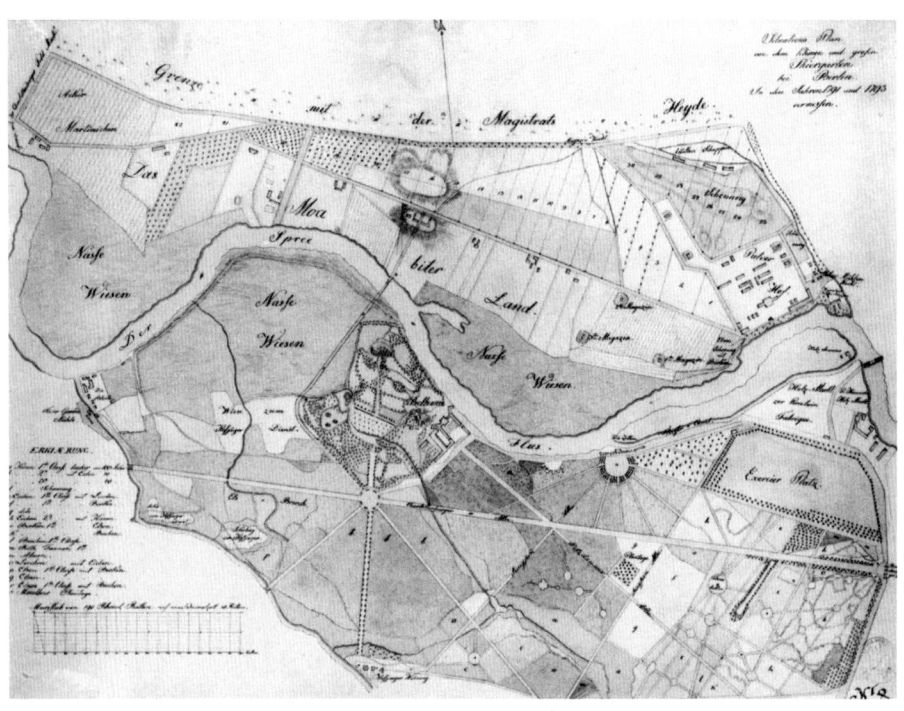

1793: PLAN OF TIERGARTEN WITH A DESCRIPTION OF AREAS AND USE

TRANSGRESSING URBANISM

2013: PICNIC IN TIERGARTEN

FAHIM AMIR

TERMITES OF TRANSNATURALITY: BAMBULE IN HABITAT HAMBURG

> Termites eat shit. Termites build with shit. There is an obvious connection between the dirt and mud and earth of termites and the abject. There is also the contradiction that termites can build and retain a certain sort of order out of shit.
> —Perdita Phillips

As urban landscapes transform across the globe, debates over urban nature and its past, present, and future forms have also introduced fundamental questions about nature's *urbanity*. This article traces the discourses around the ecologically "impossible" termite colony of the city of Hamburg back and forth in time, as a means to address questions of belonging, selfhood, and appropriation in non-innocent and non-ironic terms.[1]

There is a long tradition of literature about insects, both as models and as metaphors for human and more-than-human sociality, sexuality, morality, ingenuity, and politics: "If animals are human Others, insects are the Others of animals, intimately involved in our lives but much maligned."[2] Because of this relationship, insects also have a potential for unsettling cultural notions and imaginations of selfhood: When Africa was mapped and researched by an army of scientists in the eighteenth century, a surprise was in store for the colonialists, as it had already been colonized—by "white ants" (as termites were first called). From then on, legions of ethnographic photographers depicted seemingly "primitive" local humans and their huts next to the sophisticated architecture of these "other Africans," which resembled skyscrapers of comparatively unimaginable heights that left European engineers in perplexed envy.[3]

It was probably shortly after the German Empire had successfully orchestrated a campaign of racial and collective punishment against the Herero and Nama people in the colony of German South-West Africa (modern-day Namibia) at the beginning of the twentieth century when the colonizers themselves were colonized—by termites.[4] The "destructive, wood-munching

---

1 This text is the outcome of two incidents: firstly, it is part of the results of BauBau, a Vienna-based collaborative art research group between architect Christina Linortner and the author, which worked together in 2013 to investigate cases of Hamburg's pigeons, termites, and Shanghai hairy crabs. This research was presented in the form of a lecture-performance entitled *Habitat Hamburg – Unruly Creatures* at Live Art Festival 2013 under the theme "zoo3ooo: Occupy Species." Secondly, participation in the symposium "Tiergarten, Landscape of Transgression (This Obscure Object of Desire)" in 2015 at the Haus der Kulturen der Welt offered the possibility to reflect on the termite-related results of this research and its contexts, and was presented by the author in the talk *Ghost Dogs and Dead Men: Politics of the Habitat*. While the original research had no connection to Tiergarten in Berlin, this text has benefitted immensely from the symposium and hopes to contribute to its spirit.
2 Jake Kosek, "Ecologies of the Empire: On the New Uses of the Honeybee," *Cultural Anthropology* 25, no. 4 (2010): 653.
3 Eva Johach, "Termitewerden: Staatenbildende Insekten im Industriezeitalter," *Kultur & Gespenster* (2007): 21. Soon the otherness of termites was reframed by the "father of termitology," naturalist Henry Smeathman, using a visual rhetoric that balanced familiarity and strangeness in a tropical-pastoral setting, where analysis of the termite society modus operandi offered models of knowledge, control, and improvement also for the human realm. The exploration of these tactics not only rendered the termitarium a valuable object for the inquiries of natural historians but helped make other colonial projects of geopolitical significance intelligible. See Douglas Starr and Felix Driver, "Imagining the Tropical Colony: Henry Smeathman and the Termites of Sierra Leone," in *Tropical Visions in an Age of Empire*, ed. Felix Driver and Luciana Martins (Chicago: University of Chicago Press, 2005), 92–112.
4 For a long time, the termite population was thought to have been *Reticulitermes flavipes (Kollar)* (the Eastern subterranean termite, or in German *Gelbfußtermite*), the most common termite found in North America. Recent research suggests otherwise, and the population in Hamburg seemingly consists of its cousins from Southern Europe, *Reticulitermes lucifugus*. See Udo Sellenschlo, *Vorratsschädlinge und Hausungeziefer: Bestimmungstabellen für Mitteleuropa* (Heidelberg: Springer Verlag, 2010), 49.
5 Nel Yomtov, *From Termite Den to Office Building* (Ann Arbor: Cherry Lake Publishing, 2014), 10.

creatures"[5] were probably introduced to Hamburg through imported wood, adding the rather chilly North European city to a list of territories haunted by termites, which were by then mostly Central and South American, South and Southeast countries. While other explanations for the origin of Hamburg's infestation were initially considered by entomologists,[6] nowadays the consensus is that Germany's first own termite colony developed through the use of imported timber in the boards of a conduit in the municipal heating system.

The newly introduced termites should not have been able to survive a single winter in the cold climate of Northern Europe. Nevertheless, they did, thanks to heterotopic techno-structures newly implemented in parts of the city: 1894 saw the foundation of the Hamburgische Electricitäts-Werke, the local electricity company. The implementation of a district or municipal heating network in the urban ground meant putting otherwise "wasted" energy from the production of electricity to good use, and by 1921, waste heat was being sent through a system of pipes to governmental offices and homes.[7] This public service was not only welcomed by the humans of Hamburg but also provided the termites with a solution to the problem of the cold North European climate. As a German newspaper put it, "The barely isolated pipes warmed the earth, the wood was delicious—the termites were fine."[8] The other problem of living in too-dry wood was successfully solved by the colony itself through the extension of mud tubes into the surrounding soil, thereby providing the termitarium with the essential humidity necessary against the drying out of their thin skin and soft bodies. The termitarium became in fact an ensemble of termitaria, moving through subterranean Hamburg, chewing through wood from the inside with a thousand hungry mouths, and crossing open spaces in protective tunnels made of mud.

The termites had a healthy and thriving colony when discovered in 1937 by a construction worker who had put his jacket near the entry to the teleheating network on a pile of wood—only to see it reduced to a pile of dust, as the local urban legend goes. Not only were the teleheating pipes ideal winter resorts for the termites, they also served as subterranean guiding maps for the colonization of the city; the termites followed the grid of pipes below and worked their way to the trees in the areas of the Karolinenviertel and the Justizforum, where they have been living until today. The termites have chosen two very different habitats: while the "Karoviertel" became in recent years a trendy place to live, with all the known problems of gentrification, the time-honored Justizforum, encompassing three buildings that together form a "U," has not changed much over the years.[9] A city official even tells the story of the worst nightmare of property owners

---

6   F. J. Gay, "Species Introduced by Man," in Kumar Krishna and Frances M. Weesner, *Biology of Termites*, vol 1 (New York: Academic Press, 1969), 483.
7   According to Abraham Margolis, the chief company engineer, the driving force for the project was the high cost of fuel after World War I. But Margolis himself saw much more in district heating: socio-political gains, hygienic aspects, medical merits, and ecological aspects. After been driven out from the management of the company by National Socialists in the 1930s, Margolis settled in the United Kingdom and continued his work at another company that would bring district heating to Pimlico, a London neighborhood. See Wolfgang Mock, "Margolis, Abraham," *Neue Deutsche Biographie* no. 16 (1990): 169f. For an analysis of district heating in Pimlico as an essential part of a neighborhood that functioned as a site of an alternative social order, see Charlotte Johnson, "District Heating as Heterotopia: Tracing the Social Contract through Domestic Energy Infrastructure in Pimlico, London," *Economic Anthropology* 3, no. 1 (2016): 94–105.
8   *Hamburger Morgenpost*, "Termiten-Attacke," February 9, 2009.
9   The three parts of the "U" are Hamburg's Higher Regional Court and its Magistrate and Criminal Court.

becoming real when civil servants discovered that the termites had begun to eat up the land registration files—one thousand tiny Bakunins.[10]

While the files were swiftly relocated, the termites still posed a problem, even after a series of countermeasures taken in the course of the last ninety years, including the protection of houses via the subterranean construction of glass barricades, the use of massive heat to dry the insects out, the removal of whole houses, and the assistance of a research unit of the German Armed Forces that deployed experimental hormone therapy. Nothing helped.[11] While up until the 1980s old tactics of mass poisoning whole areas with highly toxic substances and inserting insecticides of all sorts into brick and wood were common, the newest weapon is *smart poisoning* through "homoeopathic doses" of lethal substances in concentrations low enough to be carried back to the colony and fed to the fellow termites, so that the poison can accumulate over time, unfolding its effect. Through this method, official accounts estimate that 95 percent of the Hamburg termite population was killed in certain parts of the city, but other colonized areas seem to be little affected by either old or new attempts to get rid of them. "Success is always in danger, sometimes the termites don't like the taste of the bait, sometimes a termite-free zone is infested," as it is explained in teaching material for children of age five to ten.[12]

While the termites have certainly cost the city and house owners a considerable sum, termite species have only recently been labeled "invasive." Merely twenty-seven of the 2750 determined termite species considered fall into this category, with trade being the most important single factor for their dispersal.[13] The seemingly obvious inherent quality of invasiveness of certain species is nothing simply and directly observable since it's a question of definition. Since Invasion Ecology is on the one hand a rather young field of research, established as late as 1958, and on the other hand regarded to be particularly "jargon-rich,"[14] it may not come as a surprise that the establishment of a clear-cut definition of what exactly an "invasive" species is took quite some time. It was not before 2006 that a generally accepted definition concerning "invasive species" was agreed upon: "introducing" a species now means that intentional or unintentional human agency assisted in its dispersal; therefore, an "invasive species" denotes "an organism occurring outside its natural, past or present range and dispersal potential." "Invasive" now also refers to "alien organisms that have established in a new area and are expanding their

---

10 It has been the strategic center of all Bakunist attempts of anarchist revolution to destroy as many local records of land registration and bank obligations before the central executive power could restore normal class rule; remember *Fight Club*. Ironically a contemporary anti-termite poison is marketed by BASF under the brand name Termidor®, unintentionally making a connection to Leon Trotsky's coining of thermidor for the counterrevolutionary phase of bureaucratic gains in power against revolutionary masses, as described in *The Revolution Betrayed* (1936). Thermidor was the name for the eleventh month in the French revolutionary calendar, literally meaning "the month of heat," from mid-July to mid-August, and the month in 1794 when Maximilien de Robespierre was overthrown. In the corporate newspeak presented to us on the company website, control means killing, design equals extermination, and lifetime is a registered trademark: "For the best termite control solution, turn to Termidor® HE [...] as seen on *Designing Spaces* on Lifetime®."
11 According to expert interviews with city officials at several departments, conducted by BauBau, April–May 2013.
12 Silke Klöver, *Was hat die Globalisierung mit uns zu tun? Grundwissen erwerben – Zusammenhänge erkennen* (Buxtehude: Persen Verlag, 2011), 21.
13 Theodore A. Evans, Brian T. Forschler, and Grace J. Kenneth, "Biology of Invasive Termites: A Worldwide Review," *Annual Review Entomology*, no. 58 (2012): 457.
14 Theodore A. Evans, "Invasive Termites," in *Biology of Termites: A Modern Synthesis*, ed. David Edward Bignell, Yves Roisin, and Nathan Lo (New York: Springer Verlag, 2011), 520.

range."[15] When Gay published his seminal paper "A World Review of Introduced Species of Termites" in 1967, he didn't regard termites to be "invasive" but only "introduced," since he did not find any termites in areas other than in and around human habitation and structures. For Gay, "invasive" meant that a species had established itself in nonhuman environments, i.e., "nature." This distinction is now regarded to be arbitrary, since it is considered to be only a question of time and the habits of particular species before the surrounding nature is infested too. The historically contested question of invasiveness is closely linked to the notion of habitat that was first used in Carl Linnaeus's *Systema Naturae* (1758), a work that marks the beginning of modern zoological nomenclature. But while the Latin "habitat" meant simply "he/she/it lives" and was used in the form of a verb by Linnaeus, it later ossified and acquired the meaning of a specific spatial territory that could then be trespassed or invaded by "alien, adventive, exotic, foreign, non-indigenous, non-native and novel"[16] organisms, echoing the emergence of nations with fixed, stable, and controlled boundaries. While the allocation of a "natural range" to a certain organism already *naturalizes* nature by denying the organism's social flexibility to adapt, the idea of a "dispersal potential" further reasserts the nature of nature as an atemporal matrix. But there is no nature without culture and no culture without nature, as Donna J. Haraway tirelessly reminds us with her notion of *naturecultures*.[17] In *The Biopolitics of Postmodern Bodies* (1991), Haraway explores medical theories about the immune system and stresses the striking parallels concerning models and metaphors of self-protection, recognition of the inside and outside of the body, and dangers from "within" and from "outside," both terms in use in immunology and cold war politics. Similarly the scientific language addressing natural habitats and invasive species seem to echo a "planet without visas" (Bertolt Brecht), a dubious human privilege expanded onto the nonhuman world.

The dedicated efforts against the termites of Hamburg cannot be reduced to merely rational discourses or practices. As indicated in the opening motto of this text, termites are part of an affective assemblage encompassing Western city dwellers, and their feelings of abject and uncanny affects: the problem with the Hamburg termites is that they also invade our dreams. Hugh Raffles notes in his *Insectopdedia* that "insects are without number and without end." And the nightmares they inhabit seem to be as numerous as the insects themselves. There is the nightmare of "fecundity" and "of the multitude," "of uncontrolled bodies," "of inside our bodies and all over our bodies," "of unguarded orifices" and "vulnerable places," "of foreign bodies in our bloodstream," and "of foreign bodies in our ears and our eyes and under the surface of our skin." Let's not forget "the nightmare of swarming and the nightmare of crawling," the "nightmare of beings without reason and the nightmare of being unable to communicate," "of not seeing the face," and "of not having a face." There is the nightmare "of being overrun," "of being invaded," and "of being alone," "of putting the shoe on and of taking the shoe off," "of the grotesque," "of entangled hair," and "of the open mouth," the nightmare "of randomness and the unguarded moment," "of Osama bin Laden somewhere in a cave."[18]

Both material and semiotic actors, the termites generate a nightmarishly productive

---

15   Evans, 521f.
16   Evans, "Invasive Termites," 521.
17   Donna J. Haraway, *When Species Meet* (Minneapolis, MN: University of Minnesota Press, 2008), 288–92.
18   Hugh Raffles, *Insectopedia* (New York: Pantheon, 2010), 469–73.

uneasiness that, through its temporary specificity and vague affective images, matches a "cloud in the form of a sword"[19]—a cloud that is stuck firmly in the heart of Hamburg. If mosquitoes speak, as Timothy Mitchell argues in his analysis of malaria outbreaks in colonial Egypt,[20] and tsetse flies scream, as Clapperton Mavhunga notes in the context of human and nonhuman entanglements in Zimbabwe Gonarezhou National Park,[21] then the Hamburg termites "make Bambule."[22]

By the time the termites had entered Hamburg, the discourse surrounding termites had drastically changed from admiration to disgust: research showed that, among other things, the termites not only had two stomachs, including a social stomach always ready to be emptied for any other termite of the colony but also that their feces were fed to any colleague in the colony asking for it. This digestive process includes not only otherwise indigestible wood, but also dead skin shed by living termites and the bodies of dead ones. The integrated circuit of bodily functions governing the termite state knows no waste: "From the back as from the front, the feed flows through the whole state continuously, the returning give it to those who stayed at home, the elderly give it to the young ones, in an infinite soup cycle, may the soup be a little strange though."[23] This is nothing less than the horror of total recycling.

The Belgian Nobel laureate, playwright and essayist Maurice Maeterlinck described the astonishing social metabolism of the termite state in *The Life of Termites* vividly: "You see, that's perfect communism, communism of the pharynx and the intestines, which is driven by the collectivism of shit eating. Nothing is lost in this bleak and blossoming Republic, in which the dirty ideal that nature seems to offer us realizes itself in economic terms."[24]

The silviculturist and zoologist Karl Escherich, a staunch Nazi loyalist, took up this thread in his inaugural address as the newly appointed rector of the University of Munich in 1933. His speech was titled "Termite Craze" (*Termitenwahn*), and compared the supposedly good ant system of the Third Reich, to the evil termite system of the Soviet Union.[25]

We have entered the *bestiarium* of politics and, as it seems, there is no alternative, as the historian Boria Sax elegantly points out:

---

19 This is originally Antonio Negri's poetic formulation for the tactical and ontological strengths of the swarming multitude of workers in the rising of contemporary empire, in his theatrical *Trilogy of Resistance*. See Negri, *Trilogy of Resistance* (Minneapolis, MN: University of Minnesota Press, 2011), 29. While Negri's notorious interest in "swarming" was seemingly only aimed at the liberation of humans, more recent works try to redirect the progressive energy of Negri's project also in the direction of nonhumans. See Lewis E. Tyson, "Swarm Intelligence: Rethinking the Multitude from within the Transversal Commons," *Culture, Theory and Critique* 51, no. 3 (2010): 223–38.
20 Timothy Mitchell, *Rule of Experts: Egypt, Techno-Politics, and Modernity* (Berkeley, CA: University of California Press, 2002), 19–53.
21 Clapperton Changanetsa Mavhunga, *The Mobile Workshop: Mobility, Technology, and Human-Animal Interaction in Gonarezhou (National Park), 1850–present* (dissertation, University of Michigan, 2008), 7.
22 "Bambule" was the name of a countercultural trailer park of squatters in the mentioned Karolinenviertel area, where the Hamburg termites also live. Massive protests against the clearing of the trailer park by police gained international media coverage. While "making Bambule" is a north German slang phrase meaning "to go on a rampage," a bamboula was originally a great drum and the dance accompanied by the sound of these drums. Originally from Africa, it was brought to the United States with the slave trade. Haitian revolution slaves would gather in Congo Square, at the edge of the French Quarter in New Orleans, to dance the bamboula. Later, the first swing was titled *The Bamboula*.
23 Wilhelm Bölsche, *Der Termitenstaat. Schilderung eines geheimnisvollen Volkes*, in Johach, "Termitewerden," 31. Author's translation.
24 Originally from 1926, quoted in Johach, "Termitewerden," 34.
25 From the inaugural address at Ludwig Maximilian University of Munich, November 25, 1933. Honoring Escherich's founding role in the field of study, the German Society for General and Applied Entomology has since 1986 awarded the Escherich-medal for outstanding achievements in the field of entomology.

"Every animal is a tradition, and together they are a vast part of our heritage as human beings. No animal completely lacks humanity, yet no person is ever completely human. By ourselves, we people are simply balls of protoplasm."[26]

In both traditional and contemporary political rhetoric, animals are part of greater narratives. As a metaphorical embodiment of three of the loudest war-cries of contemporary capitalism for the home front—diversity, creativity, and sustainability—the honeybee would be a worthwhile candidate for today's "good ant."[27] In a Western context, the culturally constructed and technoscientifically produced domesticity of bees make them a much more probable "poster-insect" of humanity's better management of nature than termites, who always remained alien, neither cherished as pollinators nor as honey producers.[28]

The considerable decline of honeybee populations has been much grieved for in the last years; to counteract this decline means not only fighting the loss of a much cherished genetic diversity but supporting new imperatives of sustainability that aid the honeybee's role of plant pollination and agricultural production. While in 1985 the eco-activists who publicly mounted a beehive on the roof of the Paris Opera were immediately arrested, today it seems there isn't a major cultural institution in the West left without a beehive on its roof to prove its ecological awareness. The animals' work product can also be purchased, bottled into nicely designed glass jars like those in the Haus der Kulturen der Welt museum shop in Berlin. It pays. The millenarian symbol of industriousness has a big comeback in late capitalism's "green phase." Meanwhile, the research network of the US Armed Forces is testing the possible prospects of the further employment of bees as "six-legged soldiers"[29] in the new wars to come, and "as efficient and effective homeland security detective devices,"[30] as the Los Alamos National Laboratory Stealthy Insect Sensor Project Team reports.[31]

But let's go back to our termites for mundane hope. The same year Escherich held his inaugural speech, another biologist, Jean Sutherland, published an article with the description of an unsettling microorganism living in the hindgut of the Australian termite species *Mastotermes darwiniensis* and

---

26 Boria Sax, *The Mythical Zoo: Animals in Myth, Legend, and Literature* (New York: Overlook Press, 2013).
27 Hegemonic models are instable and can suddenly tip over, as in the case of the Africanized killer bee, born in a Brazilian crossbreeding project to swarm out into nightmarish projections of uncontrollable, aggressive immigration in popular culture and beyond. See Anna L. Tsing, "Empowering Nature, or: Some Gleanings in Bee Culture," in *Naturalizing Power: Essays in Feminist Cultural Analysis*, ed. Sylvia Yanagisako and Carol Delaney (New York: Routledge 1995), 113–43.
28 However, in recent years termites have become the objects of a new discourse on artificial intelligence, such as "organic algorithms," since they were viewed as successful in building extremely complicated architectural structures that are continuously adapting, with the aid of very simple brains (see exemplary Evelyn Fox Keller, "It Is Possible to Reduce Biological Explanations to Explanations in Chemistry and/or Physics?," in Francisco José Ayala and Robert Arp, *Contemporary Debates in Philosophy of Biology* (Malden: Wiley-Blackwell, 2010), 28f. For a more pedagogical approach, see James L. Gould and Carol Grant Gould, *Animal Architects: Building and the Evolution of Intelligence* (New York: Basic Books, 2007), 99–146). These structures also increasingly become an inspiration in envisioning green architecture. See Scott Turner and Rupert Soar, *Beyond Biomimicry: What Termites Can Tell Us about Realizing the Living Building*, First International Conference on Industrialized, Intelligent Construction (I3CON), Loughborough University, May 14–16, 2008.
29 Jeffery Lockwood, *Six-Legged Soldiers: Using Insects as Weapons of War* (Oxford: Oxford University Press), 2008.
30 Kosek, "Ecologies of the Empire," 656.
31 The contemporary regional architectural trope of "learning from" is not exclusive to this field, nor it is innocent; for an exploration of ways the honeybee was made a symbolic and material resource for military technology and battlefield tactics by the US Armed Forces during the Bush administration, see Jake Kosek, "New Uses of the Honeybee," in *Global Political Ecology*, ed. Richard Peet, Paul Robbins, and Michael Watts (London: Routledge, 2011), 227–51.

named it *Mixotricha paradoxa*, meaning "the paradoxical being with mixed-up hairs."[32] While Escherich's demonization of termites based on their intestinal system is now only of historical interest, Sutherland's discovery was recently brought into the spotlight in debates about politics and culture. The paradox and recent attraction of *M. paradoxa* lies in its make up as a composite organism with four kinds of entities living inside and on it, which is why it has five genomes. As Donna J. Haraway summarizes, "This little filamentous creature makes a mockery of the notion of the bounded, defended, singular self out to protect its genetic investments. The problem our text presents is simple: what constitutes *M. paradoxa*? Where does the protist stop and somebody else start in that insect's teeming hindgut? And what does this paradoxical individuality tell us about beginnings? Finally, how might such forms of life help us imagine a usable language?"[33]

Is *M. paradoxa* one, five, or 250,000? In times where social questions are increasingly racialized and culturalized, this tiny organism "engenders key questions about the autonomy of identity."[34] *M. paradoxa* has already left the scholarly papers of natural sciences and keynote ironies of politicized conferences and entered the stage of national theaters, as in the case of René Pollesch's *Das purpurne Muttermal* (The purple birthmark) from 2006. Paraphrasing Haraway, Pollesch asks us to look into the hindgut of termites for new answers for problems of nationalism and identity politics when old answers seem to work less and less.[35]

There is the obvious danger of "biological exuberance" in seeing too much subversive potential in "nature's rainbow,"[36] but since the questions of who belongs where, who has the right to live where, and under what conditions very often take up metaphors, models, and energy from the realms of nature, these "contaminations"[37] must be met with counter-contaminations: why not look for such counter-contaminations where other contaminations have already taken hold, considering the perplexing and non-innocent complexities that come with them, as in the case of the "impossible" Hamburg colony of termites and the "companion species"[38] who have learned to live in and with them. The termites of Hamburg didn't care if they belonged to Europe or not, they also didn't care about the artificiality of the district heating that made their survival possible. There is something to learn here. While questions of political pedagogy in the narrower sense cannot be addressed here sufficiently, art-based approaches of "learning from termites" already show possible ways to continue on these paths. The curatorial collective Ethnographic Terminalia compares its own practice to the way termites "erode the planks of an old house: feeding on its structural foundations, carving out tunnels to create a self-propagating, subterranean autonomous zone, spreading slowly

---

32 Jean L. Sutherland, "Protozoa from Australian Termites," *Quarterly Journal of Microscopical Science*, vol. 2 (1933): 76.
33 Donna J. Haraway, "Otherworldly Conversations; Terran Topics; Local Terms," *Science as Culture* 3, no. 1, (1992): 94.
34 Myra Hird, *Sex, Gender and Science* (Houndmills: Palgrave Macmillan, 2004), 68.
35 Franziska Bergmann, "Enacting Theory: Zur theatralen Rezeption humanwissenschaftlicher Diskurse bei René Pollesch am Beispiel von Das purpurne Muttermal," in *Theorie und Theater: Zum Verhältnis von wissenschaftlichem Diskurs und theatraler Praxis*, ed. Astrid Hackel and Mascha Vollhardt (Wiesbaden: Springer Verlag, 2014); see *Das purpurne Muttermal* (program guide) (Vienna: Burgtheater/Akademietheater Wien, 2006), 53–68.
36 Nikki Sullivan, "The Somatechnics of Perception and the Matter of the Non/human: A Critical Response to the New Materialism," *European Journal of Women's Studies*, no. 19 (2012): 306.
37 Brian Massumi, *A User's Guide to Capitalism and Schizophrenia: Deviations from Deleuze and Guattari* (Cambridge, MA: MIT Press, 1992), 93.
38 Haraway, "Otherworldly Conversations."

and unnoticed."[39] And the artist Perdita Philipps notes: "Entangling ourselves with the alternative (destructive, cryptic, potentially immortal, coprophagous) acts of termites can open up environmental art to different emotional registers and facilitate critical hope."[40]

The notion of transculturality has recently gained traction in debates about immigration and globalization to describe cultural and social processes not in the epistemic categories of self-contained ensembles crashing against each other (as presented in Samuel Huntington's notorious *Clash of Civilisations* [1996]), but as in-it-self always already transgressing notions of purity and selfhood. The time is more than ripe for an analog theory of transnaturality[41] that promises to strengthen our ability to address questions of "nature" and "culture" as inseparable and relational— not as a new skin for the old wine of "leaving nature behind through technology," but to bring nature's resources "in" to enable us to produce more adequate accounts of the naturecultures that surround us and maybe even to envision inhabited worlds that are less exclusive and fearful.

---

39 Thomas Ross Miller, "Ethnographic Termini: Of Moments and Metaphors," *Visual Anthropology Review* 27, no. 1 (2011): 75.
40 Perdita Phillips, "Thirteen Figurings: Reflections on Termites, From Below," *Animal Studies Journal* 5, no. 1 (2016): 23.
41 Another candidate term for this politico-epistemic vector would be *hypernaturality*. While the latter comes with pop-cultural associations (for example, the famous song of the German band Scooter from 1994), the "trans" in transnaturality also transports the notion of social and political change. For discussions of global transcultural modernity in architecture and arts, see *Transcultural Modernism*, ed. Model House Research Group (Berlin: Sternberg Press, 2013) and Christian Kravagna, *Transmoderne* (Berlin: b_books, 2017).

SANDRA PARVU AND PIERO ZANINI
LANDSCAPE AS A MEANS OF QUESTIONING THE TEMPORAL FRAMES OF URBAN PLANNING

Thoughts on the city developed in the practice of landscape design have in recent years offered a new perspective on the temporal dimension inherent to any urban transformation. Our starting hypothesis is that the way landscape architects think about time provides significant food for thought with respect to urban planning. Landscape designers are not usually the most involved in the design of cities, more traditionally carried out by urban planners trained as architects.[1] However, comparing the results of various studies we have conducted over the past decade show that their approach helps emphasize in a critical and comprehensive way the current limits of large-scale planning.[2] One of the issues often missed by urban planners are the perceptions and experiences of the people living on land undergoing long-term transformation. Can they be considered as a part of the project?

The increased scale of metropolitan projects today, and the dilation of their implementation over time, raise concern among residents and are prompted as much by the expectations and hopes inspired by the project as by fears for the future of their everyday lives once the project is completed. The results of our research show a correlation between the temporal experience of landscape architects and that of residents. The operational time of the urban project is in strong contrast to both. In other words, the temporal frame in which a landscape starts making sense, in the residents' perception for instance, is not confined to the time of the project. Out of these different "times," distinct positions appear, especially in regard to the relationship between the "time of the project," the "time of construction," and the "time of maintenance." Most of the fieldwork interviews conducted with residents of Grand Paris—the name of a metropolitan area but also of an urban project with 2030 as a temporal horizon—point out the superposition and coexistence of these times. Their daily experience of this transformation has a thickness that reflects the forces at play on the territory. It follows a different logic from that imposed by budgetary constraints and administrative protocols. These two different logics, or conceptions of time, are at play: the time of the residents and landscape architects could be described as poly-chronic, and the time of urban planners and administrators could be seen as relatively more "linear" and "one-dimensional." Without ignoring the very real pressures of budgeting and administrative supervision, how can large scale planning take into account the residents' way of living through this specific period of time?

In this article, we will examine how the dialectical dimension inherent to the landscape approach mobilizes a knowledge and expertise able to probe this question. This quality of the landscape project was first discussed by Robert Smithson in "Frederick Law Olmsted and the Dialectical Landscape"[3] in the context of Central Park in New York. For him, the park "can no longer be seen as 'a-thing-in-itself', but rather as a process of ongoing relationships existing in a physical

---

1 In the current context, this is an emerging trend among landscape practitioners responsible for the design of master plans and large territorial projects, such as with James Corner in New York and Qianhai, Latz + Partner in Tel Aviv, West 8 Urban Design and Architecture in Guangzhou, and Michel Corajoud and Michel Desvigne in Lyon.
2 The research studies conducted at the Architecture and Anthropology Lab at Lavue UMR 7218 CNRS, Université Paris Ouest Nanterre to which we refer are: Alessia de Biase, Nancy Ottaviano, Piero Zanini, *Qualifying Transformation or How Is Quality of Life Designed as an Idea in the Future of the Grand Paris Project?* (Paris: Urban D/FEDER-EU, 2010–12); Sandra Parvu, *Landscape Project and Visual Culture* (post-doctorate thesis, ENSP Versailles); Alessia de Biase, Cristina Rossi, Alice Sotgia, Piero Zanini with Sandra Parvu, *Tales from a Landscape: An Anthropological Approach to the Landscape Atlas of the Seine-Saint-Denis* (DRIIE, UT93-DRIEA, CG93, 2014–16; Paris: éditions Laa Recherche, 2016).
3 Robert Smithson, "Frederick Law Olmsted and the Dialectical Landscape," *Artforum*, February 1973.

region—the park becomes a 'thing-for-us.'" The question we address is how the potential of this manifold of ongoing relationships, as unexpected and contradictory as they may appear, can be taken into account "at all levels of human activity, be it social, political or natural" in the large-scale urban project.

Several studies and social-science conferences have highlighted the various temporal horizons of expectation and logic of the actors involved in the urban project.[4] They do not however specifically explore the differences between each design discipline, and more particularly, that of landscape architecture. What is the latter made of? What does it reveal about time as an opportunity and project tool? Conversely, how does it apprehend the time constraints, often divergent, that accompany any urban project? Traditionally speaking, projects have had the purpose of "arresting time," of imposing one form, one point of view upon many, thus producing a common object of knowledge shared by a community. How do landscape architects who have the knowledge, among other things, to work with live materials, question this static dimension of form? How does that impact the understanding of urban transformation at large?

THE FORGOTTEN FRAME

Any large-scale transformation planned in the densely built and inhabited territories of the Grand Paris region entails major changes for the lives of many residents. By definition, a *project* forcefully thrusts a "vision" inscribed in the present forward into the future. The degree of violence of the jump between what exists and what is planned depends on its scale and the proportional effort of abstraction required to comprehend its proposal: the more the potential charge of the project is moved to a distant future, the higher the tension between the proposed horizon and the day-to-day lives of the residents. This tension is related to the length of time dedicated to construction, but also to the possibility of new economic and political realities generated by the project. In seeking to initiate a leap forward, planners tend to ignore the conditions of the present. This oversight coincides with a failure to integrate the current residents into the process, thus leading to unease among the latter and a lack of understanding regarding the rhythms and the periods of activity and idleness that characterize construction. Residents often express the feeling of a time that is not going anywhere, a time suspended and spent in an often incomprehensible wait.

Landscape designers are aware of what waiting means. If they are designing a garden, they know it may take years for the trees and other plants to grow and for the reality to catch up with their design. Gilles Vexlard[5] recalls that one of his concerns is

---

4   In the recent "temporal turn" taken by social sciences, and the interest in having it contribute to the development of architectural and urban research, quite a few publications and lectures address the question of time, temporality, and rhythm in urban design as an aesthetic quality or an experience to reach, but little has been said about time as a project tool. In France, a few publications and conferences have addressed the topic. Publications include: Yannis Tsiomis, *Échelles et temporalités des projets urbains* (Paris: Jean-Michel Place, 2007); Sandra Mallet, "Aménager les rythmes: politiques temporelles et urbanisme," *EspacesTemps. net*, March 14, 2013, https://www.espacestemps.net/en/articles/amenager-les-rythmes-politiques-temporelles-et-urbanisme/; *Échelles et temporalités des projets urbains: Un enjeu pluriel entre conception et perception* (PUCA, Paris, May 22–23, 2007); *Quelle(s) temporalité(s) prendre en compte dans un projet urbain durable?* (PUCA, Paris, June 10, 2013).
5   Gilles Vexlard was a cofounder in 1976 with Laurence Vacherot of the French landscape architecture practice Latitude Nord in Paris. He has received numerous awards for his work in France and Germany, including first prize from the Bund Deutscher Landschaftsarchitekten (2005), and the Topos International Urban Landscape Award (2006) for the Riemer Park in Munich, and the Grand prix national du paysage (2009).

to rapidly provide playgrounds and parks to avoid always having to tell the incoming residents that they must wait another three decades to enjoy the spaces he designs.⁶ The landscape architect is thus de facto in the position of having to think about all the time frames relevant to the project. If the promise implicit in every project sets in motion the imaginary, the performative dimension of its utterance is however not enough. Even when the promise is kept, the problem arises not so much from the gap created by the promise between a present and a future, but in the fact that this envisioned leap sets aside the continuity of an existence and the time in which lives are spent.

When this happens, feelings of uncertainty and economic insecurity increase. A recurring semantic field in the residents' testimonies emphasizes "the destabilizing character of construction works and the interim period they represent," "the feeling of insecurity," "the difficulty of finding an anchor," and the question of knowing whether "things will change or will stay like they are."⁷ For the residents subject to urban projects, it is difficult to navigate between the things that change, the time in which the change occurs, and the permanence of the structural problems that touch their everyday lives. The present becomes a temporality in which the inertia and stability of daily routines are constantly shaken by surprises, good and bad, related to programmatic changes characteristic of long-term projects. In the case of the Grand Paris project, administrators (and sometimes practitioners too) stamp their plans with dates such as 2025 for the extension of a subway line, or 2030 for the construction of the Grand Paris Express. While that does not pose any problem to them, residents do not even know whether they will be able to continue living where they are because of the rent and local tax increase connected precisely to these infrastructural developments and the logic of concentric growth specific to Paris.

Added to this is the more concrete disjunction "between the time of decision and the time of construction which often incomprehensibly extends already distant time limits."⁸ For designers, this disjunction leads to a questioning of the purpose and intentions of a project: the time span between the design of a program and its actual implementation, according to Nicolas Bonnenfant,⁹ creates obsolescence, since buildings become available ten years after they were needed for a population which may have since changed.¹⁰

CHECKING TIME

Although city planning is a discipline intended to organize the temporal aspects of urban transformation, today these times are subject to factors and changing speeds whose political dimension goes beyond the competences and authority of designers. This limitation becomes manifest in the increasing gap between the discourse of city planners, its ideals, and the ambivalent effects of their actual projects on the lives of residents. The first-hand experience of landscape architects and inhabitants alike highlight the magnitude of the gap and reveal the challenge of mastering a project on a formal as well as an economic level (as

---

6   Vexlard, interview in Parvu, *Landscape Project and Visual Culture*.
7   Interview excerpt with a resident, in de Biase et al., *Tales from a Landscape*.
8   Interview excerpt with a resident, in de Biase et al., *Qualifying Transformation*.
9   Nicolas Bonnenfant was a cofounder in 1999, with Pablo and Miguel Georgieff, of *Coloco*, a collective of landscape architects, urbanists, botanists, and gardeners based in Paris whose main specificity is to invest and accompany their projects by physical realization in situ.
10 Nicolas Bonnenfant, excerpt from an interview in Parvu, *Landscape Project and Visual Culture*.

with the dynamic evolution of incomes, land prices, and costs of living). Faced with too many uncontrollable budgetary, political, and formal changes due to the extension of projects over several years, some landscape designers have chosen to prioritize certain elements of their project, starting from the idea that everything drawn does not have the same value. To make sense of their project in the context of so many contingencies, they put in place a strategic phasing of the different stages of the worksite not so much as a means of following a construction rationale, but as a necessary tool to ensure the readability of the project in time. This position is however subject to critique by other practitioners in the landscape discipline as they find this form of planning problematic in that it continues to presuppose an unrealistic degree of control over the situation.

This is Gilles Clément's point of view. For him, in order to plan, the idea that planners make the presumption that everything between the moment they finalize their drawings and the point when they materialize is under control, and the idea that nothing will escape their intentions is an illusion. Projects are constantly derailed by unforeseen events.[11] In spite of the awareness that numerous accidents shape the transformation process, large-scale and long-term urban projects continue to be solidly anchored on this presupposition. From the opposite perspective, quite a few landscape designers think their current contribution to planning could be their capacity to drop the pretense of control in favor of the capacity to navigate between the day-to-day evolution of a situation and a longer-term intentional project. Clément's view of urban design critiques the limitations produced by the temporal organization of space within a plan. The illusion of control over the reality that emerges from the drawing board results in a belittling of the contribution of other design disciplines. In contrast to a vision of transformation he describes as technocratic, his landscape practice highlights a more tentative approach which assumes inaccuracies between what is represented and the reality on the ground.

Two positions can be therefore identified on how to conceive of time as a project tool: if in one case time is mobilized as an operational tool, in the other its purpose consists of making us take stock of the limits of any planning. The lives of residents touched by urban transformation are shaped by this tension between the mastery of time and acceptance of the diversions it produces. Faced with the unpredictable and uncertain effects brought about by radical changes of their environment, some people point to the difficulty, if not refusal, to project themselves even into the near future. To control the situation in this case means to know whether one can continue to live in one's house in the neighborhood where social ties and habits are woven.[12] As underlined by various testimonies, renovation comes at a cost and often leads to population change. While land prices rise, people fear they will be forced to move out. Thus, the apprehension is not related to urban projects as such, but given their scale and the phenomena they trigger, rather to the feeling of dispossession felt by residents and designers alike in regard to the control and monitoring of the new reality drawn by the project.

THE PRESENT CONTINUOUS

If landscape designers are sensitive to this "meanwhile"—this continuous present—how

---

11 Bonnenfant, excerpt from an interview, in Parvu, *Landscape Project and Visual Culture*.
12 Points of view expressed by various residents in interviews conducted during research, in de Biase et al., *Qualifying Transformation*.

do they attempt to position time as a way of problematizing urban planning rather than as a dimension with which one has to put up? In other words, are there ways to represent and visualize time in order to give it a consistency and materiality that enables inhabitants to work with it? Since planners and residents do not share the same temporal framework, the challenge consists not only in how to give a presence to the residents on the horizon of a long-term project but also how to make them feel part of it. In the case of the Grand Paris research, residents are not a priori against urban transformation. However, they pay attention to what they perceive of as a repetition of something already experienced in their recent past and, as a consequence, whose effects they can already predict. In this sense, they oftentimes perceive the transformations carried out by the project as a "sterile future." This perception of sterility is largely the result of the linear approach to time on the part of administrators and designers, who inevitably oversimplify reality in order to erase certain problems they do not know how to face.

One aspect of the problem of reconciling different horizons and orders of time is the unacknowledged distance between an existing reality and the project of transforming it. As discussed previously, urban projects by definition must necessarily distinguish themselves from what is there. If not, they would not be called a project and would not call for a prospective transformation. This is our architectural tradition. However, certain landscape practitioners have opted to jettison this tradition in favor of an attempt to blur the boundary between "what is" and "what will be." The shuffling of temporal frameworks is best synthesized in the following statement by Clément: "I often wondered whether I should draw my projects before or after I have built them."[13] Since most urban planners are trained architects, the relation to the existing environment is one of receiving an object that has a relation to the context, but that is distinguished from it. Most architectural curricula are based upon a distinction between process and form, place and program, context and object. Clément's statement makes these distinctions problematic insofar as they do not draw a line between what exists (the context) and the changes he wants to bring (the project).

In linguistic and cognitive sciences, context[14] is not characterized by its capacity to receive something (object or subject alike), but for its interactive dimension.[15] The context is not the site, but the project and the site growing together. The context comes out of making a project with and during the site, so to speak. Therefore a conversation can take place between forces, forms, appearances, relations, and also, times. In this sense, the idea of "'context'" acquires a generative dimension. For some landscape designers, this dimension is pushed to an extreme, as it materializes in their on-site practices through gestures such as drawings made without the mediation of scale or other support than the ground.[16] Over long periods of time, the process of thinking, designing, and drawing is intrinsically part of a dialogue with the site, because it is in its presence that all these actions are conducted and acquire their meaning. In this process, site and project literally coexist in time and space. The designer becomes one of the many

---

13 Gilles Clément, "Le geste et le jardin," *Paysage & Aménagement*, no. 7 (1986): 8–15.
14 Alessandro Duranti, and Charles Goodwin, eds., *Rethinking Context: Language as an Interactive Phenomenon* (Cambridge: Cambridge University Press, 1992).
15 Duranti and Goodwin, *Rethinking Context*.
16 Alain Freytet is a French landscape architect whose practice is based in the Limousin region, 150 km south of Paris. His practice crosses a large spectrum of scales spanning the realization of landscape atlases to the design and mapping of protected areas on the Atlantic coast and the Mediterranean.

agents contributing to the continuous dynamics of transformation that are at work in a context. For instance, Pablo Georgieff[17] describes the construction of calendars in which time becomes a tool "to provoke, build, bring into resonance, and make visible, things that can be shared."[18] The effort to visualize time in a synchronic way opens up the project to the possibility of seizing opportunities and entering into a dialogue with multiple layers and temporal registers.

"WHAT PERISHED NEED NOT ALSO BE LOST."[19]

The articulation of multiple time frames manifests itself in the research *Paysage en récit: Pour une approche anthropologique de l'atlas des paysages de la Seine-Saint-Denis* (2014–16) in which we worked with Atelier de l'île, a team of Parisian landscape architects, to produce a landscape atlas for the Seine-Saint-Denis, a territory north of Paris. Conceived by the administration as a "knowledge tool" in contrast to more operational project tools such as landscape plans, landscape atlases have to be produced and updated every ten years by a multidisciplinary team under the supervision of a landscape architect. The official method supported by the French Ministry of Environment has been the object of some discussion precisely because it seeks to introduce a boundary between the production of knowledge and the production of the project: from the point of view of designers, projects also produce knowledge and hence this distinction cannot be made. Many have criticized the landscape atlases for failing to recognize this ambiguity, underlining the fact that traditional geographic atlases are commonly conceived of as a sum of "static" knowledge synthesized at one point in time, and maintaining that landscape dynamics cannot be addressed through this lens. Participating in the production of such an atlas was for us a means of critically reflecting upon the status and role atlases should fulfill.

In the case of the Seine-Saint-Denis, this point is even more relevant, since it is a densely populated urban territory undergoing a major transformation. It becomes therefore unclear what is to be put in the atlas. What is there now? What will be there in the future? Or should we be asking a different question altogether? In this respect, we see this research as an opportunity to study the temporal conjunctions at work between residents, landscape designers, and multi-level administrators. However, the local administration invited us to join this experimental team initially in order to investigate the perception of residents and experience of the landscape from an anthropological point of view. As expected, residents recurringly describe their landscape, or what they perceive as such, as a place that awaits a transformation. They are caught in an interstitial time which articulates what is there with a more or less defined future of what will be there. Due to continual changes, places are fragile, and familiar reference points mostly disappear. In the eyes of the residents, this fragility mirrors their own feelings of uncertainty and precariousness. The rapid-paced transformation also reduces these experiences as residents feel they are confronted with an out-of-reach temporal or spatial scale, including the public media projection of negative images on a historically industrial territory inhabited by working migrant classes, long sequences of building sites, and the dismissal of the day-to-day lives of the residents in administrative decisions. All

---

17 Pablo Georgieff is a cofounder of the multidisciplinary team Coloco.
18 Georgieff, interview in Parvu, *Landscape Project and Visual Culture*.
19 Marilynne Robinson, *Housekeeping* (New York: Farrar, Straus and Giroux, 1980).

these pragmatic constraints, but also the production of mental and physical images, create a relation to the surroundings that is hostile and that rejects the possibility of a landscape experience.

More interestingly, the residents sometimes describe the experience of landscape as something originating from an immersed corporeal presence in the surrounding reality. It becomes more intense via details, even though fragile, that act like "landscape metaphors" capable of opening up a path into a world of associations and memories: in an urban context, grass blades growing in the middle of a street may lead to a landscape experience. What comes out of the research is the capacity of residents to come to terms with extremely varied temporalities. More specifically, they define the landscape as a way of finding in their active horizon traces of what has disappeared and continues to contribute to the poetry of their everyday. In the words of a resident, when people at the end of their lives have the feeling that the landscape is the opposite of what it was at the beginning, remembered landscapes become an active part of what one actually sees.[20] Numerous residents describe their experience of the landscape as something informed by the history of the changes that occurred while they lived in the Seine-Saint-Denis and contrast it with the lack of such experiences for newcomers who only see what is there in the present.

CONCLUSION

Reading in parallel the testimonies of the residents, which constitutes a significant part of our fieldwork, with the approach of landscape designers proved fruitful insofar as the different experiences and critical-thought process they share problematize urban transformation.

More specifically, at the core of their concerns is the way in which time is invested, questioned, translated, and apprehended by the rhythms, temporalities, and timeframes of large urban projects. Our investigation has enabled the identification of two poles. On the one hand, not taking into account the day-to-day presence of residents experiencing the negative impact and constant changes of their environment over long periods affects the dynamics and future livability of the territories on which these changes take place. In other words, the financial consequences and political decisions that may lead to a radical displacement of the population contribute to maintaining a superficiality of the relation residents build to the place where they live and therefore weaken these territories. On the other hand, taking into account the present tense and the already existing living conditions should not lead to a reduction of the temporal horizon, but on the contrary, to opening it up to an awareness of the tensions that may arise between contradictory temporalities at work.

---

20 Interview excerpt with a resident, from de Biase et al., *Tales from a Landscape*.

MICHAEL BAERS

TIERGARTEN: A CRIME STORY

That an urban park makes an uncanny setting for murder is the central conceit of *Blow-Up*, Michelangelo Antonioni's film from 1966, in which a fashion photographer, Thomas, thinking he is documenting frolicking lovers in a south London park, inadvertently records an assassination on film. Upon enlarging his exposures, he discovers he has captured the assassin lying in wait, concealed in some bushes, the apparent collusion of the gentleman's paramour, and some frames later, the assassinated man's dead body sprawled beneath a tree. From this point forward the film's plot revolves around a process of evidence found and evidence lost. By the time Thomas has finished in the darkroom, night has fallen. He returns to the park, finds the actual murdered body, lying as yet undiscovered, and upon returning to his studio, discovers it ransacked, and all the prints and negatives produced earlier in the day stolen, save for one grainy, nearly abstract print showing the dead man's body crumpled in a corner. Near dawn, Thomas returns to the park to find that the corpse has also disappeared. In the interim, while the filmic spectator is left in no doubt that a murder has occurred, Thomas's own sense of "the real" has become increasingly tenuous and the public urban park, that anomalous spatial typology ordinarily composed of the most decorous, docile natural forms, a kind of unnatural nature, plays a central role in his growing sense of this irreality.

This brief summary of *Blow-Up*'s plot serves as a fitting introduction to my theme, that of the phantasmatic semiotic instability of the city under the pressures of late capitalism, where the pressures of redevelopment produce all sorts of disappeared corpses. A careful watching of the film reveals this is a far from incidental concern. It is foregrounded, in fact, by Antonioni's depiction of London as a city in the midst of massive urban redevelopment, littered with wrecking balls and construction cranes, the gritty London of the industrial age in the process of being reshaped into an urban playground for the young and privileged. One can read in Antonioni's repeated use of building sites and derelict flats in constructing *Blow-Up*'s mise-en-scène that the film is, beneath its thriller pretext, a meditation on the elusive forces that shape and reshape modern cities, just as the carloads of mummers who dog Thomas throughout the film suggest how play and simulacra are becoming the building blocks of the new experiential economy of which the 1960s counterculture is the most visible example. (This dichotomy between the nineteenth-century industrial economy and the new economy of surplus sign-value production also appears in Thomas's dual role as a fashion photographer and a photojournalist who is found at the film's start exiting a doss house, a temporary shelter for vagrants, symbol of the reservoir of unskilled labor Marx pointed to as one of the prerequisites of commodity production.) The urban park Thomas visits and revisits then becomes a relatively durable spatial counterpoint to London's ceaseless mutability; a quiet space and yet, paradoxically, the place where Thomas comes to recognize, in the mummers playing their imaginary game of tennis, the essentially unreal character of the city under late capitalism.

In Europe, the urban park was a contemporaneous development with industrialization, serving in the modern era as a salubrious, heterotopic compliment to the industrialized city, its factories, commercial centers, and residential neighborhoods—both an amenity and in a time where relations between city and countryside were becoming increasingly attenuated, a necessity of sorts. Although not of the city precisely, the park shares its ambiance with cities and has even been accorded its share of modernity's social ills. That the urban park is a site of both leisure and enjoyment as well as insalubriousness is today a fairly prosaic notion, but it still requires a genealogy. It is by now firmly entrenched, perhaps more so in America than in Europe, in a social imaginary of mythic urban violence—especially from the postwar period forward—a legacy of crimes spectacular and ignominious alike.[1] But does Berlin's Tiergarten carry a criminal taint? The assumption that it would was the starting point of my investigation—that Tiergarten would today, as in the past, mirror a pervasive urban malaise. An informal survey conducted among my immediate friends and acquaintances failed, however, to discover any association whatever between Tiergarten and crime, compelling me to ask a broader, less provocative question—What types of social interactions *actually* existed in Tiergarten?— and to pursue rather more hesitantly an ancillary line of questioning: How might these quotidian social interactions, despite all evidence to the contrary, still connect to the perennial albeit phantasmatic linkages between criminality, poverty, and general social dysfunction? After all, if the park is embedded within the more conflictual terrain that is Berlin, as one of its preeminent public spaces, should not the larger problems of the city—the conflicts and tensions arising from rapid gentrification, the polarizing effects of class and wealth inequities—be visible in Tiergarten, there where they are on the surface least apparent? As Toni Morrison has written, "Invisible things are not necessarily not-there."[2]

To ask such questions suggests a fictitious, imaginary, and, indeed, spectral dimension to criminality exists alongside the factum of crime statistics, an insight that might well indeed prompt one to peer into their motive cause; that is, in the words of Janice Radway, "the extended intellectual consequences of the historically constituted divide between the social and the individual, the abstract and the concrete, the analytical and the imaginary."[3] It might lead one to allude as well to the imaginary dimension of governmentality that so often reinforces and buttresses the perception that this or that area is insalubrious, in the process subtly transforming fiction into tangible reality. To speculate thusly might also lead one to consider what is it that differentiates park space from urban space; to consider the park not precisely as a heterotopic site[4] but in accordance with Foucault's admonition that, as social beings, we live inside "a set of relations that delineates sites which are [while also being adjacent and permeable] irreducible to one another and absolutely not superimposable on one another."[5]

All of these questions, while disparate in nature, share a concern with how subjective perception effects objective, empirical facts. But having elected to concentrate less on quantifiable facts than the imaginary dimension of my observations, on site and in the moment of inquiry, in gathering data I chose to employ the tactics of the *dériviste*,

---

1   The infamous case of the Central Park Five, five young African Americans wrongly convicted of a brutal rape in 1989, is among the more prominent of such crimes. More recently, one can point to allusions of the notoriety of Baltimore's Leakin Park as a dumping ground for murdered bodies in the first series of the Serial radio podcast.
2   Toni Morrison, quoted in Avery F. Gordon, *Ghostly Matters* (Minneapolis: University of Minnesota Press, 1997), 17.
3   Janice Radway, foreword to Gordon, *Ghostly Matters*, ix.
4   Foucault's list of sites of "temporary relaxation" such as beaches and cafes, which by his account are not heterotopic, does not include the park, suggesting that if the park is heterotopic it is so to a lesser degree than, say, a cemetery or a brothel.
5   First published in October 1984 by the French journal *Architecture/Mouvement/Continuité* under the title "Des Espaces Autres," Michel Foucault's text is known to his Anglophone audience by the title "Of Other Spaces: Heterotopias." Originally drafted for a lecture Foucault presented in 1967, it was not reviewed for publication by the author and thus has remained outside the official corpus of his work, which has not kept it from being copiously and at times erroneously cited. Translated from the French by Jay Miskowiec, the manuscript was released into the public domain to facilitate its inclusion in an exhibition in Berlin shortly before Foucault's death. See page 3.

the amateur sleuth who eschews the top-down perspective of the expert in favor of the spatially situated orientation of the everyday user—a choice in keeping with my nonspecialist status as a practitioner from the field of "artistic research." I did, however, undertake my investigation with a hypothesis in mind. Given adjacency and permeability are central characteristics of urban parks, one might expect the character of the city street, the hostile, aggressive, and antagonistic stance normally directed at the urban other, the stranger encountered alone or in a crowd does not magically cease once one enters the tranquility of park space. My supposition was this cautious, defensively aggressive urban personality—one born of over-crowding, alienation, and anomie—is not absent in its historical counter-figure, the leisurely park-goer, and that social tensions typical of the urban environment persist in Tiergarten, registering on either a covert or occluded level. In other words, I wanted to attend to the process by which a street crowd transforms into a park crowd.

"The crowd—no subject was more entitled to the attention of nineteenth century writers,"[6] wrote Walter Benjamin, and one could add few subjects are as emblematic of modernity than the granular, heterogeneous yet entirely determined agglomerations of individuals one finds on city streets. The experience of the crowd in the modern city presented a series of paradoxes to early observers. It was at once a place of extreme heterogeneity—a free field of signs and a marketable mass of images, to paraphrase T. J. Clark—which made the street an elusive, transitory zone to gather social facts. It was also a zone of anomie and improvisation where the old separations that once governed class interaction had broken down for good, replaced by a "reign of generalized illusion."[7] At the same time, the street remained, in ways both easy and difficult to quantify, more stratified, more inflexibly classed and compartmentalized than ever before. The city had also become a psychological incubator, a zone of strong, at times perverse affect. For those thinkers, historical and contemporary alike, who sought to account for urbanity's salient features, the city's mythic and mythologizing anomie presents itself as at once internal psychological condition and external attribute of urban space, in which the prejudices and predilections of a given age act as barriers to objective thought. "What the myth of modernity fails to do," writes Clark, "what entitles us to call it mythical [...] is to put together its account of anomie with that of social division; it fails to map one form of social control over another."[8] This was especially true of the writers who took their involuntary reaction to urban stimuli for objective data, resolving the resulting inner confusion of terms by treating the city street as something that concerned other people. Confronted by the admixture of typologies and classes present in the city, the response of these early urban critics was both moral and aesthetic. In *The Condition of the Working Class in England*, Friedrich Engels painted the crowds of London in repugnant terms, as if his shock was so great that he could no longer distinguish between normative judgment and descriptive statement. Surveying the London street left him unhinged by the rapidity of people streaming past, a crowd in which he found a concentration of the worst aspects of society, a "distasteful," "brutally indifferent" agglomeration "of all classes and ranks," pursuing similar aims and aspirations while rushing past one another "as if they had nothing in common or were in no

---

6   Walter Benjamin, "On Some Motifs in Baudelaire," *Illuminations*, trans. Harry Zohn, (New York: Schocken Books, 1968), 166.
7   T. J. Clark, *The Painting of Modern Life* (Princeton, NJ: Princeton University Press, 1984), 36.
8   Clark, 49.

way associated with one another."⁹ It is true Engels's book dates from the final decade of the First Industrial Revolution, when the social ills stemming from a rapid influx and concentration of poorly remunerated laborers in cities ill-equipped to accommodate these new populations was glaringly apparent. Yet, it is as if Engels, the son of successful German industrialists, writes from a position of moral opprobrium, personally offended not so much by the conditions he is documenting as by the incivility witnessed. Indeed, "Not everyone can take a bath of multitude,"¹⁰ as Charles Baudelaire begins the chapter of *Paris Spleen* titled "Crowds," where he reframes Engels's apparent psychological shortcomings as a researcher into a ubiquitous character deficit. Being loathe by dint of family affluence as much as critical predilection to identify positively with urban crowds, Engels could only react defensively and critically. And lacking the facility of the *flâneur* to navigate crowded streets with a minimum of effort, he utterly missed how the modern city was creating a new type of psychology. Baudelaire, whose professional life was spent in a state of chronic impecuniousness, could ill afford Engels's lofty perspective and spent his career turning an at-times precarious proximity to the perils of the everyday into a virtue, a poetic program, culminating in a collection of brief prose works celebrating the urban experience and the kinds of psychological states it produced, in the more or less ambivalent terms one would expect of the poet laureate of the nascent modern experience. Baudelaire expressed a view of crowd phenomenon from within, as already a part of his own subjectivity, as Walter Benjamin astutely noted, and it was precisely this internalization born of his immersion in the urban life of Paris that bred in his poetry a "defensive reaction to [its] attraction and allure."¹¹ In fact, Baudelaire was among the first to describe the now commonplace experience of the city street as site and source of a barely restrained libidinal dynamism, a phantasmatic eroticism, "love—not at first sight, but at last sight. [...] of which one might not infrequently say that it was spared, rather than denied, fulfillment."¹² In Baudelaire, the internalized crowd created a poetics; in his compatriots, it bred neurasthenic frustration. In both cases it reflected the alienation the urban subject characteristically experienced toward society at large, a psychic tension who's oscillations veered dizzyingly between the wish for forms of life-affirming contact and life-preserving seclusion, with neither option proving satisfactory.

From these two positions—Engels's empirically-based critique where the shifting ambiguities of the crowd were cataloged and fixed, and Baudelaire's evocative and poetic excoriations in which the Paris crowds, while rarely named, remain omnipresent—we have inherited a modern sociological notion of the urban as at once environment and psychological construct, milieu and pathology, site for and cause of an alienated personality type—schizoid, aggressive, individualistic, disorganized—who's feelings and reactions are conditioned by social forces encountered on a daily basis. Not least by what Georg Simmel termed the "money economy," the omnipresent and overpowering hegemony of a fully matured industrial capitalism exacerbating the already alienated individual's suspicion that he or she is nothing more than "a mere cog in an enormous organization of things and powers,"¹³ transforming subjective experience into its desiccated, objectified compliment.

9   Benjamin, *Illuminations*, 167.
10 Charles Baudelaire, *The Parisian Prowler: Le Spleen de Paris. Petits Poèmes en prose*, trans. Edward K. Kaplan (Athens, GA: University of Georgia Press, 1989), 21.
11 Benjamin, *Illuminations*, 167.
12 Benjamin, 169, 170.

But the urban crowd is not an undifferentiated phenomenon. Throughout the nineteenth century, the modern city produced new types of crowds and with these crowds, new modes of comportment and new types of fear. By the end of the century, anxieties about the socially ambivalent construction of crowds on city streets—anxieties driven by the Industrial Revolution's undoing of the local commercial relations that had formerly bolstered neighborhood and class identity (a function of a single industry or a set of related trades being set in geographical proximity), dispersing trade throughout the city and anonymizing the firsthand relationships in which people at one time set considerable stock—came to encompass sites deliberately visited, such as amusement parks and café concert venues. At such locales, bourgeois families, clerks and shop assistants, workers, petty criminals, prostitutes, and pimps congregated in utter disregard for the tacit rules of separation that had formerly governed and canalized cross-class interactions, creating scenes, in the words of a contemporary observer, of great "social dishevelment."[14] In recently-created urban parks, on the contrary, strenuous efforts were made to reach a modus vivendi in which, as T. J. Clark has written, the different classes relied on an elaborate texture of controls and avoidances to maintain social hierarchies in the relatively uninflected space of a fabricated nature, "[agreeing] to ignore one another [by] marking out invisible boundaries."[15]

These invisible boundaries are the real subject of Georges Seurat's famous painting, *A Sunday on La Grande Jatte—1884* (1884–86), and Clark reinforces his point by referencing two works by the painter Roger Jourdain—*Le Dimanche* and *Le Lundi*—published six years earlier in the popular Parisian journal, *L'Illustration*. With the coming of the Paris rail system, the island of La Grand Jatte, a narrow spit lodged in the Seine between the suburbs of Asnières and Neuilly, had become a popular holiday destination, minutes away from the Clichy train station. Equally popular amongst bourgeois and worker, in Jourdain's illustration their leisure time is reassuringly segregated. A clear hierarchy is inferred, delineated first by a temporal boundary—the title of the second of Jourdain's illustrations refers to the celebration of *Saint Lundi*, a tradition among the working classes that, while archaic by the late nineteenth century, still held sufficient sentimental charge among workers to carry Jourdain's implied meaning—that a strict separation still existed between the bourgeois promenading in their finery on a Sunday afternoon and the workers who, for lack of a second-hand suit, took their leisure the day after—as well as cultural distinctions born of habitus. For the bourgeois citizen, it was a mahogany rowboat and chilled champagne taken on a grassy bank; for the worker, bottles of undistinguished *vin rouge* quaffed on rough plank benches. "Jourdain is willing and able to articulate the difference between petit bourgeois and worker," writes Clark, "because it presents itself here, at least in fantasy, as a clean separation in which each class knows its place. [...] and though both are a little absurd in their pleasures, it is clear that one is inferior to the other."[16] In Seurat's painting, on the contrary, it remains difficult to ascertain who is inferior and who superior, let alone which groupings are made up of associates and which merely the result of a temporary spatial proximity. This effect was noted by critics of the time, who saw in the

---

13 Georg Simmel, "The Metropolis and Mental Life," in *The Sociology of Georg Simmel*, trans. Kurt Wolff (New York: Free Press, 1950), 415.
14 Louis Veuillot, quoted in Clark, *The Painting of Modern Life*, 213.
15 Veuillot, quoted in Clark, 265.
16 Veuillot, quoted in Clark, 262, 263.

diversity of detail an implied revolutionary message, identifiable in Seurat's synthetic contour lines—his "uniform and as it were abstract execution"[17]—and the manner in which the painting's rigid figures are crammed together in close proximity, "as if the picture was hardly big enough to contain them."[18]

One may justifiably argue that this description of the ways social tension became legible and locatable in the debased heterotopia of urban park space is particular to a particular type of artistic modernity and a particular type of city, Paris being the metropolis where the spatial conventions that came to emblematize modernity's urban texture were developed and refined. In paintings set in Tiergarten roughly contemporaneous to *La Grand Jatte*, the park retains the formality of a brand of history painting dedicated to the staid evocation of bourgeois rectitude: the theme of class antagonism (or to be more precise, class disquiet) that dominates Seurat's work remaining entirely absent. Even in the work of a contemporaneous German painter of similarly modern aspirations such as Berlin native Max Liebermann (who, coincidentally, traveled to Paris to study painting in 1872, not long after the Paris Commune destroyed for several generations any hope the French working class held for transforming its condition, although this event appears to have left little impression on his artistic sensibility), the issue of class relations is wholly absent, or so subtle as to remain invisible.[19] Perhaps this indicates that Berlin's workers took their relaxation elsewhere—the park was at the time girdled by several fashionable neighborhoods—or perhaps it is merely a reflection of the fact that urban and cultural conditions had yet to reach a point where the particular texture of Berlin city life in itself would become a wellspring of creative ferment.[20] Or perhaps it points to an important occlusion in representation and the presence of the invisible things lurking in the aforementioned shadows Toni Morrison has written of as uncanny half-certainties, not necessarily not-there.

So it was that on a sunny midweek afternoon in early June, with Clark's text on *A Sunday on La Grande Jatte* fresh in my mind and holding in my hands a kind of psychogeographic map sketched with Sandra Bartoli's assistance, I set out for the park in order to see if I could read in Tiergarten visible signs of Clark's invisible boundaries—our inheritance from the first capitalist reorganization of urban space and its attendant recalibration of class interactions—and Morrison's invisible things, our inheritance from what came after. Any map of Tiergarten makes clear that it is divided into four distinct zones separated by major traffic arteries. On my map Sandra had also helpfully noted less clearly delineated areas—one might describe them using Situationist terminology as "zones of

---

17 Félix Fénéon, quoted in Clark, *Painting of Modern Life*, 264.
18 Fénéon, quoted in Clark, 265.
19 Certainly this is the case with a painting such as *Kinderspielplatz*, painted a year after *La Grand Jatte*, which for all its impressionistic vigor, maintains an arboreal wholesomeness, as does the biergarten depicted in *Sommerfrische im Berliner Tiergarten* from 1900, with its sedate and well-dressed patrons. Liebermann, who himself came from a successful merchant family and choose his subjects predominantly from the bourgeois world, revisited Tiergarten on other occasions, as in *Promenade im Tiergarten mit Spaziergängern* from 1925, and in no painting is a working class figure recognizable to the modern eye, although certainly some of the women in *Kinderspielplatz* could be, are very likely to have been, domestics. But the overall effect of Liebermann's work is to blend and unify rather than to isolate and distinguish.
20 In accounting for Friedich Engels repugnance to the crowds of English cities, Walter Benjamin writes: "The writer [Engels] came from a Germany that was still provincial; he may never have faced the temptation to lose himself in a stream of people. When Hegel went to Paris for the first time not long before his death, he wrote to his wife: 'When I walk through the streets, people look just as they do in Berlin; they wear the same clothes and the faces are about he same—the same aspect, but in a large crowd,'" *Illuminations*, 167.

attraction"—where different social groups gather and in which different forms of behaviors are concentrated. Approaching the park from Bahnhof Zoo, I passed, as Sandra had anticipated I would, encampments of homeless men taking advantage of the constant foot traffic to opportune passersby entering the park or visiting the Schleusenkrug café. After a quick coffee at the aforementioned café, I crossed the Landwehrkanal, entering the park proper. Turning left to negotiate a finger of the Neuer See, I circled around the Großer Weg en route to my first destination, the most socially stratified and most "problematic" area of the park from an administrative point of view—the gay cruising zone adjacent to the Löwenbrücke in the southwest. The first thing that caught my attention was a group of women with their babies encircled by prams to create a defensive perimeter, who sat beneath the shade of a tree. Behind them, a cluster of men drinking beer were gathered around a ping-pong table. From the path, I could faintly make out the latter's distinguishing characteristics, but something indefinable suggested the difference between the women on the grass and the men at the ping-pong table—varying modes of comportment I would normally have found unremarkable but in this context struck me as one example of Clark's invisible boundaries, evidence of the tacit codes of dress and behavior that continue to differentiate class-inflected modes of being.

When I reached the Löwenbrücke, the area was more or less deserted, not even a used condom to betray evidence of illicit activity. I continued east toward the so-called Fleischwiese, a kind of sunny annex to the secluded shade of the cruising area, which on this day was crowded with men in various states of undress. I then cut across Hofjägerallee to a trail that edged north along Tiergartengewässer. This southeast zone, where stands of trees are interrupted by stretches of meadow ideal for picnics or sunbathing, is the most well-groomed and tourist-oriented part of the park. On this day it was populated mostly by solitary sunbathers or parents with their children. Nothing particularly illicit was going on, although at the southern terminus of Bellevueallee I found the corpse of a small rabbit, savaged, perhaps, by a dog off its leash or a fox. My general impression was of a well-maintained space, footpaths freshly graded and maintenance crews much in evidence emptying trash receptacles and grooming foliage. People were sitting or strolling, pushing bicycles or prams, and it was easy enough to tell one type of person from another: the newness of a pair of shoes or the cut of a shirt clearly differentiated the middle-class visitor from the desultory attention to apparel evidenced by a man of perceptible alcoholic inclinations sitting on a bench smoking a cigarette, his pale and viscid calves visible below rolled-up trousers. I was only slightly perturbed when further along the path I thought I passed the same man slouched on an identical park bench in the same state of torpor as the one I had passed ten minutes before. How had he relocated so quickly—apparently unruffled by his exertions—as if he had set off on his bicycle with the sole purpose of startling me through his uncanny reappearance? This encounter struck me as all the more menacing for its apparent incongruity with the setting. I made a note that on my next visit I should arrive more toward dusk, when if something alarming were to happen, it would at least appear appropriate to the time of day.

The following week I returned around 6 p.m. to explore the park's northern zones. In particular, I was on the lookout for an area habituated by drug dealers and several other areas where trees had been cleared, both of which Sandra had indicated on her map (the tree-clearing had particularly incensed her).

I entered the park on Stülerstrasse, noting at least ten tree stumps while heading west toward the point of Strasse des 17. Juni where it passes under the S-Bahn tracks, site of a failed restaurant. Arriving, I found several homeless men taking advantage of the temporary absence of a renter to use the temporarily vacant patio as a storage space and to pursue improvised commercial activities. I didn't notice many tree stumps in the immediate vicinity—perhaps they'd already been dug up and filled in—but from a commercial standpoint it was clear the location had certain drawbacks. The nearby thoroughfare sent the sound of traffic ringing through my skull, mixing there with the smell of exhaust and the ozone haze of air pollution to color everything—the parched grass, the low ornamental shrubs and etiolated saplings, the dirty sidewalk and soot-covered walls of the S-Bahn arch—with an atmosphere of general neglect, punctuated nicely by the florid rantings of a man, apparently in the throes of a psychotic episode, circling the signpost of a bus stop like an erratic satellite.

I walked west past the S-Bahn line to the no-man's-land where the park gives way to the campus of the Technische Universität, then circled back on a path that runs along the Landwehrkanal where houseboats are picturesquely moored, and then through a tunnel cutting beneath the S-Bahn line, passing several tents pitched beside the canal. A group of boisterous drinkers reeled about on the grass outside their makeshift shelters, clutching vodka bottles in their hands. Turning north, I crossed Strasse des 17. Juni and entered the Hansaviertel district with its modernist apartment blocks. Here Sandra had indicated more felled trees, but I was unable to find them. So, circling back toward the Siegessäule monument, I crossed Altonaerstrasse to reenter the park near the Englischer Garten and the Teehaus. Here Sandra's map indicated the presence of an open-air drug market. I was disappointed again, for there was no evidence of drug dealers, although I did find three Heineken bottles carefully placed at even intervals along the path, putting me in mind of Wallace Stephen's poem about the jar on that hill in Tennessee, "which took dominion everywhere," making the wilderness slovenly.

Making my way west again, I crossed an intersection to enter Tiergarten's northwest quadrant. This is perhaps its least appealing zone. It is thickly forested, but the lush greenness gives off an appearance of foreboding rather than tranquility. Here the park appeared to be populated entirely by men, walking singly or in couples, some derelict and others quite ordinary in appearance. I passed a young man of Middle Eastern or North African descent, who fixed me with a meaningful glance. Was he one of the drug dealers Sandra had noted I might find further east? A cruising homosexual? I wasn't sure, and anyway it no longer occurred to me in my heightened state of paranoid attentiveness that he might simply be there in the park to enjoy the greenery and the hum of traffic. *He had to be there for a reason.* I reached the end of the Bremer Weg and turning back, again encountered the young man, who appeared like myself to be making a circuit of the park. This time we both fixed each other with the same meaningful glances, then moved on in silence, neither of us sure, apparently, of the other's intentions.

I seemed to have descended into a fever of suspicion. But what was it exactly that made everyone else appear suspect to me? Was it my own concentration on uncovering something suspect that lent them this appearance? Did I appear suspicious to them? If the stranger is strange to me, then quite possibly—quite probably—I in turn appear strange to the stranger. In fact, I am indeed a stranger to them, to those who do not know me and cannot be sure whether or not I harbor ulterior motives similar to those which I was ascribing to the others lingering in the park at dusk. And so the idea arose, there in the gathering gloom of a tree-covered walkway, that I myself was out of place—a stranger doubly estranged there in Tiergarten, this liminal zone between city and country, built space and vegetable life, discovered suddenly as a zone of alienation where the familiar fabric of urban space becomes derealized.[21]

Before exiting the park I passed by the Fauler See. At the water's edge a sullen-looking young man was smoking a joint while on an adjacent bench an elderly man fixed his gaze on the still, fetid pond. Confronted by this tableau, I became acutely aware of the extent to which I had maintained, despite my best intentions, the class-bound regard for the notional other it had originally been my intention to interrogate. Not wishing to interrupt their silence, and in a sense fleeing my own self-judgment, I was continuing along the trail ringing the Fauler See when I spied a narrow dirt path leading to the pond's edge. Someone had made a little cave out of the foliage, its bare dirt floor scattered with bits of refuse, vividly conveying the impression of having been only recently vacated, so strongly did it vibrate with the phantom presence of an occupant. Retracing my footsteps, I rounded a corner and came upon a misshapen man with a shock of white hair lumbering forward in heavy black orthopedic shoes, shapeless ankle-length boots made for clomping awkwardly about: the type of person who exists at the very margins of the urban scene, his pale complexion suggesting a life of reclusion.

I could imagine him dragging this ungainly footwear through the fallen leaves covering the dirt path and then along cobbled streets and up the stairs to a dirty attic studio apartment whose windows looked out upon a grimy courtyard or a deserted street faced with 1950s apartment blocks perpetually cast in the black and white of postwar austerity, where he was wont to sit, gazing out on the courtyard or street below (a view offering none of the refined delectation of the paralytic in the E. T. A. Hoffman story—one of the first works of literature to foreground the emergent scopic regime of the wholly alienated city dweller—who's vigil at his window prefigures that very modern sentiment of resentment-tinged superiority-in-isolation). The man gave me a furtive, avoidant look and quickened his step, disappearing down the darkening pathway, and with his departure, the memory of a scene from Virginia Woolf's essay "Street Haunting" surfaced, the part where Woolf observes through the shop window a young female dwarf being fitted for new boots, accompanied by two minders. The encounter calls into being for Woolf an entire "atmosphere," a parade of the halt and blind, "a hobbling, grotesque dance to which everybody in the street now conformed."[22] And now this contagion had reached across the ages to clasp me in its spell: the elderly man I passed not soon after, shuffling through the fallen leaves with the aid of a cane, now seemed not merely old but decrepitude personified; the pallid man who appeared next had a protuberant forehead of such alarming size his neck appeared to have to strain to support it. And here came a leering inebriate in his wheelchair, Sternberg beer bottle clutched in his fist, pushed along by a companion in an equally advanced state of drunkenness,

---

21 Again to quote Benjamin: "Let the many attend to their daily affairs; the man of leisure can indulge in the perambulations of the *flâneur* only if as such he is already *out of place*," *Illuminations*, 172 (my italics).
22 Virginia Woolf, "Street Haunting," in *Death of the Moth and Other Essays* (San Diego: Harcourt, Brace, Jovanovich, 1970), 25.

staggering and swaying and gripping at the wheelchair handles to remain erect.

This brief state of intensified perception in turn elicited one of those minor revelations in which the kernel of the issue one has been circling around in dim misapprehension becomes briefly illuminated. I glimpsed clearly the solitary walker in his heavy orthopedic boots returning to his lonely room, and of the broader social forces—poverty, social isolation, alcoholism, immigration—that shaped the destinies of his compatriots, who lingered here in the green twilight. Because one chief advantage of a park is it's entirely free to sit and while away the afternoon. No café server to insinuate you have overstayed your welcome after the second hour spent lingering over a cup of coffee, casting disparaging glances at your threadbare coat, your decrepit shoes—the trappings that give poverty an identifiable shape. I was reminded of a line from W. H. Auden: "The lonely are battered like pebbles into fortuitous shapes." Here the pebbles had gathered and it is the peculiar obligation of city parks to make a home for them; what Henri Lefebvre called "the right to the city"—the right of all that exists in cities to participate in "an encounter, actual or possible, of all 'objects' and 'subjects.'"[23]

What lessons had I learned? I had established early on that Tiergarten is not a dangerous place, neither in reality nor the popular imaginary of Berliners. (The most ominous anecdote I collected came from a native Berliner who grew up near Tiergarten and had reminisced about walking through the park on her way home from school, occasionally feeling "alarmed," though she failed to remember a specific incident which had prompted her trepidation, save for the normal anxiety of a child equipped with the standard faculties of imagination, making her way through the shadowy trees and bushes of a park where gardeners acted according to maintenance guidelines promoting a more wild-seeming landscape than the relatively manicured parkland one encounters in parts of today's Tiergarten.) I had found evidence of the continued maintenance of T. J. Clark's invisible boundaries, but they were more subtle than overt, perhaps a function of the two hundred years in which modern urbanism has coded and recoded precisely these type of encounters, making class division in social space at once less remarkable and more ubiquitous. Perhaps it was that the "crime" I had encountered was precisely the sort that is least remarked upon: the means power and privilege use to alienate lived space by returning the city to its inhabitants transformed into an image, a picture concordant with power's notion of what a city should look like and who should occupy it. A spectral yet embodied image, omnipresent yet retaining a connection to site and location ... as in a case of haunting. Perhaps my crime story was in fact a ghost story.

In the sociologist Avery F. Gordon's view, haunting has to do with our imaginary relationship to the real, to the way the imaginary creates a border zone that destabilizes empirical space. It is in this zone where the harms inflicted or the losses sustained in past or present instances of social violence are registered—"when the cracks and rigging are exposed, when the people who are meant to be invisible show up without any sign of leaving."[24] Through a science of haunting Gordon "imputes a kind of objectivity to ghosts [implying] that, from certain standpoints, the dialectics of visibility and invisibility involve a constant negotiation

---

23 Henri Lefebvre, *Writing on Cities*, trans. and ed. Eleonore Kofman and Elizabeth Lebas (London: Blackwell, 1996), 195.
24 Gordon, *Ghostly Matters*, xvi.

between what can be seen and what is in the shadows,"[25] the existence of the latter being, as Morrison's axiom suggests, resistant to being definitively proven or disproven. The significance of this observation in the sylvan context of the urban park rests in the way the ghosts that tie present subjects to past histories become imperceptible there, the visible traces of history and trauma to which ghosts attach themselves being inexorably subsumed by biotic process.

Just as I had sought to sensitize my perception of certain invisible thresholds demarcating social space, reading Gordon's thesis I now felt confronted with the theoretical necessity to decipher not only the synchronic traces of historically bounded modes of being and systems of occlusion and marginalization I had taken note of in Tiergarten but the diachronic shades lurking there as well. The most prominent being Rosa Luxemburg. Shot in 1919 on the Katharina-Heinroth-Ufer, which runs between the southern bank of the Landwehrkanal and the bordering Zoologischer Garten, Luxemburg's body was unceremoniously dumped into the canal by her Freikorps executioners. The site is now marked by a bronze statue that succeeds in being at once solemn and clinical to the point of affectless. Nothing remains of how the site looked in 1919—save for the canal water itself—and consequently, there is no way to build a setting for this event and its repercussions. Which might be the urban park's most characteristic attribute. Standing at the border of built and natural space, the urban park, as Thomas the photographer discovers by the end of *Blow-Up*, is a species of site where the memory and presence of trauma become inconspicuous, sociological "facts" elusive. Receding in this garden setting of summertime picnics and afternoon strolls, traumatic events stick to the shadows, gathering about them a deeper ambiguity.

25 Gordon, *Ghostly Matters*, 23.

JÖRG STOLLMANN

IN CAMPO APERTO: URBAN ENCOUNTERS IN THE OPEN FIELD

TO THE MEMORY OF VINCENZO BATTAGLIA

> I would hurry in the dusk's mud
> behind disorderly stairs, around silent scaffolds,
> through the neighborhood drenched
> in the odor of iron and of laundry
> drying, in the fetid dust,
> among shacks made of tin
> and drain pipes, new walls going up,
> with their paint already peeling,
> against a backdrop of a faded metropolis.
> —Pier Paolo Pasolini[1]

How do we conceive of open spaces in the city? How much openness do we allow? To whom are they accessible? A revisiting of Pier Paolo Pasolini's 1962 feature film *Mamma Roma* offers an aesthetic reading of an open public space that comments on the limited aesthetic scope, implicit codes, and normative standards that characterize so many urban design models of open spaces today. For instance, the model of the public park as a garden for citizens has until today prevailed in planning jargon and practice.[2] A big achievement for the livelihood of growing cities from the early nineteenth century onward, most of these public parks epitomize idyllic, peaceful, and seemingly harmonious environments. Their bourgeois pastoral aesthetics are derivatives from classical poetry and painting that idealize and depoliticize the rural vernacular.[3] In *Mamma Roma*, Pasolini opens the discourse on a fundamentally different urban landscape when he depicts an open field and an encounter between youths. Well aware of the classic repertoire of seventeenth-century Roman landscape painting, he deliberately transgresses bourgeois aesthetic codes, while aiming at a more instantaneous connection to antiquity—and therefore, one could say, to humanity. Pasolini imagines a trans-temporal landscape of human encounters, transgression, and transitivity, not free of conflict and brutality, but open—as open a space can be to the subaltern in the city.

Pasolini very consciously chose the site locations for *Mamma Roma*, especially Tuscolano II, the INA-Casa housing development located in the southeastern periphery of Rome.[4] In his journalistic writing, he argued

---

1 Pier Paolo Pasolini, *Bestemmia: Tutte le poesie*, vol. 4, ed. Graziella Chiarcossi and Walter Siti (Milan: Garzanti, 1993), 475; English translation in John David Rhodes, *Stupendous, Miserable City: Pasolini's Rome* (Minneapolis: University of Minnesota Press, 2007), 75.
2 Many aspects of today's public parks, in terms of spatial layout, aesthetic codes and "dos and don'ts," derive from European aristocratic and bourgeois cultures of the late eighteenth and early nineteenth century. In the late eighteenth century, many aristocratic gardens in Paris were opened to the public and had an impact on the later development and design of public parks. Dieter Hennebo differentiates between three phases of public park design. Present until 1840, the first phase is predominantly influenced by the English landscape garden aesthetic. At the time, public parks—also named citizens' gardens—were rather exclusive, representative leisure spaces for the bourgeoisie. In the second phase (1840 to 1900), parks opened up for sports and various activities, but only in the third phase (1900 to 1930) were they designed as people's parks and opened up to the working-class population. See Erika Schmidt, *Geschichte des Stadtgrüns. Band 3: Entwicklung des Stadtgrüns in England von den frühen Volkswiesen bis zu den öffentlichen Parks im 19. Jahrhundert* (Berlin: Patzer Verlag, 1977).
3 For eighteenth-century painting, John Barrel has convincingly argued about the ways in which painting depicted peasant life in order to become an acceptable decoration for the interiors of the powerful and wealthy. See John Barrel, *The Dark Side of the Landscape* (Cambridge: Cambridge University Press, 1980).
4 INA-Casa was a state-financed program for affordable housing in post-war Italy. It created more than 350,000 units of housing in two seven-year phases (1949–56 and 1956–63).

repeatedly that from his Marxist perspective, the neighborhoods, financed by the post-war state housing programs, were continuing a long tradition of paternalism, oppression, and social segregation by pushing the urban poor and lower middle classes out of the urban center, depriving them of material resources, social relations, and cultural identity. Thus, Tuscolano II and the whole neighborhood of Tuscolano,[5] as the context of *Mamma Roma*, form an integral part of his political discourse about the urban. This tragic story of a Roman woman and her son, their attempt at upward social movement, and their failure to integrate into the normative, petit-bourgeois state housing project and its neighborhood is a tale of societal rather than individual failure.

The main character, Mamma Roma, quits her work as a prostitute and opens a street market stall of her own. She packs with her only son Ettore, who was raised in the countryside, and moves from her apartment in a rundown 1920s housing estate to the new housing development of Tuscolano II. Both sites, the housing built under Mussolini in Piazza Tommaso de Cristoforis and the new INA-Casa complex on Largo Spartaco, are introduced cinematically in the very same manner with forward dolly long shots and reverse shots of Mamma Roma and Ettore approaching the buildings. In both walking scenes, the two characters look upward, while the buildings they are approaching are filmed from a slightly lower angle, exaggerating the architecture in scale and impressiveness. This cinematic means of drawing an equivalence between both housing projects establishes a strong connection between the two, making them more of the same thing than the characters themselves perceive. In contrast to Mamma Roma's words, "It's pretty, isn't it—our new house?" John David Rhodes has convincingly argued in his seminal book *Stupendous, Miserable City: Pasolini's Rome* that for Pasolini, both housing projects were built in the same spirit of banishing the urban poor from the inner city to encamp them in disciplinary environments.[6] In the new neighborhood, Ettore makes friends and gets a job as a waiter in the inner city. He falls in love with a local girl, Bruna. When he finds out about his mother's history as a prostitute and is bugged by his friends, Ettore is deeply disturbed. He quits his job, roams the streets with his pals and is finally jailed for petty theft. Imprisoned and feverish, he has a nervous breakdown and dies in an isolation cell. In the course of this essay, I will return to certain spaces and scenes of the movie's narrative in a non-chronological manner in order to highlight the specific role of the open field within the urban landscape constructed by Pasolini cinematically.

The housing development of Tuscolano II and the whole neighborhood of Tuscolano are not simply a carefully chosen "setting" but become an actor within the story. Mamma Roma and Ettore are not meant to fit in, and in this, they rarely differ from many of the characters they meet in their new neighborhood. Literally, the environment is directed against its inhabitants. Pasolini alludes to this in the way he portrays the building in Piazza Tommaso di Cristoforis:[7] the final shot at the end of Mamma Roma's and Ettore's walk

---

5   Tuscolano is the colloquial name for the neighborhoods of Don Bosco, Appio Claudio, and Quadraro that comprise the INA-Casa developments of Tuscolano I and Tuscolano II, situated in the southeast of Rome between Porta Furba and Cinecittà. The neighborhoods were developed along via Tuscolana, one of the antique Roman consular roads.
6   Rhodes, *Stupendous, Miserable City*, 116–17.
7   Saverio Muratori and Mario de Renzi were the authors of the urban design scheme for Tuscolano II, realized from 1952 to 1957. The main building of Largo Spartaco, with the shops on the ground floor and five floors of apartments above, was designed by Saverio Muratori.

toward their new home frames a structural column of the building symbolically as a cross. This is one of many instances where Mamma Roma is shown facing a toxic societal environment and political economy, as is materialized in the architecture of these projects.

This assigned fatality of the peripheral neighborhood to its inhabitants is hard to understand from a visit today. The INA-Casa projects in Tuscolano, designed by some of the best architects of the time, don't show signs of dereliction or social deprivation. Rather, it seems as if Neorealism's architectural mode of translating vernacular and local aesthetics into industrially produced housing has contributed positively to the societal project of Italy's urbanization.[8] Tuscolano II is based on a composition of linear buildings and high-rises. In contrast, the urban morphology of Tuscolano is predominantly characterized by very dense building blocks framing streetscapes and piazzas, developed by private speculation after the INA-Casa project.[9] Today, Cecafumo, the official name for Tuscolano, is a relaxed petit-bourgeois neighborhood with well-kept houses, public spaces, and sufficient shopping and community infrastructure.[10] From Pasolini's point of view, one would put it differently: this bourgeois project was successful at employing architecture and urban design to discipline the common people. And it was a bourgeois project throughout. In fact, the smaller INA-Casa projects provided the infrastructure for the private speculative development in Tuscolano by a small circle of wealthy landowning families.[11]

On a mission to distance himself from Neorealist cinema, which Pasolini criticized heavily for idealizing and misrepresenting Italian history and politics, it seems apt that he also deconstructs Neorealism in architecture and urbanism. After *Accattone*, his 1961 film, *Mamma Roma* forms his second and even more radical attempt to do so. Casting Anna Magnani as the movie's lead was maybe the most obvious critical hint for the general audience to grasp. She had played Pina, the heroic resistance fighter in Roberto Rossellini's iconic Neorealist movie *Roma città aperta* in 1945. Seventeen years later, Anna Magnani's main character in *Mamma Roma* is not fighting the German occupation and fascist Italian collaborators, she is fighting a society in which fascism is still present as an internal force. Instead of portraying a "good Italian," she becomes a heroine of the people, the subaltern Roman population, "stripping Italy of its mask."[12]

Also in terms of cinematic means and aesthetics, Pasolini diverges from Neorealism, and it

---

8 For a closer discussion of Neorealism as a specific attitude assigned to the work of a group of post-war Italian architects, see Bruno Reichlin, "Figures of Neorealism in Italian Architecture (Part 1)," in *Grey Room*, no. 5 (Fall 2001): 78–101, and "Figures of Neorealism in Italian Architecture (Part 2)," in *Grey Room*, no. 6 (Winter 2001): 110–33.
9 Only the project by Adalberto Libera, the first INA-Casa project in Tuscolano, radically breaks with the urban pattern integrating a slab building (Casa alta) within a low-rise high-density complex of courthouses: the *Unità di abitazione orizzontale Tuscolano* (1950–54).
10 Bruno Reichlin has pointed out that the term neorealism was derived from literature and film: "Italian architectural criticism derived the term Neorealism from literature and film once the works and authors laying claim to the term already enjoyed a certain popularity among critics and the public, and those who were designated Neorealist architects accepted the description with varying degrees of conviction and enthusiasm." Reichlin, "Figures of Neorealism," 79.
11 See Timothy Pape, "Collective Rhythm Grouping: Access to Dynamic Forms by Articulating Rhythmic Encounters in Neighborhoods of the Periphery of Rome" (PhD thesis, Centre for Cultural Studies, Goldsmiths, University of London, 2018), 130, 134.
12 Maurizio Viano makes this argument based on a discussion of cinematic means and multiple references in Maurizio Viano, *A Certain Realism: Making Use of Pasolini's Film Theory and Practice* (Berkely: University of California Press, 1993). 88 ff.

[1]

Film still from *Mamma Roma*, Pier Paolo Pasolini (1962) with a view of the neighborhood of Tuscolano / Cecafumo.

[2]

Dutch artist, after Claude Lorrain, with figures by Andries Booth, *The Campo Vaccino, Rome*, (ca. 1635–41).

TRANSGRESSING URBANISM

is here where Neorealist architecture in general, and Tuscolano in particular, come under attack. Where in cinematic Neorealism the depiction of the characters' everyday life in their "environment" makes extensive use of subjective camera positions, Pasolini instead employs and deconstructs the naive point-of-view perspective. If the subjective camera of the walks toward the two homes of Mamma Roma mentioned earlier was already irritatingly constructed and symbolic, there is an even more telling deconstruction of subjectivity, which for Rhodes is one of the main poetic cinematic means that reveals Pasolini's argument. From their new apartment window, Mamma Roma and Ettore look at the Tuscolano neighborhood with the large dome of Basilica San Giovanni Bosco, an architectural reference to Saint Peter, rising above the roofs of the apartment buildings (fig. 1). It does not matter that this is not the actual view to be seen out of any windows of the building itself. Rather telling, this very same image appears on and off in-between sequences without any reference to a subjective view and thus can be understood not as a view, but as Mamma Roma's antagonist, the main character she is fighting without knowing. This very image of Tuscolano is also the final shot of the film. When Mamma Roma learns of her son's death in prison, she leaves her market stall behind and runs to her apartment, furious and devastated, followed by the fellow market traders. At the last minute, they succeed in stopping her from throwing herself out of the window. Held by her peers, Mamma Roma stares straight out of the window in horror. When the counter-shot repeats for a last time the panorama of Tuscolano, the image has been charged with symbolic meaning to the extent that it cannot be read as a simple point-of-view shot. Instead, it is an agent for Pasolini's argument of politics embodied in urbanism and society, which further subjects and finally defeats the subaltern.

The view of Tuscolano is very likely not shot from a building within the neighborhood but from outside the development in an open field, today the Parco degli Acquedotti public park, situated in the northern part of Parco Regionale dell'Appia Antica. The first time this open field appears in the movie, it is not only introduced pictorially but also by a musical theme that will be closely linked to this particular space and Ettore throughout the whole film: the second movement of Vivaldi's Bassoon Concerto in D minor.[13] This solemn and melancholic tune frames the ordinary setting as a place of importance, especially because most other musical tunes in *Mamma Roma* consist of popular music played within the scenes, like Mamma Roma playing her favorite record, *Violino Tzigano* by Carlo Buti, or part of the ambient sound of the location.[14] In the scene, Mamma Roma and Ettore have moved into their new home, the Muratori[15] building at Tuscolano II. After Sunday mass, Ettore meets up with a group of boys from the neighborhood in front of his building and heads off with them. As the group enters what seems to be a field of fallow land right next to the new neighborhood, the music sets in: first strings and basso continuo, followed by the lyrical motive of the bassoon. The boys pass a group of girls crouching in the grass, and Ettore entertains them by pantomiming, using the ruins of a Roman building as props.[16] There is an immediate physical relationship established between Ettore and the other boys with the open field and its remnants of antiquity.

---

13 Antonio Vivaldi, Concerto no. 5 for Bassoon, Strings, and Basso continuo in D Minor, RV 481, 2nd movement.
14 The only exception being another Vivaldi piece that is related to the appearance of Carmine, Mamma Roma's pimp: Concerto for Piccolo, Strings, and Continuo in C Major, RV 443, 2nd movement – largo.
15 This building is named after architect Saverio Muratori.
16 The building, which is not discernable from the movie's mise-en-scene, is the suburban Roman Villa delle Vignacce.

Later, in one of the central scenes of *Mamma Roma*, Ettore and his sweetheart Bruna flirt with one another in a location which serves as his favorite hangout within the open field, in the shadows of a high freestanding fragment of a Roman pillar (*fig. 2*). The scene is depicted with a montage that changes in shot and counter-shot, creating the impression of Bruna and Ettore moving in a circle from one position to another while they speak. Through the cityscape in the background, the position of the field is identified as an in-between of two contrasting forms of urbanization. On Bruna's side, we see the Tuscolano neighborhood under construction with the dome of San Giovanni Bosco, very similar to the symbolic key image of Tuscolano that will also make the final shot. The background's importance is emphasized by Bruna pointing toward Tuscolano, showing Ettore where she lives. On Ettore's side, the parallel stretches of the ruins of the Claudio and Felice aqueducts appear with a row of shacks and houses closely attached, one of the many informal settlements, the *borgate spontanee*, that characterized the Roman periphery of those days.[17] While Bruna and Ettore change positions, they also change their respective backgrounds to finally meet on the side of the informal settlement.

This moment of amorous entanglement—and this is revealing about what Pasolini later described as his "certain realism," a reflective form of cinematic poetry[18]—is also a meticulous cinematic construction of how Pasolini positioned himself toward Italy's political urban economy. In this scene, he exposes the discrimination against the poor, considering state-led urban development and the associated bourgeoisie to have played a major role in it. The two models—the post-war Tuscolano development and the informal shacks of the borgate spontanee—are both the product of the same political agency of discrimination. Yet, Pasolini seems to be more sympathetic to the latter, as he writes four years before shooting *Mamma Roma*:

> In every Italian city, even in the north of the country, beyond the last kitchen garden, you will find the "concentration camps" of the poor, made up mostly of warehouses, sheds and shacks. But this reality is nowhere as impressive, complex, and I would say even grandiose, as in Rome. The Roman borgata is a thoroughly modern phenomenon that emerged out of the Fascist State, of which Rome was the capital. It is true that even today, these neighborhoods are being built. They are, in a manner of speaking, "free" neighborhoods, clusters of one- and two-story roofless shacks, which have been left unfinished for years and years, unplastered, lime-white-colored in the countryside and half-abandoned, sparkling or mud-stained like Bedouin villages. [...] The Roman countryside, along the ring road, is teeming with borgate like this one. [...] The real borgate are not these, however, the real borgate are characterized by their "official" nature. They were built by the city as part of a plan to cluster together the poor and the undesirables. This is their origin, both chronological and ideological.[19]

---

17 Pasolini describes these self-built structures along the ancient viaducts in his essay "The Shantytowns of Rome," in Pasolini, *Stories from the City of God: Sketches and Chronicles of Rome 1950–1966*, trans. Marina Harss, ed. Walter Siti (New York: Handsel Books, 2003), 177–84.
18 Viano, *A Certain Realism*, 53–54.
19 Pier Paolo Pasolini, first published in the illustrated magazine *Vie Nuove*, May 24, 1958; reprinted in Pasolini, *Stories from the City of God*, 171–76. To be fair, Pasolini overstates to a certain extent, as the borgate spontanee were already part of the Roman periphery before Mussolini came into power and they expanded rapidly in the post-war period. Nonetheless, scholars on twentieth-century Italian urbanism like Harald Bodenschatz agree on Mussolini's successful attempt to convene state power and private capital in order to orchestrate an urban development of segregation. See Pape, "Collective Rhythm Grouping," 106–16.

As much as the open field is introduced as the other to the housing developments of Tuscolano, a piece of fallow land not yet incorporated into the urban economy of housing and value production, it is not blank. It is the place where young people hang out; here Ettore encounters his friends and finds love—his first romantic and sexual experience with Bruna. It is also a place where antiquity, the aqueduct ruins, and the borgate spontanee vernacular coexist. Discussing Pasolini's aesthetics, Rhodes develops a lengthy argument about the importance of the sublime for Pasolini's work. He argues that the cinematic depiction of the urban landscape, the shapelessness and incomprehensible scale of both housing developments as well as of the scattered urban industrial landscape and wide-open fields in-between, aim at a sublime effect so that "confusion and magnitude 'incite' the viewer."[20] "Whereas the beautiful is repose, poise, ease, the sublime is discomfiture." Following Kant, he argues that Pasolini aimed at "a quickly altering attraction towards, and repulsion from, the same object."[21] Instead, I would argue that Pasolini, as much as he might have aimed at framing the housing development of Tuscolano according to the aesthetics of the sublime, exempts the open field, which, only for the sake of making the argument, would have lent itself perfectly. The musical motif defies this association as much as a closer inspection of the visual references. If an allusion to art history can be drawn, which was a great resource for Pasolini, it would rather be the Roman school of landscape painting of the seventeenth century.[22] The youth hanging out in the open field, the way they assemble around the ancient ruins, the spontaneity with which they make use of the structures (to make out) reenact a way of ease and immediacy that is found in the works of Claude Lorrain, Nicolas Poussin, and their contemporaries.[23] Ettore feels more at ease, possibly more at home, in the open field than in the housing development of Tuscolano.

On a sunny October morning in 2011, I revisited Tuscolano with my friend Susanne Heinrich, reenacting scenes from *Mamma Roma*, and was curious about what the neighborhood had become (*fig. 3*). When we entered Parco degli Acquedotti, a group gathered, barbecuing next to the ruins of Villa delle Vignacce, one of the largest suburban Roman villas. A large table carried a buffet, and while approaching, we were spontaneously invited by the group of people. Vincenzo, who was throwing a birthday dinner for a Romanian friend, became my guide through the Roman periphery for the next couple of weeks. He was a psychologist, part of a nonprofit cooperative supporting the Sinti and Roma as well as *sans-papiers*, Eastern-European migrants, and homeless Italians, while the open field in *Mamma Roma* had become part of Rome's most extensive public park, and the borgate spontanee were mostly torn down, Vincenzo opened my eyes to the large extent in which the Roman periphery still served as home to the subaltern.

20 Rhodes, *Stupendous, Miserable City*, 88.
21 "Rather, he offers us self-consciously the familiar landscape of the Romantic sublime—of Byron and Shelley, of 'arches after arches in unending lines stretching across the uninhabited wilderness, [...] masses of nameless ruins standing like rocks out of the plain'—set side by side with the 'swarming' (perhaps anti-Romantic) sublime of the peripheral cityscape." In Rhodes, *Stupendous, Miserable City*, 123.
22 Classical painting references for cinematic image compositions are very explicit in other Pasolini movies like *La ricotta* (1963). His disappointment with the Palestine landscape in *Sopralluoghi in Palestina* (1963) is revealing as he states that it does in no way resemble the depiction of biblical scenery as quintessentially as the Renaissance paintings he had in mind, making him decide to shoot the film *Il vangelo secondo Matteo* (1964) in Italy. Even in *Mamma Roma*, he shoots Ettore on his deathbed in the manner of Andrea Mantegna's painting *Lamentation over the Dead Christ* (ca. 1480).
23 Claude Lorrain, *Campo Vaccino* (1636), Dulwich Picture Gallery, London.

Together, we visited the peripheral Sinti and Roma camps—*campi abusivi* (illicit camps) (*fig. 4*)—and the newly constructed official camps (*fig. 5*) to which they were relocated by force on the basis of the Berlusconi government's Emergenza Nomadi (Nomad emergency) administration acts.[24] In January 2010, the city administration of Rome had started putting the Piano Nomadi (Nomad plan) into action, which allowed for the forced eviction of thousands of Sinti and Roma from their camps into newly built authorized camps, forcing them to leave their caravans behind and settle into confined barracks on the periphery, mostly devoid of any access to public transport. Delays in construction led to a worsening of living conditions, in comparison to the informal camps. The locations of the camps and the lack of consultation and negotiation with the affected families also led to further segregation. Shortly after our visits, the Italian council of state declared the Piano Nomadi unlawful.

Yet, even though the plan had mostly affected Sinti and Roma, it also encompassed the denomination of homeless and *sans-papiers* as "nomads." The subaltern—featured and given a voice by Pasolini in writing and film—still populate the Roman periphery's open fields in uncounted numbers (*fig. 6*). The guiding principles are still invisibility and segregation, drawing a continuous line back to the Mussolini regime and its disciplinary policies. Mussolini tolerated the borgate spontanee as long as they could not be seen from the major roads. Facing this long tradition of ignorance, suppression, and relentless political stigmatization, Pasolini's *Mamma Roma* gains in actuality and relevance. Architecture and urban design and planning seem to be at odds with creating environments for a truly open city. It seems that large parts of the urban population are as invisible to designers and planners as they are to citizens and politicians defining the political economy of the urban.

Pasolini does not give advice for planning but reminds us that the open field plays a substantial role in the creation of open and accessible cities. In *Mamma Roma*, the field is not planned, it actually exists outside the control of planning. It contains the beautiful ruins of a former empire, divested of all claims to representing power. They are available as support structures to the borgate spontanee and as hosts to ephemeral encounters. The open field is a rare combination of raw authenticity and refined beauty: it is the place in which freedom of action and interpretation is possible, independent from questions of class and social background. This model landscape is perhaps one of the key metaphors in a discussion about public space that is long overdue. The normative concept of a homogeneous and neutral public space is challenged by a multiplicity of marginal cultures and fails to be inclusive. Instances of otherness are always an opportunity to rethink public space. Instead of insisting on the stifling bourgeois social mores which still inform many parks in cities, a lesser degree of control should be encouraged to allow for cities to conceive of and comprise arcadian landscapes in which reciprocal encounters can take place.

---

24 See "Italy: Briefing to the UN Committee on the Elimination of Discrimination," *Amnesty International Report 2012: The State of the World's Human Rights* (London: Amnesty International Ltd, 2012), 190–91.

"In Campo Aperto: The Open Field," reenactment series of Pier Paolo Pasolini's *Mamma Roma* (1962) with Susanne Heinrich, 2011.

Campo abusivo La Barbuta, Rome, an informal Roma camp, 2011.

Campo ufficiale La Barbuta, Rome, the official camp planned for the relocation of most of the inhabitants of La Barbuta, 2011.

Campo abusivo, Rome, an illicit camp of Romanian migrants, 2011.

THE ENCOUNTER

I am the stranger
I come overnight
I don't have much luggage, I don't make a fuss
The next morning, I'm there
You anticipated me coming, but you did not see me

You cannot be sure if I come in peace
I understand you, but I do not speak your tongue
I know the name you assigned to me, but I do not obey
I walk your streets, but differently
You look behind me
But you will lose sight of me
I know when you sleep and when you are awake

I cut across the country, but I know where I stand
If you follow me, I vanish behind the trees
I am not afraid of chaos
Chaos is with me

You can send me wherever you want
But when and how I go, I decide
I do not need your blessing

Maybe something is missing when I am gone
Maybe I vanish silently, maybe
I go down fighting
And leave traces
In the grass

—Susanne Heinrich[25]

---

25 This poem was written as a contribution to the installation by the author, "In Campo Aperto," for the end-of-year exhibition of the German Academy in Rome, Villa Massimo, in 2011. Susanne Heinrich is a German author, singer, and film director based in Leipzig.

TRANSGRESSING ECOLOGY

141   c. *Freie Anlagen.*   142

Fig. 42.

desselben im hohen Grade steigern. Leider wird dieses immer noch nicht gehörig gewürdigt, denn man fährt fort die wenigen noch vorhandenen Wälder zu lichten oder gänzlich niederzuschlagen und macht den Boden zu Acker, beraubt ihn aber zugleich durch die Armuth an Gehölz eines grofsen Theiles seiner Fruchtbarkeit und des nöthigen Schutzes. Sicher wird nach dieser Zeit des crassen Materialismus eine bessere folgen, wo man nicht ausschliefslich nach der gegenwärtigen Ertragsfähigkeit, sondern auch nach der Lage und den Annehmlichkeiten des Landsitzes fragen und diese Vorzüge verhältnifsmäfsig höher bezahlen wird, als die Mittel sich belaufen, welche für die Verschönerungen aufgewandt wurden. Wenn endlich noch dergleichen Verschönerungen successive und grofsentheils mit den eigenen Gespannen und Arbeitskräften zu Zeiten ausgeführt werden, wo solche aus der Wirthschaft sehr gut entbehrt werden können, so sind die Kosten im Verhältnifs zu dem Nutzen und der Annehmlichkeit die man sich schafft, durchaus nur als sehr mäfsig zu erachten.

Auf Tafel XVI und XVII ist der Grundplan eines verschönerten ländlichen Wohnsitzes mit seinen Baulichkeiten, dem Park, Pleasureground und einem Theile der freien Anlagen zur bildlichen Erläuterung des Vorangehenden dargestellt worden.

**1860: JOHANN HEINRICH GUSTAV MEYER,
ILLUSTRATION FROM *LEHRBUCH DER SCHÖNEN GARTENKUNST***

1984: MAP SHOWING THE MOST VALUABLE BIOTOPES IN WEST BERLIN

2017: BEECH STUMP, TIERGARTEN

2017: WINDSTORM AFTERMATH, TIERGARTEN

KARIN REISINGER

PARK ENCOUNTERS, IN CITY CENTERS, OR TRANSPLANTED TO THE HINTERLANDS

> Why did this white woman come all the way to speak to us? Can I go to speak to the researchers of Europe?
> —Gold miner on the border of the Gorongosa National Park, Mozambique, 2011

I want to bring attention to two contrasting parks. They are situated in very different cultural and political environments as well as in different densities of constructed surrounds.[1] These examples from Russia and Mozambique show encounters between an investigation and everyday life; more relevantly, they address encounters between humans with different ideas of "nature," between humans and nonhumans, and their hierarchical dynamics. The subsequent transgressions result in new encounters: in the case of these two parks, new political encounters arise out of nature preservation practices. The subjects influence and shape each other through the encounter, and borders and divides are transgressed. In this regard, this view on the two specific areas of nature preservation is highly influenced by Donna J. Haraway's concept of "naturecultures" and its spatial context, "naturalcultural contact zones."[2]

Furthermore, transitions correlate with encounters: How did these territories become the landscapes of preservation they are today? Among nature preservationists especially, my questions about what had paved the way for the territories to *become* nature-preservation areas provoked discomfort. This practice of tracing socio-political agencies and relations within territories withheld for "nature," as well as their spatial manifestations, was neither appreciated by architects nor by ecologists or biologists. In complex landscapes, different actors, histories, conflicts, and natures collide and create a multitude of present encounters. Moreover, the ongoing existence of preserved areas is dependent on resources, forces, and energies being invested repeatedly.

In order to grasp some of the relations between the complex encounters taking place in the spatial exceptions of parks, this essay introduces two specific case studies: the urban Losiny Ostrov in Moscow and the example of Gorongosa National Park in Mozambique, which has been commonly assumed to be rural. These are two differently situated parks, embedded in one common policy but in different societies, politics, and cultural concepts of nature. With these examples, I aim to show encounters of groups busy planning the survival of the ecological environment with groups themselves busy surviving. Thus, I hope to transgress an apparently "pure" or "purified" understanding and practice of ecology to unveil its spatial, political, and cultural requirements and ramifications.

LOSINY OSTROV, MOSCOW

Like Berlin's Tiergarten, Losiny Ostrov, a national park near the Moscow city center, functions as a platform for assembling the ecological, cultural, social, and political needs of the city. One third of the national park's area lies within the city of Moscow. The population can reach the park within a short walking distance from shopping malls, train stations, and high-rise housing units. Only five metro stations stand between the

---

[1] This essay is a specific perspective on research undertaken for my dissertation *Grass Without Roots: Towards Nature Becoming Spatial Practice* (Vienna University of Technology, 2014).
[2] Donna J. Haraway, *When Species Meet* (Minneapolis: University of Minnesota Press, 2008).

Red Square and Sokolniki park, which directly merges with Losiny Ostrov. For the many tourists of Moscow, Losiny Ostrov is not a place of destination. Not even for a large number of Muscovites, as many of them describe it as dangerous. It is largely used by its neighbors for recreation and sport, as shortcuts between other parts of the city, and for illegal activities like collecting mushrooms and barbecuing. For that, built structures are unnecessary, as, for example, an improvised grill between the trees and some camping chairs completely meet the demands. The inner part of the park is subdivided into rectangular fields between streets of concrete, making the landscape especially efficient for crossing by bicycle and jogging. Snakes like to lie on the warm concrete, heated by the sun, and elks like to drink from puddles in the cracks of the pathways after the rain. Because of the rectangular grid of the streets, the area preserved for nature can easily be traversed from one part of the city to the other, and with a bit of luck, a snake could even be encountered. Followed or transgressed, a set of rules according to the preservation of nature is set in place, but what is absolutely valuable about this site is that it can be accessed easily by everybody without expensive travel costs or entrance fees (fig. 1).

The question of access is especially relevant in view of the fact that in 2014, 15.2 percent of the world's terrestrial surface consisted of nature preservation areas, whereas in 1990, it was only 8.7 percent.[3] Some scientists and nature preservationists have demanded setting up to even 50 percent under the preservation of nature.[4] Considering this massive growth, the political and social requirements for the areas primarily dedicated to nonhuman ecosystems are enormously complex and far-reaching. Looking into the genealogies of certain examples shows that it has often been difficult to withhold areas from human use. Armed conflicts, displacements, and denial of access have often lead to the discontinuation of cultural activities, easing the conversion of land in areas of nature preservation. Losiny Ostrov was founded as the exclusive hunting reserve of Grand Princes and tsars, including Ivan the Terrible. Today the park is deeply interwoven into the urban environment and, as well, offers a valuable ecological environment within a megacity. Tensions and transgressions between nature and culture are particularly visible at the border areas of the park but also within. In its history, during the Time of Troubles in the early seventeenth century,[5] resources in Losiny Ostrov were plundered and the land cultivated for self-sustenance. Today, constant recreation activities and the grilling habits of Muscovites are comparable to constant small-scale ecological crises.

Such a large park within a huge city requires a strong political will to continue to exist and requires navigating between ecological and

---

3   United Nations Statistics Division, "Millennium Development Goals, Targets and Indicators, 2015: Statistical Tables," accessed April 18, 2016, http://mdgs.un.org/unsd/mdg/Resources/Static/Products/Progress2015/StatAnnex.pdf.
4   Camilo Mora and Peter F. Sale report on scientific extension plans in "Ongoing Global Biodiversity Loss and the Need to Move Beyond Protected Areas: A Review of the Technical and Practical Shortcomings of Protected Areas on Land and Sea," *Marine Ecology Progress Series*, vol. 434 (2011): 251–66. Another demand for setting aside 50 percent for preservation comes from the evolutionary biologist Edward O. Wilson, for example in the article by Tony Hiss, "Can the World Really Set Aside Half of the Planet for Wildlife?," accessed April 19, 2016, http://www.smithsonianmag.com.
5   The term *Smuta*, "times of severe crisis" in Russia in the early seventeenth century, defines the period after Moscow's ancient ruling dynasty, which was characterized by high political instability including the uprising against serfdom, social revolution, civil war, the assassination of the new Tsar, and above all, hunger. See Chester Dunning, "Time of Troubles," in *Encyclopedia of Russian History*, vol. 4, ed. James R. Millar et al. (New York: Macmillan Reference, 2004), 1548–53.

identity politics in order to withhold the development of urban real estate for, instead, the purposes of preservation. In no other national park have I found a comparably vivid atmosphere of daily exchange and encounter. Under Stalin, people secretly held pre-political constitutional meetings in the parks of Moscow in order to escape control. Historian Karl Schlögel alludes to the indirect political function of Muscovite parks in the 1930s as being a place free from political manipulation, where the planning of revolutions was possible. From the 1930s onward recreational parks in Moscow were planned with educational and political intentions.[6] However, in practice, they also functioned as meeting points for immigrants, illicit activities, and revolutionary celebrations. Schlögel claimed the removal of bushes and underwood in the parks helped to ease security sweeps. In these complex and contradictory relationships, he defined these park areas of the non- or pre-political in a politicized society under Stalin.[7]

There was also another political park encounter, which took place in Sokolniki Park, the most "disciplined" extension of the Losiny Ostrov national park. It was here that Richard Nixon and Nikita Khrushchev held their famous "Kitchen Debate" in a model kitchen exhibited at the American National Exhibition of 1959. United States representatives at the height of the Cold War did their best to show the advantages of Western capitalism by exhibiting and distributing objects of desire and consumption, such as nylon tights and Pepsi-Cola.[8] This was accentuated by the seven-screen display of Ray and Charles Eames's *Glimpses of the USA* in Buckminster Fuller's dome, which showed connective elements between the USA and USSR, such as photographs of nature.

By definition, in a national park, the political aspect is regularly absent, and the cultural aspect is subordinate. The International Union for Conservation of Nature (IUCN), with its headquarters in Switzerland, defines national parks[9] as "large natural or near natural areas set aside to protect large-scale ecological processes, along with the complement of species and ecosystems characteristic of the area, which also provide a foundation for environmentally and culturally compatible, spiritual, scientific, educational, recreational and visitor opportunities."[10] This definition offers encounters and compatibilities but also entails hierarchies, and in practice often results in conflicts, such as in the example of imposed fines in Losiny Ostrov. The website of the national park regularly reports on violations and transgressions of the strict concept of natural heritage, even showing uncensored photographs of the offenders, which bears online testimony to unpleasant encounters.

---

6 According to Karl Marx, the removal of the distinction between city and country is one of the first conditions of the collective. This is one of many attempts of the early 1930s to translate Moscow into a new political center of socialism by redesigning the worker's everyday life. Collective recreation in large parks is one of them. For Marx's quote, see Michail O. Baršč et al., "Magnitogor'e. Zum Generalplan-Schema: 1930," in *Städtebau im Schatten Stalins*, ed. Harald Bodenschatz and Christiane Post (Berlin: Verlagshaus Braun, 2003), 361–67.
7 Karl Schlögel wrote about public space during Stalinism in "Zur Frage des öffentlichen Raums im Stalinismus," in *Stalinismus vor dem Zweiten Weltkrieg: Neue Wege der Forschung*, ed. Manfred Hildermeier and Elisabeth Müller-Luckner (Munich: R. Oldenbourg Verlag, 1998), 255–74. See also Karl Schlögel, *Moscow* (London: Reaktion, 2005).
8 Monica Rüthers, "Markt und Mangel: Geschichten der Konsumkultur vom Hoflieferanten bis zur Defizitwirtschaft," in *Moskau: Menschen Mythen Orte*, ed. Monica Rüthers and Carmen Scheide (Cologne: Böhlau Verlag Gmbh & Cie, 2003), 58–82, and especially 72–73.
9 Defined as a Protected Area Category II.
10 "Protected Areas Categories," *IUCN*, accessed April 22, 2016, http://www.iucn.org/about/work/programmes/gpap_home/gpap_quality/gpap_pacategories/.

ENCOUNTERS WITHIN EXCEPTIONS

We have seen that the state of nature is not a real epoch chronologically prior to the foundation of the City but a principle internal to the City, which appears at the moment the City is considered *tanquam dissoluta*, "as if it were dissolved" (in this sense, therefore, the state of nature is something like a state of exception).
—Giorgio Agamben, *Homo Sacer*[11]

In my examples, various states of exception alternate. To *become* nature, the dissolution of the city and of history by the enfolding of an internal principle is necessary. The national park areas examined were all disconnected from everyday society in various forms during their foundation: Losiny Ostrov in Moscow was a hunting reserve, and Gorongosa in Mozambique was a colonial hunting reserve which later housed guerrilla troops. These states of exception have clear transitional dates, with inaugurations and occupations and clear spatial borders between exceptional areas and their social and political surroundings. Whereas Agamben's definition of the state of exception was developed from a political perspective, the IUCN definition uses the words of spatial transformation, namely "set aside." It does not, however, contain a political gravity, which politicians like Jimmy Carter were completely aware of: "Politically, the creation of national parks has never been easy. Powerful forces have opposed setting aside land, calling it an impediment to the progress of power and commerce."[12] Many politicians could be quoted here with similarly ambivalent statements about forces invested in the creation of uncreated areas.

In the examined examples, natural heritage has clear precedence when it comes to decision-making—mainly made by biologists and ecologists after a political impetus, followed by political instrumentalization. Sometimes planners are involved when it comes to making spatial decisions, but often ecologists take over that task. In order to work within social and political environments, the statute of nature preservation could dynamically be redefined, reflecting on the copresence of various actors according to their different disciplines, experiences, and practices. By taking more perspectives into account, the danger of continuously separating nature and culture in the organization, use, and theorization of these exceptional areas could be reduced.[13] Instead, Haraway argues that "relations are constitutive" and that "it is time to think harder about encounter value."[14] Marie Luise Pratt witnessed the value of the "contact" perspective to emphasize "how subjects are constituted in and by their relations to each other [...] in terms of copresence, interaction, interlocking understandings and practices, often within radically asymmetrical relations of power."[15] With the ecosystems and encounters of this essay, I want to demonstrate that "pure nature" no

---

11   Giorgio Agamben, *Homo Sacer, Sovereign Power and Bare Life* (Stanford: Stanford University Press, 1998), 63. Giorgio Agamben's theory of the state of exception has formed a first basis for the theoretical understanding of the national parks I examined. Agamben describes and assembles many factors of the state of exception: the suspension of law, uncertainty, necessity, zones of undecidability, in *The State of Exception* (Chicago: University of Chicago Press, 2005).
12   Jimmy Carter, "The Finest Legacy," foreword to Kim Heacox, *An American Idea: The Making of National Parks* (Washington: National Geographic Society, 2001), 8–9.
13   This remark refers to the tradition of negotiating, discussing, and indoctrinating the dichotomies between *nature* and *culture*, or between *nature* and *nurture*—too many thinkers to be quoted here. This suggestion can also be understood as a process of unlearning.
14   Haraway, *When Species Meet*, 62. Haraway primarily focuses on trans-species encounter value.
15   Marie Louise Pratt, *Imperial Eyes: Travel Writing and Transculturation* (New York: Routledge, 1992), 7.

longer exists and that the process of purifying landscapes is based on radical power and often violence. In *Censorship Today: Violence or Ecology as a New Opium for the Masses*, Slavoj Žižek states that nature "is no longer 'natural,'" but "it now appears as a fragile mechanism which, at any point, can explode in a catastrophic direction."[16] Histories of national parks, often contaminated by histories of armed conflicts or the displacement of humans, underline this transgression.

GORONGOSA, MOZAMBIQUE

The Gorongosa National Park in Mozambique in the "hinterlands"[17] of the country stands in contrast to the urban setting of Losiny Ostrov. I will always remember this park in connection to funny families of warthogs looking for food amid tourist bungalows. Founded during colonial times, the restoration of the Gorongosa ecosystem is organized and financed by the American philanthropist Gregory Carr, who collaborates with the Mozambican government. Cultural heritage is here again subordinate to natural heritage, following the definition and migrated concept of a national park, and to tourism, following the economic pressure of the preservation project. Contrasts and radical encounters determine the exception, especially at its borders. The rich, who can afford traveling to the Mozambican hinterland, meet the poorest of the world. The hinterland becomes the center, and this encounter causes various conflictual practices and tensions. Examples are luxurious tourist bungalows and game safaris next to the daily journey of the park's service staff, transgressing the Rio Pungue river day by day. This river marks the border between the protected area, the national park, and the area of the Vinho community. It is here that people grow vegetables in the immediate neighborhood of the national park and bring food to the Chitengo campsite of the park, which is served to tourists and workers in two separate restaurants. The river becomes a border that marks a difference. The crossing is only possible by using a small ferryboat (*fig. 2*). On their way back, the same people have to pass a checkpoint where they are sometimes searched for stolen cutlery.

"Such contact zones [conservation projects] are full of complexities of different kinds of unequal power that do not always go in expected directions," writes Donna J. Haraway in *When Species Meet*.[18] This unequal power goes hand in hand with economic differences. It results in regulations, for example, and can be traced in various practices and consequent encounters. Additionally, national parks bear the danger of repeating meta-narratives and specific practices used for the stabilization of nationalities, but colliding with the micro-narratives of the inhabitants' daily lives. That conflictual relation was visible in the political unrest and violent encounters of Gorongosa. The Mozambican National Resistance (RENAMO) is the political opponent of the leading party of Mozambique, the Mozambique Liberation Front (FRELIMO). RENAMO therefore also acts as an opponent of the park, because they understand the "national" park as a political project supported

---

16 Slavoj Žižek, "Censorship Today: Violence or Ecology as a New Opium for the Masses?," *After Zero*, vol. 18 (2008), 43. Žižek goes as far as to relocate the discontent of Freud's title "Unbehagen in der Kultur" ("Civilization and its Discontents," first published in 1930) in nature.
17 Initially, I came across the term "hinterland" in the historical descriptions of the area of Gorongosa. It was used because of its position, connecting the area of former Zimbabwe to the next seaport, was a strategic position during conflicts. The position of a hinterland allowed the development of a valuable ecosystem, but precisely because of this position the same ecosystem was later destroyed during the Civil War. This divide between city and hinterland becomes clear not least through the ongoing urbanization around the park. Different from "land" and "country," the term hinterland provides an inherent connection to urbanity and politics.
18 Haraway, *When Species Meet*, 218.

by FRELIMO and as an impediment to their local cultures.[19] During the Liberation and Civil Wars, they had their bases within or near the National Park. Today, holes in the ground from weapons storage are reminders of that period. In 2011, I interviewed members of RENAMO in Vila Gorongosa at the border of the park. They expressed their fear of continuous colonization as areas are being declared part of the park with the government's support. The park is only one of many issues in the conflict between the two parties but, including its human and nonhuman participants, it became a target of continual aggression. RENAMO rebels, bearing arms in 2012, started to maliciously attack both the people and the infrastructure around the park, leading to fatalities and destruction.[20] In 2013 and 2014, their political leader hid in the mountain of the park, the area with the strongest percentage of opponents of the ruling party.[21] These are examples of political encounters in and around territories dedicated to the ecosystem.

In Losiny Ostrov, regular transgression and use of the park are dominant whereas in Gorongosa, wealthy tourists from all over the world are served by nearby villagers. The extension of the Gorongosa National Park area in 2007 caused discontent among the inhabitants of the border region. In 2011 some villages were about to be removed. Directly outside the gates of the park the population has been increasing, reaching nearly urban numbers. This situation of various encounters around the accumulation of nature has its roots in colonial times when "conservation practices outlawed indigenous survival activities – hunting, fishing, slash and burn, housing, spirituality – in certain ecosystems in Gorongosa."[22] In the aftermath of the colonial era, during the armed conflicts, thousands had fled to the National Park mountains, but in the last years, the government has attempted to "mobilize"[23] them to leave the area—due to ecological reasons. By 2010, the anthropologist Carolien Jacobs has already written about the situation of the people in Kanda at the foot of Gorongosa Mountain: "Taking the term 'invader' loosely, the Park[24] can be seen as a modern invader, who – supported by formal arrangements with government – might be able to take over political control."[25] The restoration of the park did however open a political can of worms, with a politics of ecologies that were not anticipated by the main players. Although Gregory Carr claims his activities to be apolitical and purely ecologically motivated,[26] political interaction and instrumentalization took place in a complex spatial assemblage of interests. Haraway describes "situated histories, situated naturecultures, in which all the actors become who they are *in the dance of relating*, not from scratch, not *ex nihilo*, but full of the patterns of their sometimes-joined, sometimes-separate heritages both before and lateral to *this* encounter."[27] I would argue that in the preservation areas, similar encounter dynamics simultaneously

---

19 This refers to interviews I made in 2011 in Vila Gorongosa.
20 See for example the newspapers *Moçambique para todos* and *Verdade* (online and printed).
21 "Foreigners Leave as Mozambique Tensions Rise," *New Zimbabwe*, November 10, 2013, accessed June 28, 2016, http://www.newzimbabwe.com/news-12999-ForeignersfleetenseMozambique/news.aspx.
22 Domingos Muala, "When Nature Science Despised Local Experience: Re-engineers, Destroyers, and Restorers of Wilderness in Gorongosa," (master's thesis proposal, Utah State University). Muala, a Mozambican anthropologist, accompanied me during my interviews in the villages around Gorongosa National Park in 2011.
23 "Mobilization" (or "Mobilização" in Portuguese) is the term used onsite for motivating people living within the borders of the national park or in the buffer zone to move to other areas.
24 Jacobs writes park with capital P to express the strength and the power of the park.
25 Carolien Jacobs, "Navigating Through a Landscape of Powers or Getting Lost on Mount Gorongosa," *Journal of Legal Pluralism*, no. 61 (2010): 104.
26 Interview in 2011.
27 Haraway, *When Species Meet*, 25.

take place during the encounters of different human actors or groups. The agenda of the Gorongosa Park project is determined by actual urgent ecological necessities, but it also produced relevant social and political transformations, for example by generating jobs.

With the two spatial and political national park environments, I have showed two different versions of naturecultures and their unstoppable "dances of relating." Many conflicts are caused by making decisions about spatial implementations of global ecological concepts in cities; they are often externalized, transplanted, and rerooted in the hinterlands, where they potentially lead to conflictual encounters. Transnational and transcultural influences concerned with the survival of species unavoidably meet daily local practices of sheer survival or local socio-politics. In this context, transgressing the nature-culture divide is conflictual because natural heritage practices dominate social and political environments. In any case, it is impossible to tell the complex story of Gorongosa Park in a way in which every involved being agrees.

DEAR GOLD MINERS, PLANNERS, FARMERS, RESEARCHERS, TOURISTS, ECOLOGISTS, POACHERS, AND POLITICIANS

Endangered species encounter violent pasts in specific spatial settings, actors transgress the borders, and the intermingled concepts of nature and culture blur at various scales. Urban parks like Losiny Ostrov have showed their political potential under Stalin, whereas other parks showed political meanings even if, or because of the very fact that they were transplanted to peripheral hinterlands. In addition to the ecological demands of environmental threats, national parks often unite various functions that, rather, serve the concerns and desires of the privileged instead of the local social environment. This has provoked reactions like the furious rage of the RENAMO in Mozambique.

The encounters listed in this paper are composites of my journeys in search of cultural and political encounters in apparently "purified" territories. In the landscapes of complex heritage, memoryscapes in nature preservation areas, various spatial practices and actors find themselves in competition, displacement, and hierarchy—but also in new productive encounters and naturecultures that challenge traditional dichotomies. "You're just juggling," says Gregory Carr in describing the Gorongosa restoration project.[28] The example of Losiny Ostrov in Moscow displays a vivid range of valuable encounters but also displays a great economic potential as an urban area withheld for nature: real estate projects try to transgress the borders by building close to the preserved area; illegal settlements are sometimes even built inside the preservation area. The location of parks and their connections and disconnections to the immediate environment determine the encounters on their borders—depending on who has access and who doesn't. If an area of nature preservation is located inside a city, many people have access to it. In Moscow, nature preservation is literally moved into the center, not only enabled by figures like Ivan the Terrible, but also by socialist city planning. On the other hand, the example of the Mozambican hinterland shows that the production and accumulation of nature include processes of urbanization. However, there is a complex political and cultural level of the anthropogenic practice of nature preservation; facing

---

28 Philip Gourevitch, "The Monkey and the Fish," *New Yorker*, December 21, 2009, accessed June 22, 2015, http://www.newyorker.com/magazine/2009/12/21/the-monkey-and-the-fish.

recent political global and local changes, potentially growing to 50 percent of the world surface, and becoming areas of encounters for planners and gold miners, researchers, and poachers, as well as for ecologists and politicians, the definition of such a park could become "large natural or near natural areas set aside to protect large-scale *and small-scale* ecological processes, *which include social, cultural and political processes and their daily encounters with nonhumans*, along with the complement of species and ecosystems characteristic of the area."[29] As a method of research into these territories, critically assembling many micro-encounters at the same level of meta-encounters of accepted history and stabilizing processes of ecologies and nations could help rethink and redesign the spaces from the perspective of encounters. In this critical assembling instead of debunking,[30] I seek "to disclose [...] the socio-political and cultural relations of power, discipline and appropriation"[31] within the necessary course of nature preservation, in hinterlands and in cities, and in their overlaps.[32]

29 This is my own transformation of the official IUCN definition of nature preservation areas. Words in italic replace parts of the official IUCN definition. For the original definition of national parks, see http://www.iucn.org/about/work/programmes/gpap_home/gpap_quality/gpap_pacategories/gpap_pacategory2/.
30 See Bruno Latour, "Why Has Critique Run Out of Steam? From Matters of Fact to Matters of Concern," *Critical Inquiry* 30 (Winter 2004): 225–48.
31 I borrowed Suzana Milevska's words from her lecture "Landscapes Without Bodies: Beyond the 'Innocent' Topology of Transitional Spaces," at the symposium *In Transitional Landscapes* at Packhaus Vienna, on January 16, 2015.
32 This essay was written in Spring 2016. More than one year later, political tensions in Gorongosa have intensified, and new ceasefires have been arranged. Economic pressure on the land of Losiny Ostrov increased. Rewriting this essay in 2017 demanded taking new perspectives into account and giving voice to new human and nonhuman refugees and pioneers. In the presentation "Connective Oscillations: Architectures between the Devil and the Deep Blue Sea" at the MORE Congress in Florence, January 26–28, 2016, I focused on the nonhuman perspective of such encounters (forthcoming in the anthology *More. Expanding Architecture from a Gender-based Perspective*, Didapress, 2018).

Film stills INTO the Losiny Ostrov park in Moscow, 2014. Film: Karin Reisinger.

[1]

Film stills INTO the Gorongosa park, Mozambique, 2011. Film: Karin Reisinger.

EVA HAYWARD

RADIANCE OF CARDINALS, SHIVER OF SHARKS: MULTIPLICITIES, AESTHETICS, AND THE LIMITS OF ETHICS

> *Limitrophy* is therefore my subject. Not just because it will concern what sprouts or grows at the limit, around the limit, by maintaining the limit, but also what feeds the limit, generates it, raises it, and complicates it. Everything I'll say will consist, certainly not in effacing the limit, but in multiplying its figures, in complicating, thickening, delinearizing, folding, and dividing the line precisely by making it increase and multiply.... [The limit] has an abyss: The discussion is worth undertaking once it is a matter of determining the number, form, sense, or structure, the foliated consistency, of this abyssal limit, these edges, this plural and repeatedly folded frontier.
> —Jacques Derrida, *The Animal that Therefore I Am*

This spring I taught an undergraduate Animal Studies course, which did the usual things that such courses now do: get students to question the categories of Man and Animal.[1] We discussed the artificial nature of these categories—how these designations *do not* represent ontological states, but *the logic of ontology* itself. Man is a promise, an assurance of human inclusion, however this promise has functioned as a foreclosure, a technology for ensuring that *not* all humans are made Man. Recall Frantz Fanon's assertion, "Colonial racism is no different from any other racism. Anti-Semitism hits me head-on: I am enraged, I am bled white by an appalling battle, I am deprived of the possibility of being a man."[2] Racism, Fanon argues, is what made Man. The Animal, in contrast, administrates this inequality; that is to say, the Animal is both punishment and the apparatus of punishment. If you are animalized, your manhood is refused. These seeming ontologies are operations, technologies of violence, and their primary goal is to stabilize anthropocentrism through technologies of race and sex. While keenly aware of these operations, we also wanted to take up Jacques Derrida's notion of "limitrophy," or the "abyssal limit," which has come to define our relationship with other sentient life. Knowing that the Man/Animal "divide" is a misnomer—one that obscures foreclosure through a discourse of speciation—my class also wanted to hold open the unknowable, to consider the agential force of organismal life that has been misrecognized as Animal. In this, we had to ask: What is at stake in wanting to attend to animal life? Subsequently, how we consider these lives—let alone the question of ethics—without returning to their Animal knowability?

In our discussions on animal rights and critiques of speciesism—where we examined how the Animal is mobilized through human rights discourse, and in this way, animal rights is a racial project, that, somewhat ironically, reaffirms the Man (and the racial supremacy it concretizes)—I was struck by my students' belief that seeing "animals" as individuals is necessary for engendering empathy, identification, and an ethics of care. Only the intersubjective look—a reach that folds in the Other—through eyes of recognition, familiarity, pupil-to-pupil, proffered *real* resistance to hierarchical domination. Speciesism, they were suggesting, is the inability to see "animals" as "*this* animal." Extending Derrida's neologism *l'animot*[3]—a species designation that recognizes differences between kinds

---

1 Our discussion of Man as a metaphysical and ideological construct was informed by our reading of Sylvia Wynter and Katheine McKittrick's "Unparalleled Catastrophe for Our Species? Or, to Give Humanness a Different Future: Conversations," in McKittrick's edited collection *Sylvia Wynter: On Being Human as Praxis* (Durham, NC: Duke University Press, 2015).
2 Frantz Fanon, *The Wretched of the Earth* (New York: Grove Press, 2005).
3 Jacques Derrida, *The Animal that Therefore I Am*, ed. Marie-Louis Mallet, trans. David Willis (New York: Fordham University Press, 2008).

of animals; grasshoppers are not sparrows, but under the gross designation "the animal" they are enfolded, entombed, enclosed—might not the proximity of *this*[4] grasshopper (*her* eyes; *his* antennae) resolve an over-arching assumption about grasshoppers (in the plural form)? *This* grasshopper might resolve (as Derrida also does with his cat—*this* cat is "she," he tells us) the indeterminate pronoun "it," which is an abjected pronoun for Man—"what is it?" to query the sexually ambiguous.[5] "It" may index *this* ("*This* cat, *it* is looking at me") as an act of not assuming sex (what we might call an ethical act), even as it still signifies failed humanness ("Man? Woman? It.") for the sexually ambiguous.[6] *This* animal, my students surmised, is a radical break with both anthropocentrism ("the animal") and speciesism (*l'animot*)—what is afforded the liberal humanist subject (selfhood, and its presumption of ontology) is conferred to *this* animal. The inward noir of the pupil, those tiny voids—the dark edge of the eye—is a limit and an abyss, and as my students questioned: Might this abyssal limit be the opening toward care, empathy, and ethics?

At one register, of course, we see *this* impulse as a desire to be responsible for the oppression and suffering of sentient life. Specificity (species-specific), then, becomes an ethical register, a domain of know-ability. In part, know-ability is a capacity to make meaningful, but the ethical interrogative of *this* animal (*this* indexing a register of proximity and closeness) also requires a degree of identification (however capacious). The ethical gesture—attention to specificity—is subtended by a degree of *like*-ness, a degree of recognition to confer individuality. Embedded in the proposal of individuation is the presumption of ontology—if the Man is assured an ontological status, then surely the Animal—as an ethical act—is also ontological (rather than operation of ontology). This is an understandable proposition—after all, my students represent the neoliberalization of universities in the United States. But, at another register, one I counter-proposed to my students, we can see this as an anthropocentric—and in this, ultimately a racist—demand: "If you are like me, then (and only then) you are worthy of my care." After all, is not anthropocentrism another word for narcissism? And if anthropocentrism reveals itself as an investment in the racial ordering of the Man, then this narcissism takes up white supremacy as its function. The common-sense certainty of my students—or more generally, and more problematically, animal rights activists and advocates—about face-to-face, pupil-to-pupil ethics, left me wondering about problems with individuality, ontology, and identification in thinking ethically about sentience.

My curiosity is often guided by art; to think, I turn to paintings, sculptures, and photographs. This is a "turn" fueled as much by pleasure as it is a methodological turn. As if a turn toward the world—the world as it is *felt*—is always a turning toward the indexical stroke of a brush or the texture of a line or the umbilicus of light between referent and photo.[7] Or, how art—that assumed sole enterprise of Man—enacts the receptive and tenuous force that sensuousness is. Art impinges on us from beyond our will, our making, or our ability to anticipate—as such, it has a privileged relationship with the psyche. Formalism—as one kind of creative attention to artful impingement or imposition—emphasizes the form as the locus of this charge. How color and line moves my eye across an artwork, for instance, demonstrates a compositional affront (*affronté*) that demands a response. Form/alism is about the inextricable force of materiality and subjectivity

---

7   Roland Barthes *Camera Lucida: Reflections on Photography*, trans Richard Howard (New York: Hill and Wang, 1982).

(psychical life), and how these forces coterminous. All at once, this thickness of paint is a charge, a substance, and a politic. Form draws limits, as Jacques Derrida has it; it is always a complication and a differentiation.

In the opening epigraph, Derrida describes the limiting function between the Man and the Animal. For Derrida, this limit is both an abyss and an effect of the abyss, a loss and its symptom. Derrida is not indexing the racial function of the Man and the Animal, not what Frank Wilderson will call a by-product of "the Human/Black divide," in which the Man is antiblack, is racist.[8] The abyss and its effect, in Derrida's terms, are what produce the Man, the absence (another Lack) that creates a generative edge (castration). Limitrophy, his neologism, describes the proliferating symptom that is the Animal (and for Derrida, animals), symptoms that make up the precarity of subjectivity. The subject is an effect of not only what it is not, but also what it can never know. The Animal is permanently unknown; consequently, our relation with animals is symptomatic.[9] Unknow-ability is a limit, a refrain that generates form, structure, and arrangement.

As an abstraction, minimalist painting illustrates form as a philosophical limit. What is minimal is still in excess, in plentitude, but limit is the refrain of such abundance. The limit compresses so as to ignite, "complicating, thickening, delinearizing, folding, and dividing the line precisely by making it increase and multiply." It is the artwork of Charley Harper, an American Modernist—who described his own style as "minimal realism"—that has me wondering about the limits of eye-to-eye ethics and the possibility that formalism (aesthetics) offers another approach to ethics. Harper said:

> When I look at a wildlife or nature subject, I don't see the feathers in the wings I just count the wings. I see exciting shapes, color combinations, patterns, textures, fascinating behavior and endless possibilities for making interesting pictures. I regard the picture as an ecosystem in which all the elements are interrelated, interdependent, perfectly balanced, without trimming or unutilized parts; and herein lies the lure of painting; in a world of chaos, the picture is one small rectangle in which the artist can create an ordered universe.[10]

Minimal realism is an encounter with an intensifying formalism; and for Harper, a formal approach that is importantly ecological and discursive. Harper's paintings compress (through leaving out) life into excited geometry that is "interrelated, interdependent." Pattern, as opposed to individuation, carries the expressive charge of an environment, its discursification. Far from simply disciplinary, this formalism suggests an attention to the force of life (life drive, Eros). Minimal realism is a limit, a frame that feeds and complicates itself. About minimal realism, Harper says: "I don't try to put everything in, I try to leave everything out." The effort "to leave everything out" is a limit and its provocation. The exclusion produces another register of excitation, but to the degree that intensity is predicated on the exclusion itself. Harper extends his stylistic approach to the problem of species, and even more intriguing, the

---

8   Frank Wilderson, *Red, White & Black: Cinema and the Structure of US Antagonisms* (Durham, NC: Duke University Press, 2010).
9   Consider in English the word "pet." In noun form, it is a domesticated animal, a nonhuman being that enters the familial, the intimate space of the home. In verb, it is a sexually charged act, as in "heavy petting." The word pet reveals something about the unknowability of the Animal as an effect of sexual repression.
10 Springfield Museum of Art, "The Nature of Charley Harper," September 18, 2010, https://www.springfieldart.net/?exhibition=the-nature-of-charley-harper.

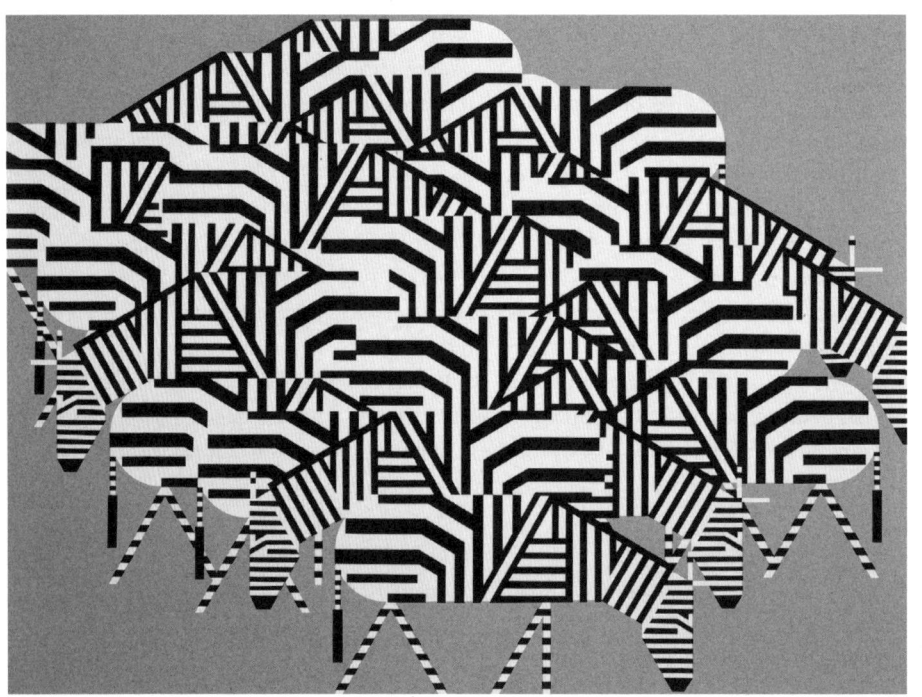

Charley Harper, *Serengeti Spaghetti* (1979).

problem of animals as ontologically discrete life forms. For Harper, the individual, the singular—"the feathers in the wings"—both reifies a misunderstanding of species as biological isolates (islands unto themselves) and reinforces the anthropocentric conceit of like-ness or same-ness as an imperative for empathy and an ethics of care. Instead, species are "plural and repeatedly folded frontier[s]"; species are expressive and thickening limits (Derrida).

In this painting, "Serengeti Spaghetti" (1979) (*fig. 1*)—a playful alliteration that also references the staggering patterns as lineaments (or a distinctive feature) of zebras, and also, the collective noun for zebras is a "zeal"—zebras are not carefully rendered, not translated into portraits that reveal the nuances of a particular individual. Instead, this zeal is literally zeal (as in energy, liveliness). Toward the center of the painting, individuality is lost to radiating rays of back and white angles—a geometry rendered in *chiaroscuro*. There is no aim to capture inner subjective states—the intersubjective imperative of pupil-to-pupil and opening-to-opening is abandoned—instead, we are pulled into a maze of radiation. At the edge of this zeal, a few tiny black triangles mark the eyes, but these eyes are not to be looked into, not to find that spiral of selfhood; zeal (Eros) replaces the individual animal. The painting proposes that the individual animal (*this* animal, or these *animals*) only serves to reinforce anthropocentrism and its presumptive ontological authority. The dizzying vertigo of black and white lines and angles suggest something about the syncopation of this zeal, the multiplying multiplicity of pattern and movement. It would be too simple to turn this herd into a scaled-up singularity; that is, the herd as an individual. This desire to turn the multiple into the singular is anthropomorphic, but for now let us focus on the ethics of face (face-to-face) and the implications of *losing face* in Harper's painting.

Emanuel Levinas describes a face-to-face mode of ethical encounter, and although other philosophies of ethics have emerged, many still carry Levinas's aesthetics of faciality, coherence, and singularity. About face-to-face ethics, Levinas writes: "There is first the very uprightness of the face, its upright exposure, without defense. The skin of the face is that which stays most naked, most destitute. The face is meaning all by itself [...] it leads you beyond."[11] For him the face *faces* to express meaning. More than express, "there are no meanings without a blank wall on which signs are inscribed and effaced; there is no self-conscious consciousness without black holes [pupils] where its states of pleasure and displeasure turn."[12] Levinas continues: "The face speaks. It speaks, it is in this that it renders possible and begins all discourse. [...] The first word of the face is the 'Thou shalt not kill.' It is an order. There is a commandment in the appearance of the face, as if a master spoke to me." For Levinas, the face is a signboard for meaning—for to face an Other is to question one another. By question, I mean attention, a focus that imposes a directive. The blank screen of the face and its abyssal pupils are invitations and accusations, limits and their effects. The meanings from the Other facing us—aligning their actions upon us—enter the black holes of our face, through which our outer sensations are invaginated into sexual and subjective lives. A face is a field that accepts some expressions and connections and neutralizes others. In other words, in facing one another, we require responsibility; face-to-face encounters inaugurate the ethical impulse.

---

11 Emmanuel Levinas, *Ethics and Infinity*, trans. Richard A. Cohen (Pittsburgh: Duquesne University Press, 1995).
12 Alphonso Lingis, *Dangerous Emotions* (Berkeley: University of California Press, 2000).

It is important to note that the full meaning of Levinas's face is not literally the face—the face, for Levinas, is dynamic—but the phenomenological starting point of Levinas's face is decidedly anthropocentric. And consequently, as Judith Butler argues in her reading of Levinas's facing ethics, raises the facelessness—who or what is denied a face?[13] And in this question, Butler worries that face is predicated on race—about this she writes, "He [Levinas] was of course the one who claimed in an interview that the Palestinian had no face, that he only meant to extend ethical obligations to those who were bound together by his version of Judeo-Christian and classical Greek origins." Whether or not Levinas is specifically addressing Palestinian facelessness, as Butler supposes, the "face" itself reveals another order of racial thinking, one that assumes the Man *as* face. That is to say, the Man exists in order to face, in order to be ethical. In this, we find ourselves returning to Wilderson's assertion that the Man (and the whole of its ontological operations) is firstly an effect of racism. Following Butler and Wilderson, if face and its ethical imperative are xenophobic and racist, then we can see how anthropocentrism serves these goals. To be clear, this is not to confuse the Palestinian or the Black and the Animal—a project we see happen in both racist rhetoric and, curiously, in animal rights discourse—but to understand how anthropocentrism shores up racial thinking.

Face-to-face ethics reinforces anthropocentrism, reasserts the *knowability* (limitlessness) of the Animal, and thus assures the Man of himself. The question we are left with is: Can we extend the reach of ethics to those without face, without anthropocentric singularity? Or, are the multiple and the faceless the limits of Levinasian ethics? This question, really two questions—one about multiplicity, another about facelessness—exceed the space and time I have here today, so I will offer a few thoughts about these questions in conversation with Harper's work. Harper writes:

> Remember that I didn't start out to paint a bird – the bird already existed. I started out to paint a picture of a bird, a picture which didn't exist before I came along, a picture which gives me a chance to share with you my thoughts about the bird. Once you accept this seemingly simplistic but really quite profound premise, you will appreciate the many varied approaches to the making of pictures, all of which start where realism leaves off, but all of which require an understanding of realism for their successful execution.[14]

In this painting, we have a radiance of cardinals, radiance as radiation, emitting rays of energy and multiplicity (*fig. 2*). Eyes are deranged, literally "moved from orderly rows," and are pixelated among triangulations of beaks, wings, markings, and tails. Rather than finding an individual, even in the collector of the seed, this painting confuses the eye by pulsing vision with patterned radiations. Even the angularity of lines and shapes disallows us from projecting our curved bodies onto these birds. Pushed even further, beyond the immediate question of identification and face-to-face ethics, we are no longer seeing the visualization of radiance, but are kinesthetically irradiated by this radiance. Again, this is not simply about speciation or species difference, not about biological essentialism (animals as empiricism), but about sensuousness that exceeds the protocols of identity/identification, face-to-face arrangements, and their ontological imperatives.

---

13   Judith Butler, Parting Ways: *Jewishness and the Critique of Zionism* (New York: Columbia University Press, 2012).
14   Roger Gregory, "Bird Artist Charley Harper's Lasting Legacy" (blog), May 16, 2011, https://rogergregory.wordpress.com/2011/05/16/bird-artist-charley-harpers-lasting-legacy/.

Charley Harper, *Last Sunflower Seed* (1973).

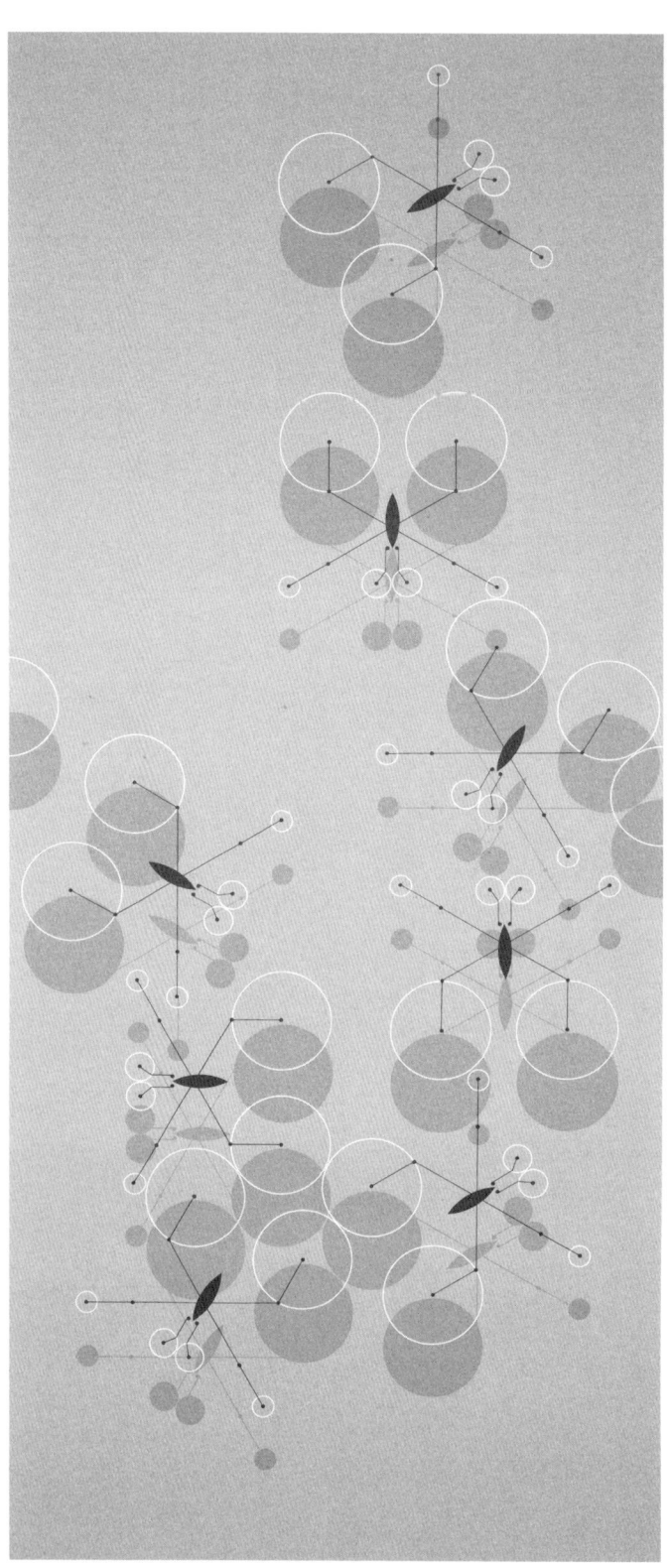

Charley Harper, *Jesus Bugs* (1969).

As this painting shows, the surface of identification, where meaning is displayed, is effaced. Multiplicity is not rendered facial, is not organized by relays of identification, empathy, and so forth—instead we are held in flight lines (see literally the profusion of lines marking the *movement* of wings), in radiation without total administration. Importantly, radiation in this instance is not metaphorical, or not that alone. It is a composite of sensation and aesthetics through minimal realism. Sensation, because Harper translates behavioral tendencies in organisms (cardinals, in this instance) into patterns, into iterative fields of expression. Aesthetic, because the multiple exposes a crisis in meaning-making, in making face, in making an individual so as to harness the apparatus of ethics. It is not that Harper forgoes ethics—indeed his playfulness and humor is an ethical gesture; consider the crisis of one seed among a radiance of cardinals—but his artwork reveals the problem with ethics that is predicated on an aesthetics of anthropomorphic singularity.

Jesus bugs, water striders, pond skaters—covered in hydrophobic hairs, these insects walk on water. The soul taken from the Animal is returned here through a rejoinder: If the insect has no soul, then does Jesus? Harper paints these insects as geometric, capturing the insect's refracted shadow as a doppelganger in this proliferating equation (*fig. 3*). Striders skate the surface of still water, their movements synchronized by their shadow but in deranged aggregates, such that which shadow belongs to which strider is disordered. The eye moves around the painting in search of order, but cannot settle easily onto an individual. The holiness of walking on water spectacularizes another aesthetic problem inherent to ethics, an insectile limit that is also a different order of the limit of facelessness. Of course, water striders do have heads and sensory organs associated with those heads, though at a scale and shape that has no obvious correspondence to ours. Abjected are those whose face appears to lack faciality, lack the capacity to reflect our identificatory regimes. Abjection, here, is the aesthetic configuration of disgust, of what is outside (another limit) the self as a threat to the self. It too is abyssal but is so through the function of an intimate threat. The "I" is threatened by some*thing* it finds too close, too intimate, too proximate—and the *thing* reveals (through, importantly, intimacy) the I's object-hood. The Insect is often rendered meaningful through these operations.

The articulated bodies of antennae, compound eyes, mandibles, and exoskeletons are not, generally speaking, anthropocentrically integrated to solicit responsibility. For Levinas, we find our identity in facing others, existing, and acting under accusation. Facial coherence is the necessary refrain for allowing bodily intensities to be marshaled and detached so that the blank wall of the face displays meaning. We can see an architectural impulse in Levinas's ethics—the face is a threshold, a frame through which expressive capacities are orchestrated and aperture-d to encounter some other. For the Insect (capitalization indexes its metaphysical function), the frame is irresponsibly rendered, deranged, leaving the Insect outside of ethics. More could be said about the abjection of the Insect, but I want to stay focused on the question of collectivities.

What is interesting about Harper's *Jesus Bugs* is that he situates the abjected facelessness of these insects *as* their life force. Multiplicity does not resolve abjection or facelessness but reframes the problem with face-to-face ethics by exposing the aesthetic substrate of ethics itself. Man is an aesthetic category, and through aestheticization, it renders itself ontological and, retroactively, prior to aestheticization. This is the presumptive problem of "the face" and its ethical capacity. With regard to Harper's bugs, consider the collective nouns of other insects: an army of ants, an intrusion of cockroaches, a plague of locusts, and a scourge of mosquitos. These nouns reveal how ethology manage aesthetic discomfort—to recognize animal behaviors, lifeways, and bodily capacities—but only to administer, not resolve, abjection. In fact, we need to ask what role scientism has in the reification of unethical engagement, rather than its resolution.

One of the ways ethology intervenes, perhaps unintentionally, is to consolidate hives of bees, shivers of sharks, murmurations of starlings, and schools of fish into behavioral collectivities, a collection of agents that can act in concert to produce phenomena governed by the group. Scientism installs behavioralism as generalization; in this way, individualism (a face) is replaced, but anthropocentrism reasserts itself through generalization. As in Harper's painting, a school of fish moves in concert, patterns within patterns, ripples with ripples (fig. 4). On the left-hand side of the painting, an open-mouthed fish swims underneath as a threat to the collective. Of course, to some degree, Harper is expressing the ethological tendencies of organisms to school, perhaps a protective measure of the small against the threat of the large. But, it is the formal aspect of the identical qualities of fish in Harper's school that dislocate identification—perhaps with exception to the opened-mouth fish below the school, whose red eyes situate the unfolding drama—and our eye is drawn to the patterns of involvement.

What serves as over-aestheticization—waves upon waves, fish upon fish, all of it refracted in mirroring shadows—turns individualization into excessive geometry, and curiously, it is the "joke" of the painting that is revealing. Circling white ripples over a black circle—a threatening mouth of a larger fish, but also a punning bullseye. This is not an aesthetic gesture that aims at beautifying but instead abstracts life through formal limits. The joke reframes the ethological, and the repetitive symmetry refuses identification and its attachment to the individual. Here, in a playful gesture, Levinas's face is exposed as insufficiently ethical, and more seriously, asks us if ethics function beyond reifying Man and its idealization. This is to ask: What if the ethical gesture is only an ennobling of humanism? If so, if ethics are anthropocentric, then is there any way to attend, to address, or to consider sentient life?

Harper does not save face for the individuals of this school but percusses bodies, relations, and forces for the purposes of experiencing sensation, which is not the same as responsibility. Sensation, which is firstly affective, is movement between forms and against sensitivities. Sensation is not necessarily about identification, as in "I am like you," nor even about difference, the imperative of ethical consideration, but sensation is excitation before conceptualization. For Harper, this is about expressiveness over and against the authority of the singular or the behavioral collective. If otherness is predicated on *familiar* difference—a philosophy of similar-enough difference that enables the ethical gesture—then radical alterity, an unfamiliar (uncanny) difference, is the unencompassable that remains outside order and ethical response. Perhaps alterity—that which is outside and cannot be properly ordered—resonates with the sensuous registers in Harper's paintings.

To conclude these ruminations on limits of ethics, the problem of multiplicity, and the role of sensation in sentience, I want to look at Harper's "Bark Eyes" (fig. 5). Black, white, and gray lines divide this noir setting—yellowed and dotted, birch leaves fall, cascading

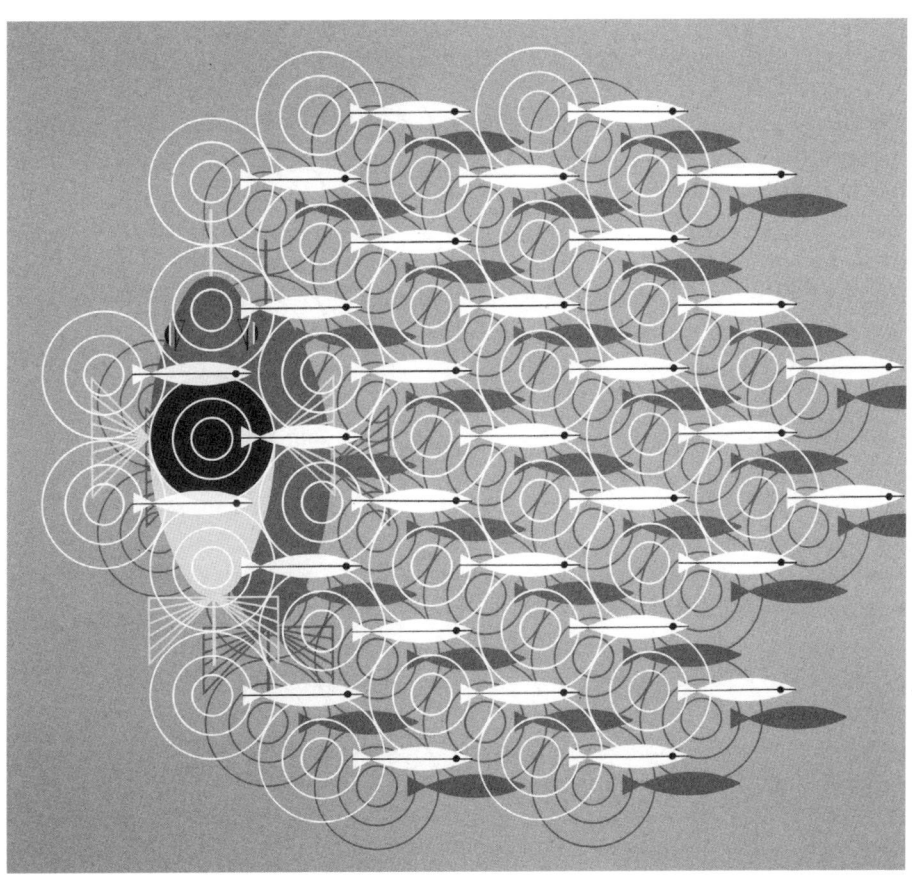

Charley Harper, *Skipping School* (1977).

angling lines. Eyes have been distributed throughout: owl eyes, tree eyes (remember that birch trees and their many knots are called a "thousand-eyed tree"), and disembodied eye-shine scattered throughout the dark woods: sometimes in pairs, sometimes as a single eye, sometimes situated sideways. Sometimes the knot "eyes" of the birch trees meet up with the knots of neighboring trees, giving them a shared look. The dark pinholes on the white bark—like the holes on the leaves and the pupils of those yellow night eyes—confuses *who is seeing* with *what is seeing*. That is to say, it is not that this painting is about looking into the eyes of an individual, but rather those radiating pupils become a visual texture, a tactile feeling of the work. It is, as I have described elsewhere, *fingeryeyes*[15]—or tactility made from eyes turned into patterns—that has me wondering if sensation might offer an alternative—or at least to question the presumption of the reductive problems of scientism and ethics.

Remember, as Alphonso Lingis[16] teaches us, sensations are amalgamations, made of percepts and affects that shape the energetic relay between sensitivities, sometimes called subjects and objects. Perception, in other words, does not precede affect; in fact, affect is what makes and shapes our sensorium, our experience of our environment. By affect, I mean excitation, a psychical charge, an effect of sexuality (and its repression). Sensuous bodies, then, are both repressions and provocations of perception, with excitation (affect) unleashing and binding bodily order. As such, sensation is not a direct exchange between our environment and the capacity of our nervous systems. Which is not to say that we do not *feel* our environment—we do—but this *feel* is psychical as much as it is physical. Through sensitivity, the psychical (sexual) mediates the physical, pressuring us to feel our cohabitation in a sensible environment that opens us outward and differently. Might the sensuous, the sensational, offer us an alternative approach to humanistic ethics, one that is attentive to both limits and the excitable effects of those limits?

Harper's paintings, as I hope I have demonstrated today, reveal the anthropocentric problem of ethics and their aesthetic substrates, while also proffering some tentative insights into theorizing our sensuous rapport with environments. To be clear, I am not suggesting that aesthetics are the problem *per se*—obviously Harper's paintings are aesthetic—but that face-to-face ethics presumes an order of Man, which conceals how aesthetics function within this humanist endeavor. So, rather than sidestepping the aesthetic, these paintings lean into aesthetic consideration so as to offer a robustly sensuous study of the limits of ethics. In doing so, Harper demonstrates how sentient lives (us all) are visitors of our senses, not because sensations are outside the body, transcendental, but because sensation is always distributed psychically and materially. So, it is not only that a zeal of zebras or a radiance of cardinals expose the aesthetics of ethics, but they expose a sensuous (and ultimately sexual) plentitude that exceeds ethics. Which is to ask, how do a shiver of sharks and a parliament of owls put into question our understanding of responsibility? How might attention to psychical forces helps us to understand, differently, ecology and our place in it? And, perhaps most radically, do we yet know how to attend to other sentient lives and their radical unfamiliarity? If ethics can only reify Man and its technologies of anthropocentrism, then we must ask if we have *ever* responded to environments and cohabitants with deference?

---

15 Eva Hayward, "Fingeryeyes: Impressions of Cup Corals," *Cultural Anthropology* 25, no. 4 (2010): 577–99.
16 Alphonso Lingis, *Sensation: Intelligibility in Sensibility* (New York: Humanity Books, 1996).

Charley Harper, *Bark Eyes* (1986).

TRANSGRESSING HUMANISM

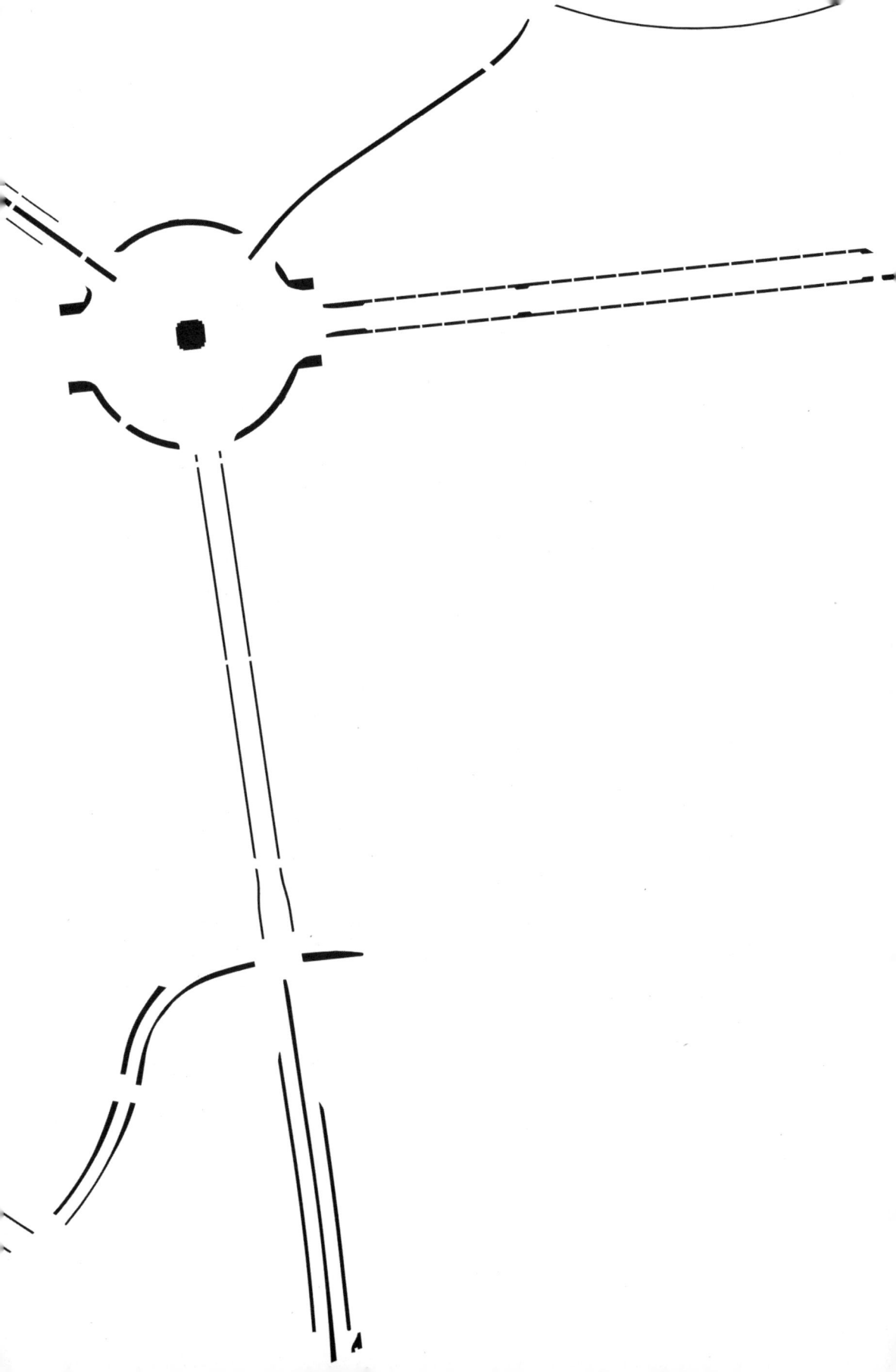

1930: BOBBY THE GORILLA, ZOO BERLIN ICON

TRANSGRESSING HUMANISM

2013: BIRD THING, TIERGARTEN

2015: *FAGUS SYLVATICA*, TIERGARTEN

TRANSGRESSING HUMANISM

2017: MINING BEE NEST, TIERGARTEN

2018: POPLAR TREE STUMP, YEW BUSH, AND HUMAN COUPLE

2017: WINDSTORM AFTERMATH, TIERGARTEN

2014: KULTURFORUM

TRANSGRESSING HUMANISM

2015: ANCIENT BEECH, TIERGARTEN

STEFANO MANCUSO

GREEN THEREFORE SMART: INTELLIGENCE AND CONSCIOUSNESS IN PLANTS

I consider the organization of this project extremely transgressive for including botany in a discussion about transgression. In fact, it is most timely for botany and transgression to be combined in the same sentence.

There are many things that have been spoken about Tiergarten—except for the subject of plants, which is the physical matter of which Tiergarten is made of. This text is not focused on the park, but about plants, which in fact constitute the most abundant organism on Earth. Conventionally, the idea of the plant is one of a passive organism, and this is a very ancient notion. Plants are rarely mentioned in the history of humanity. Even in the book of Genesis, when God tells Noah to save all creatures and bring them onto his Ark, plants are not mentioned despite the fact they are living creatures as much as animals.

In a basic psychological test that rapidly shows an audience four slides depicting plants together with animals, and one last slide of plants with two humans, 96 percent of viewers said that they saw animals, and for the last slide, 99 percent said that it showed only a man and a woman. There was no mention of plants in either test result—however, 80 percent of the slides were filled with images of plants. Plants encompass the environment but, nonetheless, people don't seem to notice them. And yet plants are not so different from animals. In fact, they are even much more successful! What I mean by successful is that 99.7 percent of the biomass on Earth is composed of plants. This is an incredible percentage, and people are rarely aware of it. This also means that animals altogether account for just 0.3 percent of the biomass. Animals are only traces. On Earth, life is mainly green. It's a green planet, and there is something really strange in the fact that we never discuss plants and never consider the largest mass of life on the planet and how it functions.

When we talk about plants, the general idea about them isn't different from what is depicted in the engraving "Pyramid of Being" in the *Liber de sapiente* (*Book of Wisdom*) of 1509 by Charles de Bovelles. This was a Renaissance model showing the order of nature, which is in this case very simplistic. There is *petra*—rocks—that exist; they *est* (are), and that's all. The next step immediately after the rocks are the plants that *vivit*, so they are alive: living organisms. Above the plants, there are the animals that are able to feel sensations (they sense), and at the top of the creation pyramid there is man, and in fact, the studying man (*Homo studiosus*), who is endowed with intelligence.

Nothing much has changed since then. Many people think that plants are not able to sense, or else they make allowances that plants are able to sense the environment or other organisms in some naive way. The truth is that plants are incredibly more sensitive than animals. These preconceptions are also trivial: when something changes in the environment, an animal can run away, whereas a plant's only chance of survival is to detect every change in the environment in a very precise and intricate way. Therefore, plants need to be much more sensitive than animals, and this is a proven reality. Normally they sense at least twenty different physical and chemical parameters like light, gravity, and vibration, to mention a few. This is something that we all share with plants—the ability to sense—except they are also able to sense chemical, electric, and magnetic gradients. Moreover, plants are able to sense other organisms and even pathogens in the environment around them; they are like some kind of superhero with super powers when compared to animals. However, the story about intelligence, or the lack of, is in itself a stupid one. Every living organism is in fact intelligent, but the definition was originally drawn from the human mind. By now, there is a much more inclusive definition of intelligence, which is the ability to solve problems. There is no possibility to survive without solving problems so every organism, not only human or animal, is intelligent.

There is another false idea about plants in that they are a very ancient organism that appeared on the earth far, far before humans and mammals. That's normally true, except that the angiosperms, the flowering plants, are in reality modern organisms, appearing on Earth much after mammals. Why are we unable to understand that plants are such sophisticated organisms? Possibly because they are incredibly different from animals: they have no face and unlike many animals, possess an organization without a common center, which constitutes an advantage for plants. It is also because they cannot escape from the place where they live that they are subjected to predation. Therefore, their "body" is built in a specific way that resists this. Plants, in this way, are not "individuals," a latent term that means "not divisible." If I cut into a cat, I would normally kill the cat; but if I cut a plant into a hundred pieces I don't kill the plant, and often I can even propagate it. Plants are made by "multiplication." They are very modern organisms, made by reiterated structures. Somehow they resemble a colony, like insects or worms, except for living inside of the same body.

Another false idea is that plants don't move. Plants actually move a lot, but on a different timescale. As an example, the fastest movement in nature by a living organism is the opening of the bunchberry flower. The movement of plants is something that has been known since antiquity, but it was for the first time demonstrated in 1898 by Wilhelm Pfeffer, a German botanist. Only two years after Auguste and Louis Lumière invented cinema, Pfeffer created the technique of time-lapse photography, discovering that by accelerating the footage captured, one can observe that a plant makes many movements and shows many behaviors.

Plants have become models of research in recent advanced technology because they are incredibly good at not wasting energy. For example, there are many passive movements, like the opening and closing of the pine cone, that is dependent on the level of humidity in the air. This is a phenomenon that has been studied in engineering in order to develop new materials able to open and close according to environmental conditions, such as light or humidity levels. Another extraordinary form of passive movement is that of the dandelion, which exhibits a double movement with the opening of the flower followed by the opening of a feathery canopy "parachute" that allows the seed to float and travel. Every single one of these seeds is able to open and close according to humidity. In my institute, the International Laboratory of Plant Neurobiology (LINV), we conducted a study for the European Space Agency into the seed of *Pelargonium carnosum*, which is capable of a passive helical movement that helps it to burrow into the earth. This study had the purpose of developing devices to explore the soil of extraterrestrial planets. I cannot point out enough that this is a passive movement and *only* a passive movement: this plant is able to make a wonderful helical movement without using any energy.

Active movement is also present in plants— even very fast movement—for example like that of the carnivorous *Dionaea muscipula*, the Venus flytrap. Today we know that all five hundred different species of carnivorous plants are capable of moving. In observing the movement of a group of sunflower seedlings, it is not immediately recognizable that they are in fact "playing." But sunflowers are social plants that in the first moments of their lives need to interact with each other, a similar behavior that we normally call play in young animals.

Plants also have many more abilities we are not commonly aware of. For example, they are able to detect sound. This is something that we demonstrated at LINV just a couple of years ago. All roots turn toward sources of sound. Capable of detecting the sound of water, they grow resolutely toward the source. They are also able to produce sound; the amplified sound from a growing root is a compellingly heavy click.

Another example of spatial awareness in plants comes from a unicellular organism, *Physarum polycephalum*, a multi-nucleate whose common name is slime mold. This plant, which has many nuclei but is just one cell, grows outward from a single point searching for food sources and is uniquely able to design and create the optimum network of pathways and transport for food between two given points. In an experiment lead by researchers in England and Japan in 2010, when slime mold was given the criteria of the population density and distance of Tokyo, it was able to spatially replicate the pathways of the existing transport network of the region. After watching how slime mold also replicated highway systems in China, Netherlands, and Italy, scientists contended that observing models based on slime mold behavior can lead to a more efficient way to design transportation networks.

We can also observe the awareness of space in parasitic plants, such as *Cuscuta europaea*. This plant needs to find a host very quickly after germination, and by swerving its seedling around it can immediately detect a nearby plant using chemical cues, such as a tomato, and then start to parasitize it. *C. europaea* can even distinguish between different species of plants and, if given a choice, such as tomato or wheat, it has been shown to prefer the tomato—a favorite; in the case where there is no tomato, the wheat will also do.

We also observed and filmed beans in my lab. As beans like to grow on a support, one can easily see that they are aware of where the support is—there is no doubt about that. The bean tries to reach the support through the best of its efforts (*fig. 1*). (If you watch the film, you can see and almost "feel" its efforts. It takes the plant a couple of tries, but it already makes a hook in the right direction, finally reaching the support.) This is plain evidence; there's not much more to say. In another film from our laboratory, we have seen how plants are able to detect a support, which proves that they know what is in the environment around them. This film shows one support placed between two beans, who start to compete against each other to reach it, somehow in a similar way to animals. Once one reaches the support, the other one immediately changes direction and tries to find an alternative, in this case, to grasp something on the ground. This demonstrates even something more, not only that a plant is able to detect objects around it, but that it is also aware of what other plants in the same proximity are doing.

Roots are the most important and interesting part of plants because it has been revealed that the possible common center, what for mammals is the brain, resides in plants in the tip of the roots. This ultimately demonstrates that intelligence and consciousness belong not only to human and animal minds but constitute biological phenomena in and of themselves and, as such, they can be found and studied in plants as in any other organism.

For all of this wonderful behavior to take place one needs consciousness. What is its definition? Today there is a huge debate about consciousness in machines but, paradoxically, it is much easier to convince people that machines, rather than plants, are conscious. The first person to define consciousness was John Locke in "An Essay Concerning Human Understanding" (1690), who wrote that it is "the perception of what passes in a man's own mind." Consciousness was believed to be that simple: it was something that pertained to humans exclusively. In 2012 however, at the Cambridge Declaration on Consciousness, many prominent neurobiologists stated: "We decided to reach a consensus and make a statement directed to the public. It's obvious to everyone in the room that animals have consciousness, but it is not obvious to the rest of the world. [...] Convergent evidence indicates that non-human animals, [...] including all mammals and birds, and other creatures, [...] have the necessary neural substrates of consciousness." The definition was expanded: not only humans but every animal with neural substrates, has consciousness.

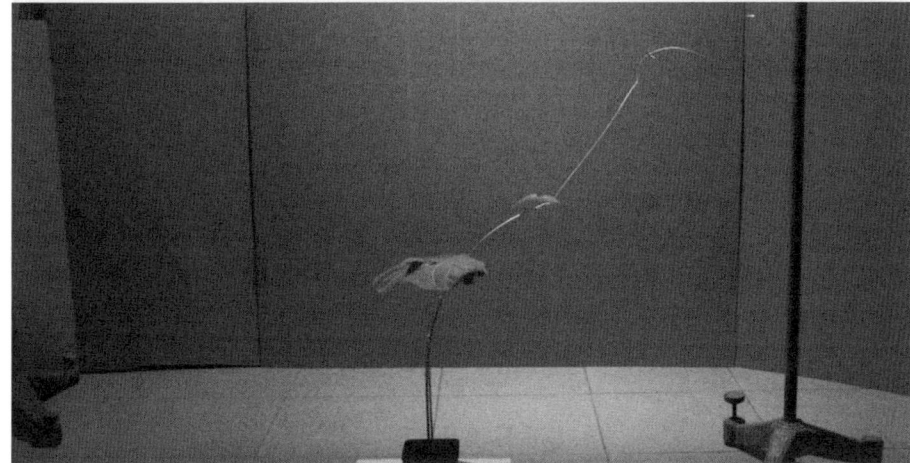

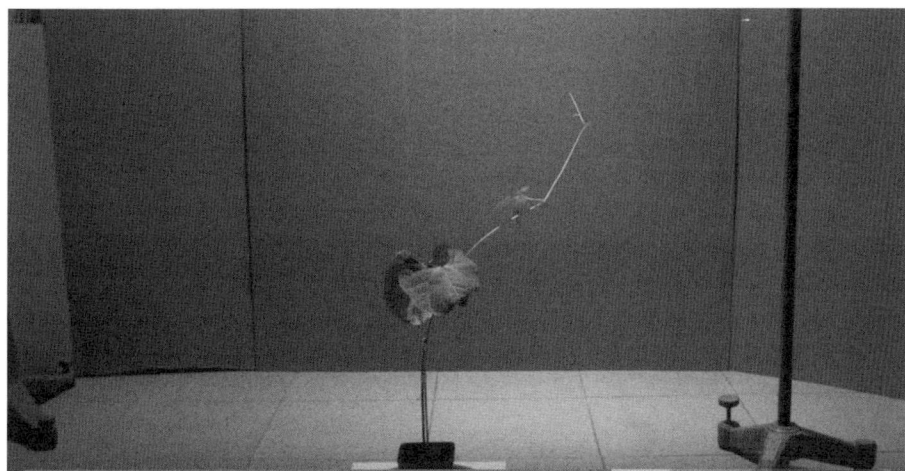

Film stills of an exploring bean plant, International Laboratory of Plant Neurobiology, Firenze, 2010.

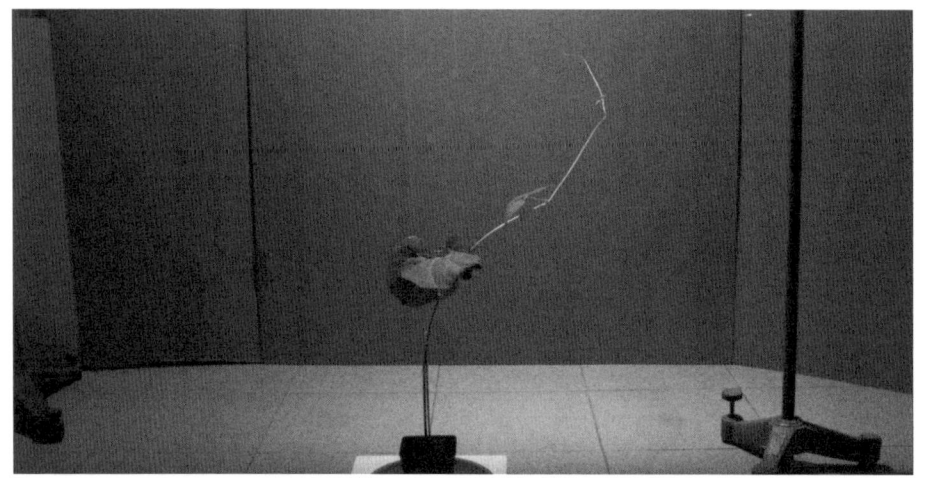

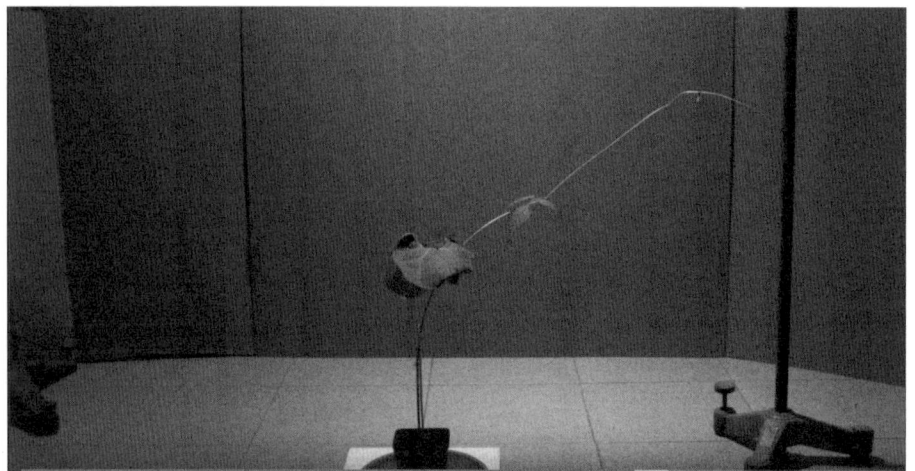

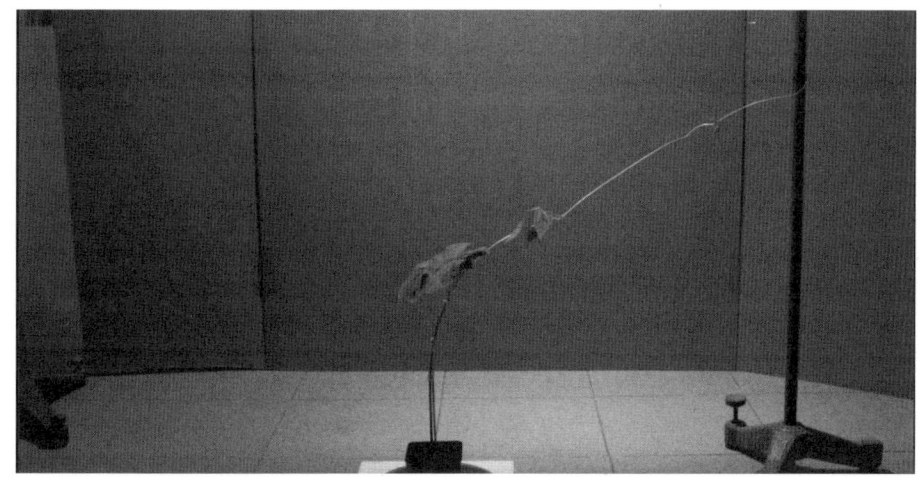

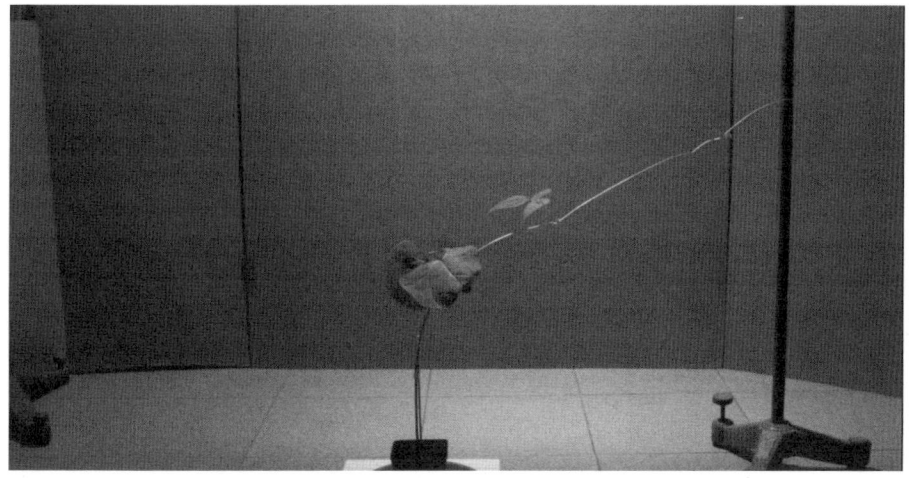

CHRIS WILBERT

MORE-THAN-HUMAN HERITAGE SPACES: ANIMAL-HUMAN STORIES FROM HOO TO TIERGARTEN

HOO

Forty or so kilometres southeast of London, on the north Kent coast, lies the Hoo Peninsula extending out into the Thames Estuary. On land associated in many minds, and some tourism marketing, with the opening scene of Charles Dickens's book *Great Expectations*, we can find Lodge Hill—an abandoned military training school dating from 1870. A 2012 survey showed it to be the summer home to about eighty male breeding nightingales (*Luscinia megarhynchos*) and an unspecified number of females. These nightingales over-winter in west Africa and come to England to breed from April to August.

This area of the Hoo Peninsula is a hybrid landscape, neither just social or natural, a landscape of potentiality, some of which are being acted out by non-human animals. Hoo is also not the kind of bucolic landscape typical of tourism marketing of this region. The opening chapter of *Great Expectations* is thought to be set in St. Mary's churchyard in Cooling on the eastern edge of the peninsula, where the orphan boy Pip is accosted by an escapee from a prison ship.[1] Such ships—convict hulks—were moored in the Medway and Thames Estuary off the north Kent coast in the early nineteenth century at the time of the Napoleonic Wars and after, while there was also a prison on St. Mary's Island in the Medway.

In Dickens's time, Hoo was a malarial-infested marsh landscape until its improvement by drainage to become a more agricultural space. Now it is crisscrossed by electricity power lines from the power generating stations, and railway lines that deliver coal and take out mined aggregate. In amongst this industrial landscape, it is still partly rural with farmland, woodlands, and nature reserves but significant numbers of houses. In short, it is a complex mixed landscape, with a long and contested, often militarised history. The Lodge Hill site is also a landscape of potentiality in that military use can seemingly be traded for housing development.

The local Medway Council and site owners, the Government Ministry of Defence and its developers, made plans to build about five thousand homes, two schools, and the infrastructure that such a site requires. Opposition to the development came from conservation charities and many local people. Planning permission was given by the Council in September 2014. However, the development plans were ruled as being unsound by an independent planning inspector, and it has now been "called in" by central government and were made the subject of a public inquiry in June 2016.[2]

Part of this site, and another nearby, was recently designated as a Site of Special Scientific Interest by the unfortunately named Natural England, the government's advisers on the natural environment, purely to safeguard the nightingales. Such sites are not meant to be developed. However, under current planning rules, such a Site of Special Scientific Interest (SSSI) can be developed if alternative habitat is offered for the endangered wildlife involved.[3] This kind of tradability of sites, known as biodiversity offsetting—where damage done in one place is supposedly made good by creating "habitat" elsewhere—is controversial,

---

1   See the opening sequence of David Lean's 1946 adaptation of *Great Expectations* at: https://www.youtube.com/watch?v=eXyo68s-f1E.
2   "Lodge Hill," *Kent Wildlife Trust*, accessed March 25, 2016, http://www.kentwildlifetrust.org.uk/what-we-do/planning/lodge-hill.
3   "Guiding Principles for Biodiversity Offsetting," *Department for Environment & Food and Rural Affairs* (*DEFRA*), accessed June 15, 2015, http://www.defra.gov.uk.

though many local councils and some conservation organisations do support it, at least as a final resort.[4]

NIGHTINGALES AND OBSERVATION

Conservation work is often caught up in all kinds of contradictory policies and valuations of what is too often seen as a singular nature, though it is much more complicated in practice than its public discourses often allow. Steve Hinchliffe argues that the facts with which conservationists work are often unfinished matters.[5]

At a basic level conservation work often involves knowing what animals or plants are present or not present in places, and this process can often be far from clear.[6] This in turn involves forms of surveillance, and indeed this has become increasingly sophisticated in recent years, with even drones being utilised in some cases, as well as satellite transmitters, alongside the old-fashioned surveys done through sightings.[7] Hinchliffe and Stephanie Lavau have undertaken ethnographies of the UK avian influenza wild bird's survey, and in doing so, have sought to tease apart the more positive aspects of observational sciences from the synonymous grouping of surveillance and control as a controlling form of biopolitics.[8] Here they follow Michel Serres's distinction between surveillant societies and observant societies, with the latter being seen as more open to difference and less likely to assume mastery or control. This position is one of a range of positive views of scientific observation that have emerged in science studies and human-animal studies over the past few decades. Hinchliffe argues: "To observe and to observe well is to learn to be affected by the world [...] to be attuned to it [...] to engage in building a sensorium and, in doing so, to make differences."[9]

Hinchliffe's and Lavau's work might just ask us to see scientific and conservation observational work in more positive ways as something that is open to difference that makes for "useful, curious, and surprising relations."[10] But we can also see how things like observations and surveys are very often caught up within policy processes where how birds or animals are viewed is already circumscribed. We can ask questions about how nightingales are being asked questions here. And moreover, what are the questions being asked by, and of, ornithologists, farmers, tourists, and housing developers.

At Lodge Hill, two surveys have been done by the British Trust for Ornithology. One was a survey of bird numbers that had to be undertaken in spring and early summer when male birds sing to attract mates, as hearing their songs is the only way they can be counted because they are very rarely seen. The other survey was "Factors Potentially Affecting the Viability and Success of Biodiversity Offsetting to Compensate for Nightingale

---

4   Martin Harper, "The Battle of Lodge Hill (Part 5–The Full Story)," *RSPB*, accessed March 15, 2016, http://www.rspb.org.uk/community/ourwork/b/martinharper/archive/2014/01/24/the-battle-of-lodge-hill-part-5-the-full-story.aspx; "Biodiversity Offsetting," *Essex Wildlife Trust*, accessed June 10, 2015, http://www.essexwt.org.uk/news/2013/12/19/biodiversity-offsetting.
5   Steve Hinchliffe, *Geographies of Nature* (London: Sage, 2007), 147.
6   Hinchliffe, *Geographies of Nature*.
7   Rafi Youatt, "Counting Species: Biopower and the Global Biodiversity Census," *Environmental Values* 17, no. 3 (August 2008): 393–417.
8   Steve Hinchliffe and Stephanie Lavau, "Differentiated Circuits: The Ecologies of Knowing and Securing Life," *Environment & Planning D: Society & Space* 31, no. 2 (2013): 259–74.
9   Steve Hinchliffe, "Sensory Biopolitics: Knowing Birds and a Biopolitics of Life," in *Humans, Animals, Biopolitics*, ed. Kristin Asdal, Tone Druglitrø, and Steve Hinchliffe (London: Routledge, 2017).
10 Hinchliffe, *Geographies of Nature*, 147.

Habitat Loss."[11] Here is the closest place we get to an answer about who will "tell" the nightingales that this site may be developed. The authors discuss the needs for a new site to compensate the nightingales and how it must already be in existence, otherwise suitable habitat might take fifteen years or more to be developed. They also argue it should be near to the current site for colonization to be likely. One way of attracting the birds to a new site that is briefly discussed is "tape luring"—using tape recordings of songs to lure birds to suitable new habitat—though how to do it, which vocalizations to use, and the ethics of doing this seem to thwart any serious development of this idea.

MULTISPECIES STORIES

Here, a matter of concern emerges—struggles over landscapes, with differing groups seeking to speak for differing localities, including the birds and other wildlife that have benefited from this enclosed, inaccessible, disused military site. The geographer Kevin Grove reminds us here that the hybridity of landscape is not just an *ontological* condition, it is also *political*. Realization of some potentialities can only occur through the negation of others.[12]

So let us think of these absent and present nightingales. Who will tell the nightingales that they will have to move, that it will be dangerous for them to stay, or how to find the new site designated for them? Will they go? Do nightingales have an attachment to places as communities and even as individuals?

Nightingales, we are told, live up to about five years, but they do show *great site fidelity*, meaning they return to the same site and pass this on to offspring. The British Trust for Ornithology tracked a bird migrating from eastern England recently using a small geolocator attached to the bird and a year later captured it fifty metres from where it was caught the previous year.[13] Site fidelity is not at all unusual for migrating birds or for a huge range of creatures, from garden snails to flying foxes and limpets.[14] It might be that this characteristic has been undervalued in our imaginaries and in the questions we ask non-human animals, in the same ways place has tended to be undervalued in more radical politicising in recent years.

Thom van Dooren and Deborah Bird-Rose argue that story-making is an example of how animals weave experiences into a meaningful sequence so as to, for example, determine if a predator is drawing nearer or farther away and on this basis make a decision on what to do.[15] Such experiences rendered meaningful by non-human animals then "might be recognized and thought about through the familiar lens of 'narrative.'"[16] This account of what they term storying and narrative can then be applied to our understanding of some animals' engagements with places.

Van Dooren and Bird-Rose note that the term "habitat" seems to imply a purely physical set of relationships and features, and in this context seems to emerge as a largely interchangeable place, as a kind of locality that is transferable to other similar localities defined as suitable habitat.[17] They go on

---

11 Robert J. Fuller and Chris M. Hewson, *Factors Potentially Affecting the Viability and Success of Biodiversity Offsetting to Compensate for Nightingale Habitat Loss* (Thetford: British Trust for Ornithology, 2012).
12 Kevin Grove, "Rethinking the Nature of Urban Environmental Politics: Security, Subjectivity and the Non-Human," *Geoforum* 40, no. 2 (March 2009): 207–16.
13 Paul Stancliffe, "Tagged!," *Bird Watching* (2011): 68–69.
14 Ruth Brooks, *A Slow Passion: Snails, My Garden and Me* (London: Bloomsbury, 2013).
15 Deborah Bird-Rose and Thom van Dooren, "Storied Places in a Multispecies City," *Humanimalia* 3, no. 2 (2012): 4.
16 Bird-Rose and van Dooren, "Storied Places in a Multispecies City."
17 Bird-Rose and van Dooren, 10.

to query such a view by pointing to how, in the case of little penguins in Sydney, it can be seen that penguins and landscape shape each other. Penguins return to the same place, even the same burrow, year after year. A connection is made with a place that is in some way remembered, reconfigured, and passed on to the next generation of penguins. Moreover, any piece of land that meets their behavioural requirements is not as good as any other; there is something special about the places they do breed in.[18]

Therefore, taking a multispecies approach to stories of place involves the willingness to recognise storied-experience in non-human places and to accept non-humans as narrative subjects, with all the risks that entails—of, for example, projecting narrativity on to their behavioural experiences in an anthropomorphising form.[19]

We might learn from this place attachment and perhaps see that this opening to multispecies storying is still needed more in our work, our day-to-day lives, and in our political theories and practices. We might also ask where do the knowledges come from to put narratives together in multispecies narrative? Certainly, the sciences have increasingly taken on the mantle of spokespersons for non-human animals, and science-studies work has sought to show how this occurs. As mentioned earlier there is more room needed for more ordinary narratives of the engagement of people with non-humans, animals in shared spaces, for reflection upon such narratives, of what people know of non-humans and how these knowledges filter into the sciences, their practices, and beyond.

In a similar vein, Katrin Anna Lund and Karl Benediktsson have used the metaphor of "conversation" to get into wider multispecies aspects of landscapes.[20] But they also note that how one is situated in this conversation has a bearing on what kinds of viewpoints can be brought in and what kinds of understandings are brought about, so conversations do not always flow smoothly.

SPACES AND PHILOSOPHICAL ETHOLOGIES

The recent challenge of animal studies has been seen to encompass three needs, according to the geographer Henry Buller:

1. to recognize and demonstrate impacts of the purposefulness and agency of animals both in our co-habited worlds and in resistance to them;
2. to destabilize dualistic approaches through a more fluid, and relational human/animal ontological reconfiguration of cultural practice, spatial formations and ultimately de-centred subjectivities;
3. and, finally, to create a more radical politics that might accommodate all of this complexity and the inherent variations within it.[21]

Just as practically every discipline that engages with animals is in the midst of a reconfiguration of concepts and operating assumptions, a lot of interesting ideas on spaces of human-animal relations are now starting to emerge from the sciences of animal life such as cognitive ethology.[22] Ethology has, we are told, gone through something of a transformation in terms of

---

18 Bird-Rose and van Dooren.
19 Bird-Rose and van Dooren, 4.
20 Katrin Anna Lund and Karl Benediktsson, "Introduction: Starting a Conversation with Landscape," in *Conversations With Landscape*, ed. Katrin Anna Lund and Karl Benediktsson (Farnham: Ashgate Publishing, 2010).
21 Henry Buller "Animal Geographies II," *Progress in Human Geography* 39, no. 3 (2015): 374–84.
22 Brett Buchanan, Jeffrey Bussolini, and Mathew Chrulew, "General Introduction: Philosophical Ethology," *Angelaki* 19, no. 3 (November 2014): 1–3.

theory, methods, and epistemologies in recent years. And we have also recently seen the emergence of what has been termed philosophical ethology—which strongly embraces phenomenological descriptions of the lives and experiences of non-human animals. This renewed and supposedly animalised phenomenology is argued to be distinct from the theorisations of twentieth-century phenomenology, which struggled to describe the animal dimension of humanity by which humanity is constructed through "inclusive exclusion" of its animality.[23] Dominique Lestel, for example has argued that phenomenology is the most effective means for moving beyond what he terms a realist-Cartesian ethology, which tended to reduce animal life to behaviours and behaviours to causal mechanisms.[24]

According to Lestel and others, behaviourist ethology has continually denigrated the importance of shared life and social dimensions of observational situations by seeking to produce and perpetuate a separation of animals from humans. Moreover, Cartesian ethology and ecology have "reduced the notion of environment to an extremely poor naturalistic ecology. Animals here become organisms deterministically adapted to a set of objective conditions. Their subjective construction of their milieu is effaced."[25]

Lestel has thus developed what he calls a bi-constructivist ethology, so called "because it must develop ways for humans to construct the ways that animals construct their worlds. [...] An animal gives meaning to what happens as part of its 'behaviour,' but there is no reason to believe that there is only one meaning in each case."[26] The new ethology here is re-characterised as the science of the human interpretation of animal interpretations, with the aim of enriching our zoological imagination by enhancing and deepening our capacity for the perception, interpretation, and sharing of animal lives.[27] This would include *carefully* using anecdotal and other "folk" and "amateur" evidence normally excluded from "scientific" approaches to help elucidate cultures and behaviours of animals, though explaining behavioural characteristics is not a main trajectory here; rather, it is the responsive activity of making meanings in their environmental interactions.[28]

What I understand from this is that meaning has too often been denied as an aspect of the social environment (milieu) of animals, and that meaning-making needs to be put at the centre of a new ethology, one which draws on both the natural and social sciences to do this, hence the notion of etho-ethnographical phenomenological methods to study human-animal shared lives. This new field of study focuses on hybrid communities of humans, animals, and technologies, where meaning, interests, and affects are shared.[29] As they argue, hybrid communities rest on a threefold interpretation process: "The animals' interpretations, the human interpretations of what the animals do and 'think,' and lastly, the humans' interpretations of the interpretations other humans have of the

---

23 Ted Toadvine, "The Time of Animal Voices," *Konturen*, no. 6 (2014), accessed September 12, 2017, http://journals.oregondigital.org/konturen/article/view/3532/3257.
24 Jeffrey Bussolini, Matthew Chrulew, and Dominique Lestel, "The Phenomenology of Animal Life," *Environmental Humanities* 5 (2014): 127.
25 Bussolini, Chrulew, and Lestel, "The Phenomenology of Animal Life," 128.
26 Bussolini, Chrulew, and Lestel.
27 Bussolini, Chrulew, and Lestel, 128, 130.
28 Bussolini, Chrulew, and Lestel, 128, 129.
29 Florence Brunois, Florence Gaunet, and Dominique Lestel, "Etho-ethnology and Ethno-ethology," *Social Science Information* 45, no. 2 (2006).

animals and other humans."[30] Going further, Lestel asks: "The central question posed by the notion of hybrid communities is the following: what does the idea of a 'social contract' mean between beings where some speak, and others barely communicate, but where they all share interests and meaning?"[31] And: "Similarly, while humans have constituted various kinds of communities, humans and animals have also, over the centuries, woven a surprising diversity of mixed and interspecific communities."[32] However, the importance of these communities has been downplayed, ignored, and ridiculed.

In viewing how shared life with non-human animals is withering, we get a powerful view of the role of the imagination. For Lestel, imagination is a collective activity "resting largely on the spaces of possibles revealed to us by the species with which we share our life."[33] So, when we exterminate our cohabiting species, we reduce our imagination dramatically and limit our existential potential to become actualized human beings. We end up with a pathological imagination in a kind of dialectic where human actions in exterminating animals transform humans, affecting human subjectivity for the worse.

Lestel seems to share with philosophical phenomenology the view that "all beings experience their worlds through unique embodied sensory perspectives."[34] Yet, in their outline of "the phenomenology of animal life," there is not much sense of how to deal with the subject-centred approach of phenomenology and how to move to one of experience.[35] However, Lestel's threefold interpretation process of hybrid communities seems to offer more than his attempts at phenomenology, especially in rethinking spaces of encounters, of shared values and meaningful spaces between diverse people and diverse animals.

TIERGARTEN

In early July 2015, the heat of Berlin was excessive, so I retreated into Tiergarten and wandered and wandered along paths through landscapes of trees, and listened and saw, and sat and read about this place. These are incredible spaces to have in the centre of a city, a capital city. There are nightingales—*nachtigallen*—here I am told, but in July it is long past the times when they sing.

The symposium I attended mentioned that the ways the park was used and managed was somewhat threatened by a desire to see more tourists use this space and by ideas that perhaps parts of the park could be managed using income from corporate bodies who were having to pay for certain building activities at the edges of the park. Here, it seems ideas of "restoration" of heritage views were being contemplated in similar ways to other suggestions for heritage landscapes like Hampstead Heath in London. For example, in 2013 English Heritage was exploring the possibilities through public consultation of removing regenerated woodlands and restoring landscape views around Kenwood House on the Heath to ones that could be seen in the nineteenth century.

But the idea of "encouraging" more tourists to visit the park is an intriguing one, and one

---

30   Brunois, Gaunet, and Lestel, "Etho-ethnology and Ethno-ethology," 167.
31   Dominique Lestel, "Hybrid Communities," *Angelaki* 19, no. 3 (November 2014): 61–73, 68.
32   Lestel, "Hybrid Communities," 63.
33   Dominique Lestel, "The Withering of Shared Life through the Loss of Biodiversity," *Social Science Information* 52, no. 2 (2013): 311.
34   Traci Warkentin, "Whale Agency: Affordances and Acts of Resistance in Captive Environments," in *Animals and Agency*, ed. Ryan Hediger and Sarah E. MacFarland (Leiden: Brill, 2009): 23–44.
35   Lestel, Bussolini, and Chrulew, "The Phenomenology of Animal Life."

that can often throw up all kinds of tensions between people who live and work in a city and those who visit. Often this can be a false dichotomy, because even residents behave quite like tourists a lot of the time in cities: they visit attractions, museums, cafes, restaurants, theatres, clubs, use public transport, and frequent public spaces; and often tourists are itching to get off the beaten track to experience everyday city life.[36] Moreover, where tensions are to be found, it can often be around what businesses and local authorities think that tourists want, and in seeking to provide this in ways that give rise to antagonism from other users, often including some other tourists.

More than this, if Tiergarten can be seen as an aspect of that ever-expanding notion of heritage and as a historic park as I think it can, then we can point to it being not just a heritage of and for people, but something more—a more-than-human heritage landscape. Heritage policies and discourses tend to make distinctions between cultural heritage and natural heritage, or to speak of natural and cultural landscapes. However, such distinctions have long been seen to create a false division of nature and culture that is idealistic, Eurocentric, and practically simplistic. This is even more so when we turn to urban parks like Tiergarten.

Rodney Harrison has called for an expanded field of heritage, one beyond nature-culture dualisms that are more dialogic and characterised by connectivity ethics that acknowledge our implications within and vulnerability to changes that effect other parts of the collectives we are enmeshed within.[37] Harrison draws our attention to how heritage has little to do with the past and much much more with practices that are fundamentally concerned with assembling and designing the future: "Heritage involves working with the tangible and intangible traces of the past to both materially and discursively remake both ourselves and the world in the present, in anticipation of an outcome that will help constitute a specific (social, economic, or ecological) resource in and for the future."[38]

Harrison's point is a good one and expands the notion of heritage away from being about conserving to being about making futures, and these futures can and should include diverse peoples and diverse non-humans. Typically, we hear that Tiergarten has a history dictated by kings, court gardeners, directors, and then latterly, the people of Berlin in the immediate post-1945 period when most trees were felled, and the directors and council responsible for allowing its regrowth and replanting. Through all of this period, such a park, like any landscape, might be best seen as a process of co-productions between differing people, their plans, labours, practical uses, and wider ecological and geological entities and their practical doings. Sometimes it is with a future in mind, at other times less so.

If we take the aforementioned arguments for multispecies storying of places and learning to make room for animals (and plants, trees, mosses, insects, soils, and more—but I will limit my argument here, for now, to non-human animals), then we can perhaps seek to extend what is valued here to include the kinds of stories that Sandra Bartoli has begun to put together regarding Tiergarten, to include human-animal stories. Like the

---

36 Robert Maitland, "Culture, City Users, and the Creation of New Tourism Areas in Cities," in *Tourism, Culture, and Regeneration*, ed. Melanie K. Smith (Wallingford: CABI Publishers, 2007).
37 Rodney Harrison, "Beyond 'Natural' and 'Cultural' Heritage: Toward an Otological Politics of Heritage in the Age of the Anthropocene," *Heritage & Society* 8, no. 1 (2015): 32.
38 Harrison, "Beyond 'Natural,'" 35.

research stories told by Domique Lestel and his colleagues, these are people-animal stories of something that might be termed hybrid communities, but stories where the questions asked of animals, the ways of telling stories are not reduced to behaviouralism or other reductive theories that have tended to dominate ethology as well as popular natural history television documentaries. We can learn from Lestel that a *careful* use of anecdote and other knowings can inform a wider sense of seeking better understandings of animals' interpretations, the human interpretations of what the animals do and "think," and the humans' interpretations of the interpretations other humans have of the animals and other humans activity.

ANIMAL COMMODIFICATION

In amongst Tiergarten is the Zoo Berlin, opened in 1844. In recent years with the increasingly serious consideration of animals as part of human living spaces, we have seen an emerging storying of places like zoos.[39] Zoos have of course become much more commercialised spaces in the late twentieth and early twenty-first centuries. So storying of the human-animal lived spaces around us needs to include these practices. They need to take seriously the politics of spaces—and that commodification is rife—whilst still acknowledging that many people-animal relations are not wholly commercialised.

Like all other forms of the worlds around us, non-human animals have increasingly been drawn into the circuits of capital in wide-ranging ways. Some, such as the meat industry, are immense, brutal, and in many ways can be seen to be one of the drivers of real subsumption through the manipulations of biological processes.[40] Others, such as the example of migrating nightingales whose habitat may be built upon, are less obviously violent, but still carry severe repercussions for some beings.

But how are non-human animals to be characterised in differing encounters within circuits of capital? Much of the political economic and urban political ecology work in geography for example has focused on the new regulation of neoliberal natures or human-animal relations, where neoliberalism is seen to be locally plural and diverse in form. Work from political economic approaches here has tended to define nature and animals like fish or wildlife as a resource often narrowly circumscribed as primary commodities.[41] As such, in these approaches we find most economic or socio-ecological practices, relationships, or effects—good or bad—being related back to the same central driver: capitalism or neoliberal capitalism.[42] As Karen Bakker has argued: "Political economic values are but one aspect of meaning to take into consideration in potential and actual transformations of environments. There are various cultural dimensions of valuation that are also important, and then added to this we have the possibility of seeking to understand nonhuman animal meanings."

So, does an engagement of multispecies storying get us closer to aiding how a radical

---

[39] Eric Baratay and Elisabeth Hardouin-Fugier, *Zoo: A History of Zoological Gardens in the West* (London: Reaktion, 2004); and William A. Deiss and R. J. Hoage, eds., *New Worlds, New Animals: From Menagerie to Zoological Park in the Nineteenth Century* (London: Johns Hopkins University Press, 1996).
[40] Nicole Shukin, *Animal Capital: Rendering Life in Biopolitical Times* (Minneapolis: University of Minnesota Press, 2009).
[41] Karen Bakker, "The Limit of 'Neoliberal Natures': Debating Green Neoliberalism," *Progress in Human Geography* 34, no. 6 (2010): 717.
[42] Janelle Cornwell, cited in Brian J. Burke and Boone Shear, eds., "Non-Capitalist Political Ecologies," special section, *Journal of Political Ecology* 21, nos. 6–11 (2014): 132, accessed September 12, 2017, http://ipe.library.arizona.edu/Volume21/Volume_21.html.

politics engages with animals, or does this look like some liberal extension of who should be included within politics? It is necessary to include animals as active beings in what occurs in our lives, and much of this storying and phenomenological-influenced work discusses respectfulness, conversation, and openness. But focusing on the spaces and places of people with animals and other entities means also engaging with things like capitalism, markets, and histories of land changes and the forces involved.

Many but not all of our interactions with non-human animals are inevitably capitalist, driven by markets, as commodities, and exploitative, violent, and often hidden. But, then capitalism is not disembodied: we are also the subjects of capitalism. The current perception is that these incorporations into circuits of capital are massively extending—to the extent where even welfare of farm animals is increasingly commodified in terms of value-added "welfare" foods; or where "supposed 'green' energy is developed from the animal waste from factory farming systems."[43]

But, as an experiment, we might begin to see that even in our own localities many other relations with non-human animals remain to all intents and purposes non-market based, semi- or non-commodified. The latter encompasses a whole gamut of differing relations from what Lestel calls "friendships" between people and animals based on spaces of living together,[44] to the more violent relations of non-commercial hunting, with so much in between. Even pet-keeping—though a multi-billion dollar industry in one sense—cannot just be taken to be a wholly commodified relation, as it is enormously varied. Even tourism—though a multi-billion dollar industry—cannot just be taken to be a wholly commodified relation when it includes interactions with animals and landscapes. We could go on.

Here, I just want to suggest that we might take seriously J. K. Gibson-Graham's take on how we ourselves imagine and engage with capitalism. Too often, like some urban political ecology and political economy approaches to natures, capitalism becomes all-encompassing, and that to which all other things can be related back. Such perspectives are too often indifferent to the contributions of alternative ways of economic life. We need to continually critique capitalism, but we also need to be open to seeing other possibilities, and not to simply condemn them to inevitable failure. This goes for how we engage with non-human animals. Here we might take up Gibson-Graham's notion of resubjectivation—that is, "the difficult process of cultivating subjects (ourselves and others) who can desire and inhabit noncapitalist economic spaces."[45]

---

43 Henry Buller and Emma Roe, "Commodifying Animal Welfare," *Animal Welfare* 21(S1) (2012); Eliza Barclay, "China Turns to Biogas to Ease Impact of Factory Farms," *Yale Environment 360*, November 11, 2010, http://e360.yale.edu/features/china_turns_to_ecological_biogas_production_to_ease_impact_of_factory_livestock_farms; Shukin, *Animal Capital*, 66ff on waste and capitalism.
44 Dominique Lestel, "The Friends of My Friends: On Animal Friendship," trans. Jeffrey Bussolini, *Angelaki* 19 no. 3 (November 2014).
45 J. K. Gibson-Graham, *The End of Capitalism As We Knew It: A Feminist Critique of Political Economy*, 2nd ed. (Minneapolis: University of Minnesota Press, 2006).

SANDRA BARTOLI

FROM TIERGARTEN'S PLANT SOCIETIES AND BERLIN'S BIOTOPE MAP TO A MAP OF NEGLECT

> A walk in Tiergarten in the time between 1946 and 1949 meant that one would stare into a horizon of endless ruins, no matter from which side of the park one would start, and Tiergarten itself, or better, what constituted its beauty, which is its forest growth, had all disappeared.
> —Willy Alverdes, "Der große Tiergarten zu Berlin im Wiederaufbau" (1958)

The necessity of a plan for taking things away from the city, to make space, or even to accept and embrace the decaying cycle of architecture are all relatively unexplored ideas, if not completely taboo. Rem Koolhaas, in a panel discussion at the Venice Architecture Biennale in 2010, makes a productive statement about the relationship between ecology and the city:

> We are becoming more and more concerned with what we leave behind as a species. Heritage has become a right, which is a very bizarre condition. One of the interesting statistics is that if you look at everything that is preserved now by UNESCO, about 40 percent is in Europe, but then if you see everything in the pipeline, there is a drastic adjustment. 20 percent for Europe, 20 percent for Africa, etc., so heritage has become a politically correct issue. If you look everywhere where there is preservation, we count 12 percent of the surface of the earth, including the water surface. So all our discussions about ecology, [...] about the city, have to take into account perhaps a new regime where part of us has to live with radical change, and the other part has to live with what we call radical stasis [where] things will stay the same. And I think we haven't even begun to consider the consequences of that, [...] to consider the implications of preservation at this scale. Or the simple livelihood of cities. As a counterpart to this enormous attempt at remaining stable, we [OMA/AMO] rewrote the UN charter and tried to propose a series of norms we could use to take things out. Because I think what we'll soon face is this need, a philosophy, a theory, to take things away.[1]

What I report in this text is Tiergarten's unique qualities in relation to a specific moment in Berlin, when a destroyed city gave impulse to a new concept of ecology born out of the overlapping of human and natural history. In this moment, the classic concept of the duality of nature and city started to dissolve in a very concrete way.

Tiergarten is a structured forest and park. Its beautiful massive construct is an interval of clearings and small thick forests, which are a combination of plant societies planted after World War II—beeches, oaks, alders, pine trees, and so on—but also of wild saplings filling the gaps and middle ground of these island forests with yew and English dogwood plants. This renders these inner territories inaccessible to people, especially in the summer, and instead, they become the habitat of low-ground nesting birds and many other animals. The soft and wide edges of these forests, left alone by the lawnmower, make another textured lower horizon. Constructed by a variety of long grasses and wild plants spreading toward the adjacent clearings, they are like low liminal membranes that make the best of both worlds at the interface of shady forests and open and sunny meadows. This structure of interlacing vegetation

---

1   **Rem Koolhaas,** *Ecological Urbanism* (panel discussion at the Venice Architecture Biennale, August 26, 2010).

forms regions and islands that are at times open and free for human use and at other times perfectly inscrutable: spatial singularities crawling with animal sound and movement. This particular architectural quality of Tiergarten is also the reason for such a high coexistence of the wild and the human.

But there are reconstruction projects both already realized and in proposal by the monument department of the Berlin municipality that are counter to the spatial quality of Tiergarten, that constrain the park in reproducing a partial and hegemonic history of the city,[2] and that undermine the visible coexistence of human and natural history.[3]

Furthermore, many aspects of the new Parkpflegewerk, the park management plan drafted in 2016, apply a strict correctional approach to this place;[4] loaded with human exceptionalism, the plan intends to maximize human accessibility, clearing away the perceived "unruly" wilderness and diminishing the essential ecological and cultural value of this spatial model of co-species.[5] Under the view of a uniquely combined human, animal, and vegetal heritage that transgresses their respective jurisdictions—and which has led to an urban construct of "natural" territories effortlessly overlapping and intensely used by different species—it is now urgent to retrace the origins and transformations of Tiergarten.

---

[2] Klaus Lingenauber of the Landesdenkmalamt, Berlin's monuments department responsible for historical reconstructions and changes, seems to be using a narrow set of cultural references partial only to specific moments in the history of Berlin: as an example, that of Kaiser Wilhelm II, a regent focused on a military empire leading directly to World War I. Wilhelm II commissioned Hermann Geitner, Tiergarten inspector at the time, to refurbish the Siegesallee, the allée of victory, in a grand commemoration of military power. Lingenauber, coauthor of a plaque near the Reichstag commemorating Geitner, writes highly of Geitner's accomplishments, including the fact that he became the Royal Tiergarten director after finishing the refurbishment and, as he was also responsible for extensive tree felling in Tiergarten, even going so far as to quote Wilhelm II's motto, "Im Park muss die Axt regieren" (In the park the ax must rule).
  Perhaps this plaque can be seen as a symbol of the political climate currently reshaping Tiergarten, which is further confirmed by the former director of the Landesdenkmalamt, Klaus von Krosigk, who has publicly stated his wishes for a Tiergarten director with direct decisional power on the park: "A highly competent man who can tell the Senate: My way or the highway!" See the report of the symposium of November 16, 2012, at the Akademie der Künste, *Tiergarten Dialoge 3*, Senatsverwaltung für Stadtentwicklung und Umwelt Berlin (available at https://www.berlin.de/ba-mitte/politik-und-verwaltung/.../id-2501_geitner.pdf, p. 19).
[3] The landscape planner and ecologist Angela von Lührte, during an excursion in May 2014, was showing a group of architecture students a large beech tree a little to the north side of the Sternallee. The tree displayed round crevices out of which one could hear the sound of bird chicks, probably woodpeckers. This was just meters away from the Siegessäule and can be seen as a poetic comment on the coexistence of an instance of dark human history with natural history, as the Siegessäule was placed here by the National Socialists after moving it from Platz der Republik to the enlarged Großer Stern roundabout. This kind of circumstance of a large old tree, not aligned with the axis of the allée reconstructed in the late 1980s, is the fruit of time and a loving indifference to cultural hierarchies. It is now April 2018, and the tree is gone, as the new management plan for Tiergarten, in progress since 2016, instead foresaw the redesign of this allée with rows of young linden trees of the same size and shape planted at an even distance; all exceptions to this design, such as many of the existing old trees, encountered zero tolerance and were removed.
[4] The new Parkpflegewerk is highly problematic because it conceptually starts from the premise that Tiergarten is a flawed park in need of correction in order to compete with parks of much higher touristic performance, such as Central Park in New York or Hyde Park in London. In this way, the new management plan jettisons not only the ecological role of Tiergarten, which exhibits a much higher biodiversity than any other famous urban park, but also the evident spatial qualities that are directly related to this. Since 2009, there has been a steady increase of new paths and the shrinking and felling of forests, also in protecting areas like the edges that form a front toward the strong and often devastating west winds and along the major roads. The new plan of 2016 foresaw a wide range of interventions of this kind, opening areas of access through the forest, as an example, toward Tiergartenstrasse and the new luxury gated quarter of the Diplomatenviertel, or the proposal to build several bridges between the inaccessible islands of the Neuer See, thus destroying these bird sanctuaries and conveniently providing even more accessibility to the popular Cafe am Neuen See near the Spanish embassy.
[5] This view, applied to the architectural spatial context of Tiergarten, is inspired by Donna J. Haraway's notion of co-species. See Haraway, *When Species Meet* (Minneapolis: University of Minnesota Press, 2007).

TIERGARTEN: A LUSH FOREST THROUGHOUT THE CENTURIES DESPITE ITS DESTRUCTION

The ecologist-landscape planners and botanists Angela von Lührte and Maria-Sofie Rohner, in their essay "Der Große Tiergarten – Botanisch-historische Exkursion in Berlin-Mitte am 1. Juni 2008," make essential points about understanding Tiergarten as both a place of ongoing relevant ecological research and of possessing a rich botanical heritage, which had been broadly acknowledged, appreciated, and documented throughout the centuries. Giving various examples of this natural heritage and its interlacing with human history, von Lührte and Rohner mention that the first reports in the sixteenth century about Tiergarten describe a forest of diversified structured swamps and bogs lying south of the Spree river, the result of the most recent ice age in the glacial valley flowing from Warsaw to Berlin.[6] When Tiergarten was transformed between 1740 and 1786 into a Baroque park for the public, it retained these swampy and boggy characteristics in its forest. In fact, the Baroque aesthetics were very simply applied by carving geometric rooms, salons, and labyrinths out of the woods, while the untouched marshes were pragmatically integrated into the space.

By 1742, Tiergarten had ceased to be a royal hunting ground when its perimeter fence was removed, transforming it, under the guidance of Georg Wenzeslau von Knobelsdorf (the new superintendent of the royal palaces and gardens at the time), into a forest with a park-like character.[7] Von Lührte and Rohner further mention that during the mid-eighteenth century, the botanist and physician Johann Gottlieb Gleditsch led weekly botanical excursions through the park for the benefit of medical students. During this work, he documented seventy-eight species of trees specific to Tiergarten.[8] In 1786, the writer Friedrich Nicolai gave a rich description of the vegetation in Tiergarten after a strong and invigorating rain shower. Through his writing, he described a forest of dark pine trees, slender elms, bright birches, and smooth honey locust between centuries-old oaks and defined the different spaces through elements of both architecture and mood, such as "melancholic corridors" formed by lines of densely grown larch and "dusky" small trees of English yew leading to large plazas and green salons delineated by hedges of oaks and evergreen conifers.

Among these historical descriptions and observations reported by von Lührte and Rohner was also a significant text by a young Alexander von Humboldt. In a letter to a friend at the end of February 1789, after collecting moss and lichen specimens during one of his "frequent solitary walks in this place," he wrote of Tiergarten as a rainforest, describing the "sonic universe" of creatures that surrounded him, keeping him company, and which made him think of Leibniz's principle of the soul,[9] a system where life and matter are seen as one.[10]

---

6   Angela von Lührte and Maria-Sofie Rohner, "Der Große Tiergarten – Botanisch-historische Exkursion in Berlin-Mitte am 1. Juni 2008," in *Verhandlungen des Botanischen Vereins Berlin Brandenburg* 142 (June 2009): 251–84; von Lührte and Rohner are also landscape planners who studied and collaborated on several projects with the founder of the urban ecology department at the Technische Universität Berlin, Herbert Sukopp. This essay was published in a collection edited, among others, by Sukopp.
7   See Folkwin Wendland, "Die historische Entwicklung des Großen Tiergartens in Berlin," in *Der Berliner Tiergarten. Vergangenheit und Zukunft*, ed. Landesdenkmalamt Berlin (Berlin: 1996), 10.
8   Von Lührte and Rohner, "Der Große Tiergarten," 252. The botanist Carl Ludwig Willdenow introduced Humboldt to the love of the science of plants. For Tiergarten, he compiled a list of 170 plants, 34 mosses, 19 fungi, and 44 kinds of trees in his "Florae Berolinensis Prodromus" (1787). See also von Lührte and Rohner, 253.
9   Von Lührte and Rohner, 253.
10 The term "principle of the soul" refers to Leibniz's metaphysics.

Von Lührte and Rohner go on to report that between 1833 and 1838, the work of landscape architect Peter Joseph Lenné transformed Tiergarten into a "landscape park" that resulted in the loss of some of the forest's character not only through the thinning of thick forest to make wide clearings, but also through the reshaping of extensive tree groves with thick sub-layers of bushes and the draining of large swamp areas. The transformation of Tiergarten by Lenné, however, is also seen by botanist Wolfram Kunick as careful, simple, and sparing in its consideration. For example, Kunick writes that Lenné introduced a new waterway and drainage system that took advantage of the slight gradient between the Landwehrkanal and the Spree river, and included many old trees and existing sub-forest plants that formed dense islands of wild bosquets and interconnected long-grass clearings.[11] In Kunick's dissertation of 1974, a survey assessing the transformation of the vegetation of West Berlin, the result of a review of Tiergarten's transformation throughout the centuries was that the main characteristics of the park's floodplain were partially retained, which helped define the specific quality and variety of vegetation, such as oaks, beeches, birches, maples, linden trees, chestnut trees, etc.[12]

In the twentieth century, as a consequence of World War II, Tiergarten lost its forest. This however did not happen during the war, but right after, throughout the winters of 1946 and 1947 when the British Army gave permission to the population of Berlin to fell 200,000 trees for firewood. Of these old trees, only 700 of them remained.[13] Immediately after the felling, a large part of the area was turned into vegetable gardens and potato fields, especially on the east side, to cope with the general state of famine. The writer Max Frisch in his diary of 1946 compares Tiergarten to a vast open steppe due to its sandy soil, which was a natural and successional transformation of the place once the trees were felled. Heavy sandstorms resulted from the lack of trees, and the widespread presence of rubble mounds was the tipping point for a replantation of Tiergarten, which started as early as 1949 with the appointment of the new park director Willy Alverdes.[14]

NONHUMAN HERITAGE/ BIOCENTRICISM

The plan drafted by Alverdes in 1952 for the replantation of Tiergarten immediately after the war retraced the general scheme of Lenné's plan, but it was far from a historic "reconstruction." Alverdes's plan differentiated itself in many ways: it was a layout substantially affected by post-war conditions, and it was also the product of a pragmatic approach drawn by an economy of means and the necessity to regrow the Tiergarten forest in the most rapid way. The sandstorms hitting the city were a clear issue, but so was the early recognition of the scarcity of green areas after the division of the city.

11   In the two excursions in Tiergarten of 2013 and 2014, von Lührte mentions how many of the old trees in Tiergarten suffering from severe drought became sick between 1935 and 1939 when the large-scale works for the Germania plan by Albert Speer provoked the sinking of the groundwater. The same problem occurred during the building of Potsdamer Platz between 1991 and 2000. Von Lührte was able to read these critical moments by analyzing the rings of old trees with a core sample.
12   Wolfram Kunick, *Veränderung von Flora und Vegetation einer Großstadt dargestellt am Beispiel von Berlin (West)* (dissertation, Technische Universität Berlin, 1974), 105.
13   Willy Alverdes, "Der Große Tiergarten," *Garten und Landschaft*, no. 10 (1952).
14   Alverdes was gardener, horticulturist, and landscape architect. He was also responsible for the design of many lushly planted public places, characteristic of Berlin, such as the Kleiner Tiergarten in Moabit, the public landscape (green areas) of the Hansaviertel, the Ottopark, the Fritz-Schloss-Park, the greenways along the Landwehrkanal, the Spree river, and Nordhafen.

In his writings, Alverdes insisted on the existential necessity for offering Berliners a place of leisure by concealing the city's ruins using Tiergarten's sprouting mass of fresh vegetation. Ideologically, Alverdes's plan worked from a point of zero history and drew direct references from the ancient natural history of the city. The plan was also exceptionally long-term from an ecological perspective. One could speculate that his work was influenced by the radical "biocentric" narratives of some of the culture of life reform of the early twentieth century.[15]

What is relevant to the case of the replantation of Tiergarten was Alverdes's intention to develop holistic models that integrated scientific studies about botany in order to inform practical planning. As the result of a philosophy of ecology and planning decisions set in motion in the 1950s, it is important to understand that this was perhaps one of the most dominant paradigms present in Tiergarten. The other main paradigm was the transformation set out by decisions at the legislative level in the late 1970s.[16]

Alverdes, who was an exceptional horticulturist and botanist, writing about Tiergarten in the 1950s, insisted on the belief of the innate human necessity for finding nature in the city (and, therefore, of the "well-being" that is drawn from this encounter). In her essay about Alverdes, landscape architect Katrin Lesser-Sayrac writes that Alverdes believed in the power of plants: his conviction was that their form and way of life would be able to offer essential "experiences" to people and enhance "life awareness" (*Lebensgefühl*). In his work, each plant was considered an individual, thereby adamantly opposing the gardening practice "to regiment plants" by forcing them into specific shapes. He countered this by studying and understanding the life cycles and natural growth of plants and was fascinated by their ability to create complex vegetation systems sustaining each other that were, in an architectural and typological way, visible landscape habitats.[17]

The plan for Tiergarten was to achieve an experience of full immersion for the visitors walking in this new forest, and the principle was implemented at all scales, from large long-grass clearings to the denser and more contained groves within the park. Alverdes, adhering to the political climate at the time, declined the reconstruction of historical areas that had been built to glorify the late nineteenth-century German Empire as well as of the Baroque path system that was based on axes. He instead invested in the spatial structure of the canopy forests, the rich forest undergrowth, the wide lower edges of small plants, and the large meadows, which he opened for all kinds of use (that were, since the time of Lenné,

---

15 Early on, Alverdes recognized the importance of every single open green area—even the smallest fragments—in West Berlin, a city surrounded by the Wall where the *Lebensraum* (space for life) to experience *Lebensgefühl* (the feeling of being alive) was limited and therefore precious. These specific terms of *Lebensraum* and *Lebensgefühl* were the vocabulary of many of the reform movements of the early twentieth century, which were biocentric at their core and combined biology with aesthetics. In fact, Alverdes had been part of the first wave of the Wandervögel movement, before World War I. The "wandering birds," or "vagabonds," was a student movement that, in reaction to industrialization and the stifling conservatism of the Kaiser Reich of Wilhelm II, was interested in a new understanding of life and in returning to nature. The group was anti-authoritative, critical of societal conventions, and involved in pedagogical reform and naturism. Some historians include the Wandervögel as among the first hippies.
16 Kunick, *Veränderung von Flora und Vegetation*, 103–7.
17 Alverdes thought that plants, as individual creatures, should be free to grow, never controlled by being constrained to military pathways: "We are sick and tired of constrictions and we should not impose on plants what we now refuse for ourselves." Katrin Lesser-Sayrac, "Willy Alverdes – sein Werk als Gartenarchitekt und seine Verdienste für den Großen Tiergarten in Berlin," *Der Berliner Tiergarten – Vergangenheit und Zukunft* (Berlin: Landesdenkmalamt Berlin, 1996), 38. My translation.

previously forbidden). While plants were allowed to flourish, all military monuments were ordered to be destroyed.[18] The density and articulation of plants in this emulation of a natural state were key elements for the replanting as well as differentiation of green spaces, to the point that Alverdes saw the modernity of landscape architecture specifically in the implementation of the discoveries about plant sociology in natural science.[19]

Furthermore, conceived also as a nature park by Alverdes,[20] the narrow trails meandered through thick forests and rhododendron groves in order to simulate a walk through nature in a virgin state. This was an unusual design for an urban park, and Alverdes's intention was not only to achieve variety in the green texture, but also to give the wildlife more quiet recesses, for which he introduced deep niches in the vegetation and reworked the slight topography to form secret spaces as well as used yew bushes along larger promenades to naturally shield plant and animal territories from paths of intense human use[21] (*fig. 1*). In the gardening practices for the park, he also encouraged the inclusion of spontaneous wild plants such as *Verbascum thapsus* (p. 21)[22] and praised the quality of planting schemes that were assigned to turn parts of Tiergarten into "wilderness," for instance in the islands of the Neuer See[23] (*fig. 8*).

PLANT COMMUNITIES IN TIERGARTEN

By planting the forest with a natural low, middle, and top layer (respectively, forest floor and grasses, shrub layers, and canopies), Alverdes set the conditions for species to self-complicate over time. He used a number of different kinds of plant societies[24] for which the planting was informed by the quality of the soil, the topography, and the water conditions: as an example, societies of black alder forest were used in narrow areas along the water shores; willow, poplar, and ash floodplain forests were planted at the end of each water segment; areas with a consistent high waterbed and deep soil were suitable for forests of English oak-hornbeam, which also included red beech, mountain and pointed maple, winter linden-hornbeam, and pussy willow; and places of deep waterbed and poor soil, like the east side of Tiergarten up to Brandenburger Tor, were planted with sessile oak, hornbeam, and birch forests, while other plants of this group included pine trees, winter linden, silver birch, and European mountain ash.

In order to establish good conditions for more fragile and slower growing trees, Alverdes used methods analogous to the successional fields of the plant societies, where pioneer plants played an essential role in establishing the right soil and climate for

---

18 By 2018, the axes will be entirely reconstructed, as an example, around the Großer Stern, which will be completed with the restoration and, in large part, reconstruction of nineteenth-century monuments dedicated to the military and stately commemoration of generals and royals.
19 Alverdes studied the indications in the published research paper "Vorschläge für die Wiederbepflanzung der Grünanlagen und Schaffung von Windschutzpflanzungen auf pflanzensoziologischer Grundlage im Landschaftsraum Groß-Berlin" by Prof. Dr. Kurt Hueck, Institut für Landwirtschaftliche Botanik der Universität Berlin. Alverdes, "Der Große Tiergarten," 10–11.
20 "Berlin wanted [...] a nearly natural forest park, something from the landscape of Mark Brandenburg and as attractive as nature can be far away from the city," Alverdes, "Der Große Tiergarten," 10. My translation.
21 Willy Alverdes, "Rhododendron im Großen Tiergarten Berlin," *Garten und Landschaft*, no. 10 (1959): 292.
22 Willy Alverdes, "Die Neubepflanzung des Großen Tiergarten zu Berlin," *Garten und Landschaft*, no. 1 (1955): 2.
23 Alverdes, "Rhododendron im Großen Tiergarten Berlin," 292.
24 Plant societies are abstract plant communities defined through botanical research that catalog the ability of groups of plants to create a relatively stable biotope type from ground cover up to the trees while holding a certain equilibrium and consistency throughout time. Fritz Runge, *Die Pflanzengesellschaften Mitteleuropa* (Münster: Aschendorff Verlag, 1994).

other plants, by planting fast-growing softwood trees such as hybrid poplars *(Populus robusta)*—also nicknamed *Populus berolinensis,* or Berlin poplar—every six to eight meters. In very dry areas east of Tiergarten, black alder was assigned to help the poplars, while red oak eased the growth of red beech. Together with the planting of the underforest and middle-forest layers with the plants of corresponding societies, within a few years, these species provided the spatial and microclimatic quality of a full mass of vegetation. Special care was devoted to planting these layers on the edges of Tiergarten to protect it from the winds.[25]

The immediate purpose of Alverdes's plan was to achieve a series of diversified groves with characteristic forests that were "intensely interconnected ecologically" within the 240 hectares of Tiergarten.[26] The long-term plan was to gradually cut down the fast-growing trees after thirty years in order to leave space for the slow-growing ones. Tiergarten's space is, up until today, structured mainly through these sets of plants. The subtle diversity of Alverdes's plant communities can be easily read as the basis of the social diversity for this place and the prerequisite for a multiplicity of species and uses.[27]

THE BIOTOPE MAP AND ITS READING OF TIERGARTEN

If Alverdes's approach to the replantation of Tiergarten was inspired by the natural world and its systems, another important movement born out of the unique conditions of West Berlin after the war added a paradigm shift not only to the park but altogether to the worth of the urban wild in the city. This was the pioneer fieldwork that led to the Berlin Biotope Map of 1984 *(pp. 241–53).*

In cities like London and Berlin after World War II, over a few years the bombed and derelict areas became wild gardens of plants completely exotic to the city that grew on rubble and empty lots. The bombs in this specific context turned out to be time machines

---

25   Alverdes, "Die Neubepflanzung," 4.
26   Willy Alverdes, "Der Große Tiergarten Berlin – Neugestaltung einer historisch bedeutungsvollen Anlage," *Garten und Landschaft,* no. 2 (1964): 50.
27   Examples of use in Tiergarten; scenes:
A compact pine tree group on a mound in an open grass field alternately evokes ancient high grounds from the last glacial period, the place for an improvised small tent, or one person's temporary camp in a sleeping bag spread out on the soft dry needle floor. The air is full of the smell of moss and resin; it is one of those rare isolated places offering prospects and refuge at the same time. Southwest of the Großer Stern (Siegessäule) and through the shiny deep green of the rhododendron grove, the outrageous felling of two old beeches gives way to a sudden clearing. Their long, smooth, elegant trunks hold a crew of four people: a young one models in the center, the camera snaps and quickly flashes; another one is kneeling below, holding a round reflective screen with outstretched arms.
Naked except for his suspensory scrotal support, a thin, tall man jogs loosely along the wide gravel path of the Großer Weg, his hair knotted back as tightly as his jockstrap thong.
2018: A New Zealander photographer dressed in a light-brown down jacket and pants spends a good part of a seriously freezing February 2018 photographing the many goshawks of Tiergarten and their breeding habits. He hides in the glowing beige winter foliage and shrubs, holding an extremely large zoom lens between yews, while chainsaws are clearing sights to an invented historical axis, dubiously relevant, drawn as a dilettante web of arrows that betrays more insanity than any other in the new park management plan. The New Zealander is fascinated by the state of the goshawks in Tiergarten and refers to another similar place, a nature reserve, back home in Wellington.
Hurricanes in Berlin, 2017: severe windstorms had been more frequent in past years. The one that happened last week ripped out trees which were then lying on trails; large branches flew, crashing into the crowns of other trees, their buoyancy taking everything down. The day after is crisp, wet, and everything is emerald and blue haze. It smells fresh, like in a real forest. But then what is real?—Tiergarten is as real inside the city. Drops of fresh water, mist; it is autumn. Broken trees and shattered branches are scattered everywhere; the paths are covered with mounds of leaves and twigs. The birds, tits, nuthatches, and blackbirds, are rushing, swirling fast above, often in groups, to find insects in every fresh crack and interstice. Larch tree groups are tall, and many of their branches are gone.

when plant seeds, buried for centuries, were brought to the surface and germinated; some of these plants were hard to find even in the countryside. This extraordinary phenomenon drew the attention of naturalists, botanists, and ecologists.[28]

Furthermore, until 1961, botanists and ecologists in Berlin were accustomed to doing their research in the countryside. After the division of the city, they reverted to the urban space not only because of the special insular condition of West Berlin, but also because the urban realm had turned into an unprecedented, exotic, and exciting field of research. This phenomenon grew to the point that West Berlin became internationally known as a city at the forefront of urban ecology. This was the context that produced original research and a corresponding new body of legislation.

POLICIES

A city enclosed by a wall sets a very peculiar psychological situation where all open green areas are viewed and cherished as a precious anomaly. Summarizing the situation of West Berlin with an existential analogy, architect Irenée Scalbert wrote, "In a kind of reversal Robinson Crusoe, who builds a fence to enclose what could be saved for civilization, the city responded to its island condition within East Germany by looking to encompass nature within the confines of its own urban boundary."[29]

These distinctive conditions of West Berlin set the ground for new policies of ecology that were supported by a political climate influenced by the emergence of a growing environmental awareness (for instance, the Alternative Liste für Demokratie und Umweltschutz, what later became the German Green Party, was founded in West Berlin in 1978). As an example, between 1975 and 1976, the Berlin House of Representatives decided that each tree-felling proposal in Tiergarten from the park department needed the official permission of the district assembly. This political decision aimed to turn Tiergarten into an approximation of a "rainforest" by considerably slowing down and sometimes even stopping for several years the tree-felling program that had been planned by Alverdes.[30] This decree, together with the fact that Tiergarten was a frontier area adjacent to the Berlin Wall, increased the unique wilderness of the place already set in motion by Alverdes's plant societies.

Furthermore, Tiergarten, until then a space dedicated to the purpose of human recreation and culture, was redefined as a biotope, which meant that the management practices of the gardeners were accountable to helping improve biodiversity—instead of jeopardizing it with conventional embellishment practices that interrupt natural processes and perpetuate a distaste for apparent dirt and disarray, such as the removal of deadwood and the preference for short-grass

---

28 The artists Helen Mayer Harrison and Newton Harrison proposed that the site of the Topography of Terror should be kept permanently in its current state, with its debris mounds covered with wild vegetation.
29 Irenée Scalbert, "London after the Green Belt," *AA Files*, no. 66 (Spring 2013): 1–15.
30 This information comes from several interviews conducted with Christoph Schaaf (former Parkleiter GFA Mitte) between 2013 and 2016, and with Reiner Haase (Bezirksamt Mitte von Berlin – Abteilung Weiterbildung, Kultur, Umwelt, Naturschutz, Umwelt- und Naturschutzamt) in June 2016. Schaaf also mentions that around 1975–76, there had been an opportunity to list Tiergarten under the category of a nature conservation area (*Naturschutz*), a much stricter regulation than a landscape conservation area. In 1991, Tiergarten was then instead declared a heritage monument; this placed ecology on a secondary level of importance and was somehow fatal to the park, spinning a series of unjustified projects of historical reconstruction that had no real historical substance in Tiergarten to begin with (such as the Venus Basin, for example). This direction is by now exacerbated by a new management plan for Tiergarten that is absolutely partial to a retrograde understanding of heritage, with little consideration, if not straight contempt, for the ecology of the place.

lawns over long-grass meadows. The approval by the House of Representatives of the nature conservation act of January 30, 1979 bound the Berlin Senate to develop a landscape program together with a species protection program, or Artenschutzprogramm. This conservation act was prepared by a large team of ecologists, botanists, and landscape planners with the support of many citizen-naturalists. The latter is an important detail as regular citizens volunteered in doing census work for many years, out of their own interest for the wild landscape of Berlin. Produced at the department for the research of ecological systems and botanical survey at the Technische Universität (TU) Berlin, the project became a city-wide endeavor that was not only confined to academia. The preface of the published fundamentals of the Artenschutzprogramm stated that this was the first ever drafted for a West German city and, most importantly, it was also applied to the *entire* city.[31] This meant that all West Berlin was under nature protection law. Furthermore, within the program, the category of the protection of nature, *Naturschutz*, was applied comprehensively to the city in parallel to the land-use plan, which was a radical approach; for instance, in the case of industrial or housing areas, nothing was excluded. This unique alignment of conservation claims by ecologists with problem claims of green policy[32] led to the charting of the entire city as a construct of different biotopes in an extensive map.

THE BIOTOPE MAP

The practical effect of the Wall moved botanists to revert to the urban space for their research. The condition of the city, full of empty plots of land, also produced a radical new understanding of ecology and of the city itself. Berlin, with its wealth of wild zones covered with extraordinary plants, became the forefront of the study of urban ecology. This was a term that Herbert Sukopp, the head of the department for the research of ecological systems and botanical survey at TU Berlin, started using to describe this peculiar situation, and in so doing, redefining the understanding of ecology in an urban context.[33] Plant species for Sukopp were straightforward indicators of the quality of urban life, and one needed a map charting this information. Sukopp's scheme, the compiling of a biotope map based on Berlin featuring "flora, fauna, and other ecological factors throughout the different zones of the city," was radical because it structured the city through botanical and zoological

31 In the preface of the published fundaments of the Artenschutzprogramm, written by Sukopp, there is a quote from the new nature conservation act saying that the program's purpose is "the preparation, implementation, and control of policies for the conservation and care of wild plants and wild animals" in the city. Herbert Sukopp, Axel Auhagen, Hedemarie Frank, Ludwig Trepl, *Grundlagen für das Artenschutzprogramm Berlin* (Berlin: Technische Universität Berlin, 1984), 3. My translation.
32 Jens Lachmund, *Greening Berlin: The Co-Production of Science, Politics, and Urban Nature* (Cambridge, MA: MIT Press, 2013), 90.
33 The term "urban ecology" was, until the shift in its understanding as a result of its use in Berlin, previously used in the field of sociology by the Chicago school, a group of scholars during the 1920s and '30s, to describe the systems of energy consumption and flow of resources affected by observations of the industrial process of the production line. Terms like "social urban ecology" dealt with the cure of the city's "pathologies" (pollution, crime, etc.) for the improvement of the quality of urban human life and the control of behavior: "It was the rise of ecosystem theory that gave a new twist to the development of urban ecology. The term *ecosystem* had been coined by the British biologist Arthur Tansley in 1935, but was significantly elaborated in the 1950s and 1960s by North American ecologists such as Raymond Lindeman, Stanley Auerbach, Howard Odum, and Eugene Odum. [...] In their hands it became a cybernetic model that represented organisms (including human beings) and their physical environments in terms of self-regulating flows of materials and energy. [...] Quantitative measurements of energy consumption and material flows and the representation of the results in schematic diagrams became the hallmarks of the new research practice that they introduced in their discipline. [...] This approach [...] was subsequently extended to the study of [...] environmental problems." See Lachmund, *Greening Berlin*, 82–85.

categories[34] and defined a larger system of nature in an anthropogenic environment: a bombed area between housing blocks, generally perceived as a wasteland, became a compelling new kind of natural space, developed out of a human-made environment.

For the first time, the purpose of a plan for the city was to protect and foster wildlife species, while many of the conventional policies of maintenance became a threat to biodiversity. Going beyond the city's open areas and including all built structures and buildings also meant laying claims of nature conservation throughout the entire city. This also became the first time that a map was drafted for this purpose, and the spatial visualization of this program was key to its implementation and political power.[35]

The primary assignment of the species protection program developed by the Berlin Senate was for the protection, care, and development of the city's biotopes of flora and fauna.[36] All this work, commissioned and published by the Senate, sanctioned the structures of the urban biotope as directives of management and planning for the administration. There were new and wildly sounding biotope names promising hybrid types of spaces that merged human and natural history: for example, there was the Autobahnbiotop (the highway biotope), the Strassenbiotop (the street biotope), the Rieselfelderbiotop (the sewage-farm biotope), and the Brachebiotop (the fallow-land biotope). There was also a section of the program that showed the juxtaposition of these different biotopes for each region of the city and provided a set of guidelines for their conservation, support, and growth.[37] For example, in the category of the Biotope der geschlossenen Bebauung (the biotope of closed blocks), a team of ecologists was tasked with marking all building blocks in West Berlin, making recommendations not only to introduce the greening of the facades and roofs of houses, but also to support and

---

34 Ecologists and citizens in West Berlin were reframing derelict areas as "new environmental entities," the prototypes of new urban ecosystems: "It was a nature that was largely determined by the human-made environmental conditions of the city." See Lachmund, *Greening Berlin*, 68. "Beginning with the late 1970s, [ecologists] aimed at a comprehensive structuring of the Berlin territory according to ecological criteria. [These] fieldwork practices resulted in spatial classifications, statistical indicators, and cartographic renderings that together represented Berlin as variegated complex of flora, fauna, and living spaces. [...] They also helped to establish the city [...] as a generic object of ecological knowledge." See Lachmund, *Greening Berlin*, 72.

35 Wolfram Kunick, in his dissertation *Veränderung von Flora und Vegetation einer Großstadt dargestellt am Beispiel von Berlin (West)*, was the first to lay down a comprehensive botanical survey onto a regular map of the city, and in this way, redefining West Berlin through plant categories found in specific urban situations. Berlin, a built environment, was understood for the first time as a place with its own set of biotopes, climate, and nature. To make this large project manageable, Kunick subdivided West Berlin into four basic urban structures that corresponded to four zones of different plant compositions: a) closed building blocks/high-density areas (*geschlossene Bebauung*), b) loose building compounds/low-density areas (*aufgelockerte Bebauung*), c) interior city periphery (*innerer Stadtrand*), and d) exterior city periphery (*äusserer Stadtrand*). This analysis was drafted on a ground-figure map of Berlin at a scale of 1:50,000, which was provided by the city council.

36 Sukopp et al., *Artenschutzprogramm*, 5–6.

37 *Entwicklung*, or development, a term normally used for building expansion, was highjacked for the ecological agenda of the program.

38 An official document and a compelling instrument of planning, this biotope map responds, as Jens Lachmund points out, to interpretative and practical needs of ecology and administration in a fascinating way, including, among other things, a definition of fifty-seven biotope types and eighteen "Organismengruppen" (i.e., fern and flowering plants, mosses, lichens, fungi, algae, mammals, birds, reptiles, amphibia, fishes, butterflies, bats, beetles, Heteroptera, grasshoppers, dragonflies, spiders, and mollusks; for each individual group there is a set of program-support guidelines), an IUCN Red List of endangered species, a Red List of biotopes for West Berlin, and a set of maps surveying the conditions of the biotopes with proposals for development and planning (plan 2 is for maintenance and development of biotopes, plan 3 for conservation areas, plan 4 for the priority areas for nature conservation, and plan 5 maps the entire city as a space of the development for biotopes; accordingly, different priorities are placed for the development of biotopes).

foster animal life like birds, bats, moths, and spiders in attics, and field mice in cellars.[38] Most importantly, the biotope map was a document that showed a fundamental paradigm shift where the conventional antagonism between city and nature was dissolved.

TIERGARTEN IN THE BIOTOPE MAP

In the assessment of the biotope map, Tiergarten was considered one of the few nearly natural areas and relics of the Spree river's alluvial valley in the extraordinary situation of a densely built urban context. Considered a unique biotope, Tiergarten was given primary importance as a refuge for species living on water, for floodplain forests, for its long-grass meadows, and for its fragmentary layers of soil original to the floodplain's ancient geological time, still carrying wet meadows and floodplain shrubs—all worthy of support maintenance and expansion.[39] Tiergarten was defined as part of a larger regional space within the Artenschutzprogramm's development of the Spree river valley.[40] The southern part of Tiergarten in the map was also classified as among the most valuable biotopes,[41] counting for its 212 hectares some 437 plant species, of which 31 were endangered.[42] Tiergarten was charted as the habitat of more than 22 mammal species, the highest number compared to any other area within West Berlin, with a range of old trees and decrepit buildings housing a high number of mammals.[43]

Based on Kunick's survey of 1974, the Artenschutzprogramm proposed designating Tiergarten under the category of a landscape conservation area—a Landschaftsschutzgebiet.[44] A telling detail from the program reported very matter of factly that dry grasses, extremely precious from the ecological point of view, could be found in landscape parks of unique conditions such as Tiergarten and Pfaueninsel (Peacock Island), but also in the premises of new social housing where areas are given very little maintenance (neither watered nor enriched with fertilizer),[45] which suggested that all green areas in the city could be biodiverse if they are left derelict enough. The Artenschutzprogramm also validated Tiergarten as an island of cooler temperatures, generated by the three-layer structure of the plant societies laid out in the 1950s that pulled in winds from south to north throughout the city, establishing an urban microclimate up to seven degrees lower than the surroundings.[46]

---

39   Sukopp et al., *Artenschutzprogramm*, 725.
40   Sukopp et al., 577.
41   "Among many planning recommendations, there are the further reduction of paved areas and, between Schlosspark Charlottenburg and Tiergarten along the canalized Spree river, the design of potential connections for species in the form of green areas with 'species-trails' (*Artenwanderwege*)." Sukopp et al., 698–99. My translation.
42   In Pfaueninsel (Peacock Island), 453 species were documented, of which 100 are endangered. See Sukopp, "Bäume und Sträucher der Pfaueninsel," in *Grundlagen für das Artenschutzprogramm Berlin*, 348. Currently, Tiergarten holds 616 species of plants (including ferns and flowering plants), which is a very high level of diversity compared to Central Park in New York, which carries approximately 300 plant species. See the website *Naturschutz und Denkmalpflege*, http://naturschutz-und-denkmalpflege.projekte.tu-berlin.de/pages/modellanlagen/grosser-tiergarten.php. In the Artenschutzprogramm report, Tiergarten is also recorded as including several old species of grass planted before 1890 in a mixture from southwest middle-Europe and southern France. Large expanses of dry grassland in Tiergarten had formed after World War II, and twenty species were found for each survey section compared to Pfaueninsel's 140-year-old dry grasses, where the number of species is over forty. The older the dry-grass fields, the more diversity they acquire.
43   Some of the mammals living in old trees in Tiergarten include the muskrat, the tree marten, a variety of bats (the water and frans bat, the rare wide-wing bat, the dwarf bat, and the brown long-eared bat). While Tiergarten has twenty-two species of mammals, Pfaueninsel has thirty. See Sukopp et al., *Artenschutzprogramm*, 352.
44   Sukopp et al., 362–63.
45   Sukopp et al., 443.

A MAP FOR PLANNING NEGLECT

The Artenschutzprogramm recommended keeping aside areas that were considered by the administration as reserves for building development, such as ruderal areas (*Brache*, or fallow land), former railway areas, empty lots, and allotment gardens (*Schrebergärten* and *Kleingartenanlagen*), as essential for plant, insect, and mammal species. This had the consequence of a highly stabilizing effect for nature in the core of the city (figs. 3, 4, and 5). These areas included Gleisdreick, Südgelände, and rubble areas south of Tiergarten, but also areas not apt for development, such as the slopes and fragments of green near the railroad, canals, streets, in parks, and other open areas and gardens. Here, the Artenschutzprogramm suggested that maintenance care should be kept to a minimum: it proposed all kinds of devices for a program of neglect that cherished a multiplicity of life in the city, such as areas without a prescribed use, where heaps of leaves are left on the ground and trees can grow old without being brutally amputated so that they can develop tree hollows and crevices for animals to nest. The program also stipulated that the use of biocides should never be allowed throughout the city. For Tiergarten, as an example, they suggested that shrubs and trees grow "unkept and free"[47] in areas that are relatively natural, spared from maintenance care.[48] Among the achievements of the biotope map are the many parks in the city exclusively made of spontaneous ruderal plants requiring spartan management care, such as the beautiful, wild Park auf dem Anhalter Bahnhof south of Tempodrom (figs. 5, 6, and 7), the park on Möckernstrasse, and Natur-Park Südgelände.

Today, the vast urban wild, presented in the biotope map and praised for its unexpected beauty, is in part still present in Berlin despite the rampant urban densification. But its existence, and with this, the unique and beautiful ecology of the city, are endangered and depend on a caring level of forgetting and indifference, especially from the side of the city's administration. The park department managing the city is currently prioritizing an ideological line of heritage preservation that privileges dilettantish reconstructions over ecological considerations. Spontaneous vegetation and unplanned green areas, whose vast appreciation was one of the achievements of urban ecology in the 1970s and '80s, are today considered worthless areas of wild, uncontrolled growth—*Wildwuchs*.[49] The planning of neglect was also a big part of the strategies of the Artenschutzprogramm,[50] and the biotope map was a retrospective map of studied neglect. Tiergarten experienced a relatively long existence of loving indifference and forgetting from 1960 up to 2006, the results of a *laisser pousser* attitude that generated this highly architectural and diversely textured place, richly layered in human and natural history.

---

46 Manfred Horbert and Annette Kirchgeorg, "Stadtklima und innerstädtische Freiräume am Beispiel des Großen Tiergartens in Berlin," *Stadtbauwelt* 67 (September 1980), 270–76.
47 Sukopp et al., 776.
48 Christoph Schaaf, the chief gardener from the 1960s up to 1990, reports on the many initiatives taken by the gardeners under his lead to improve the ecological diversity of Tiergarten, as an example, by transplanting an ant nest in Tiergarten, an experimental project in collaboration with the rangers of the Grünewald forest, or the initiative to plant reed beds in the proximity of water near the Rhododendron Hain (a rhododendron grove south of Siegessäule on the Bremenweg) in order to help purify the water. Many of the meadows were only mowed once a year, especially on the east side of Tiergarten, a very dry area of sandy soil that developed into a biotope of high diversity, which was registered as among the most valuable in West Berlin in the biotope map of 1984. This information comes from a number of interviews I made with Christoph Schaaf between 2016 and 2018.
49 Silvan Linden, "Wildwuchs, or the Worth of the Urban Wild," in *Intercalations 4: The Word for World Is Still Forest*, ed. Anna-Sophie Springer and Etienne Turpin (Berlin: K Verlag, 2017), 169–77.

The approach of indifference and forgetting also looks at a city made extensively of microbiotopes that are repositories of life's diversity. Areas that might look derelict and lacking value are revealed as "nature reserves," like the numerous lichens and mosses blooming in February in the cracks of the sidewalks. These are vivid micro-landscapes of complexity; the gardener, ecologist, and botanist Gilles Clément calls these areas of indifference "gene reservoir gardens." In a time in which every empty lot is disappearing in Berlin, these areas of neglect, the repositories of a natural diversity, are most endangered. The densification of the city should be accompanied by a set of guidelines of indifference and forgetting, which carries its own degree of development: the development of the urban wild. Going even further, in a time of mass extinction and ecological collapse, I propose that a plan of neglect for the city should be accompanied by a plan of decay and destruction, taking things away from the city and freeing space.[51]

---

50 The Artenschutzprogramm already proposes simple rules of neglect by planning for diversity and intensity of use and frequency: given the fact that many species can live in industrial and urban conditions, the design task was to create inconspicuous and low-disturbance areas of refuge which can be integrated in parks, for instance, without the need of fences, allowing for a higher level of coexistence. Human visitors can be distracted and lead away from and around these areas with trails, paths, sports fields, and planted vegetation. Sukopp et al., *Artenschutzprogramm*, 59–60.

51 An example would be a plan of destruction and decay for obsolete structures, such as car parks and, polemically, the Berliner Dome. Koolhaas addresses the question of preservation and what can be taken away from the city in this way: "There are two opposing ideologies at the core of preservation [...]: John Ruskin's [ideology], because Ruskin is perhaps one of the most profound thinkers concerned about aging in general and [...] authenticity, and one of the most aggressive ones to think about the issue of what it means not to change, and what it means simply to decay. The opposing ideology [...] is represented by Viollet-le-Duc, who felt that in order to preserve the past, it has to be in its most splendid form. If one currently looks at how the virtual and the digital are working, it is perhaps a return to Viollet-le-Duc, with the perfect Roman forum, and the perfect antiquity in its form. Personally I'm on the side of Ruskin, but that is a very inconvenient side to be on as an architect. [...] It's obviously a very utopian position." Koolhaas, *Ecological Urbanism*.

A grove of beech trees with underforest in Tiergarten, 2017.

Spontaneous trees (*Ailanthus altissima*) in a courtyard used as a parking lot, Berlin. 2018.

The banks of the Landwehrkanal, treated with low maintenance and ecologically sound principles by the district of Kreuzberg, Berlin, 2018.

Poplar grove, Potsdamer Platz, 2018.

Park auf dem Anhalter Bahnhof, 2018.

Park auf dem Anhalter Bahnhof, with visible old tracks, 2018.

Park auf dem Anhalter Bahnhof, 2018.

An island grown wild to effect on the Neuer See in Tiergarten, 2017.

Artenschutzprogramm | **BERLIN**
zum Landschaftsprogramm   Entwurf

Entwicklungs- und Maßnahmenprogramm

Teilplan 2
Pflege- und Entwicklungsmaßnahmen für Biotoptypen

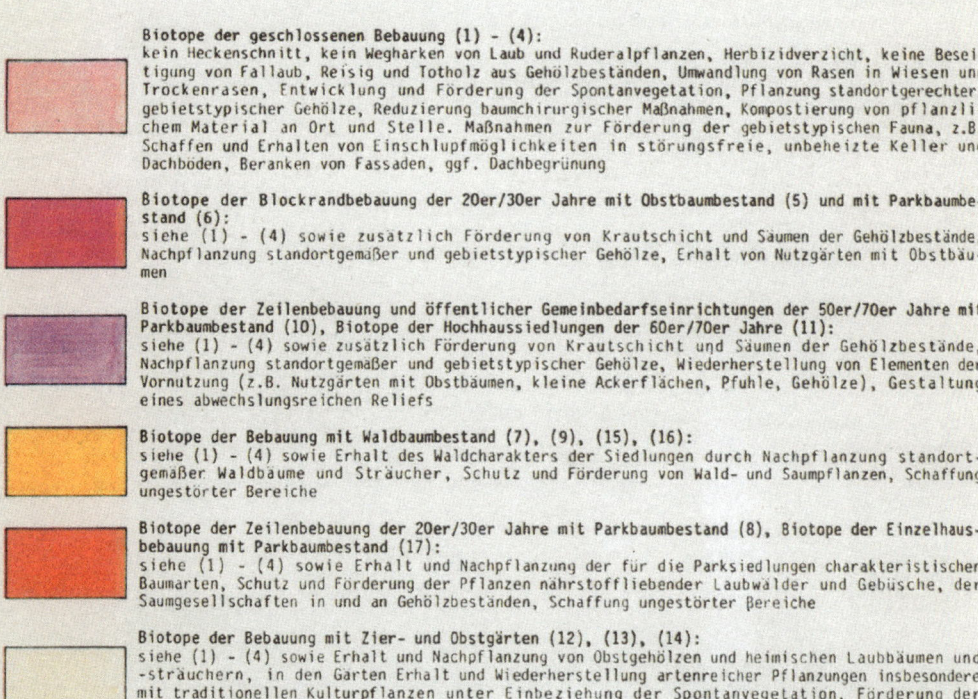

Biotope der geschlossenen Bebauung (1) - (4):
kein Heckenschnitt, kein Wegharken von Laub und Ruderalpflanzen, Herbizidverzicht, keine Beseitigung von Fallaub, Reisig und Totholz aus Gehölzbeständen, Umwandlung von Rasen in Wiesen und Trockenrasen, Entwicklung und Förderung der Spontanvegetation, Pflanzung standortgerechter, gebietstypischer Gehölze, Reduzierung baumchirurgischer Maßnahmen, Kompostierung von pflanzlichem Material an Ort und Stelle. Maßnahmen zur Förderung der gebietstypischen Fauna, z.B. Schaffen und Erhalten von Einschlupfmöglichkeiten in störungsfreie, unbeheizte Keller und Dachböden, Beranken von Fassaden, ggf. Dachbegrünung

Biotope der Blockrandbebauung der 20er/30er Jahre mit Obstbaumbestand (5) und mit Parkbaumbestand (6):
siehe (1) - (4) sowie zusätzlich Förderung von Krautschicht und Säumen der Gehölzbestände, Nachpflanzung standortgemäßer und gebietstypischer Gehölze, Erhalt von Nutzgärten mit Obstbäumen

Biotope der Zeilenbebauung und öffentlicher Gemeinbedarfseinrichtungen der 50er/70er Jahre mit Parkbaumbestand (10), Biotope der Hochhaussiedlungen der 60er/70er Jahre (11):
siehe (1) - (4) sowie zusätzlich Förderung von Krautschicht und Säumen der Gehölzbestände, Nachpflanzung standortgemäßer und gebietstypischer Gehölze, Wiederherstellung von Elementen der Vornutzung (z.B. Nutzgärten mit Obstbäumen, kleine Ackerflächen, Pfuhle, Gehölze), Gestaltung eines abwechslungsreichen Reliefs

Biotope der Bebauung mit Waldbaumbestand (7), (9), (15), (16):
siehe (1) - (4) sowie Erhalt des Waldcharakters der Siedlungen durch Nachpflanzung standortgemäßer Waldbäume und Sträucher, Schutz und Förderung von Wald- und Saumpflanzen, Schaffung ungestörter Bereiche

Biotope der Zeilenbebauung der 20er/30er Jahre mit Parkbaumbestand (8), Biotope der Einzelhausbebauung mit Parkbaumbestand (17):
siehe (1) - (4) sowie Erhalt und Nachpflanzung der für die Parksiedlungen charakteristischen Baumarten, Schutz und Förderung der Pflanzen nährstoffliebender Laubwälder und Gebüsche, der Saumgesellschaften in und an Gehölzbeständen, Schaffung ungestörter Bereiche

Biotope der Bebauung mit Zier- und Obstgärten (12), (13), (14):
siehe (1) - (4) sowie Erhalt und Nachpflanzung von Obstgehölzen und heimischen Laubbäumen und -sträuchern, in den Gärten Erhalt und Wiederherstellung artenreicher Pflanzungen insbesondere mit traditionellen Kulturpflanzen unter Einbeziehung der Spontanvegetation, Förderung der Krautschicht und der Säume von Hecken und Gebüschen, Schaffung ungestörter Teilbereiche auf einzelnen brachliegenden Parzellen sowie Maßnahmen zur Förderung der gebietstypischen Fauna

Biotope der Industrie- und Gewerbegebiete sowie der Hafenanlagen (20):
siehe (1)-(4) sowie für gärtnerisch gepflegte Flächen sowie keinerlei Pflege für ungenutzte Flächen, Erschließung einiger Brachflächen für eine extensive Erholung, in Planungsverfahren Behandlung vegetationsbedeckter Flächen als Grünflächen, Schutz für wertvolle Biotope vor industriell-gewerblicher Nutzung, Erhalt einiger Flächen als Versuchsflächen für Bioindikation

Biotope der in Betrieb befindlichen Gleisanlagen und Güterbahnhöfe (21), Stadtbrachen (35):
siehe (1) - (4) für gärtnerisch gepflegte Flächen, z.B. bei Einbeziehung junger Brachflächen (Baulücken) für Erholung und Kinderspiel, vorrangige Erhaltung großer innerstädtischer Ruderalflächen, teilweise Freigabe zur extensiven Erholungsnutzung, daneben Ausweisung von repräsentativen Naturschutzgebieten von mindestens 5 ha Größe, zum Erhalt von Pionierstadien. Offenhalten von Böden im 5-Jahres-Rhythmus

Höhlen (22):
Schutz und Erhalt vorhandener Fledermausquartiere, Schutz vor Störungen, Erhöhung der Quartierkapazität durch Anbringen von Hohlblocksteinen etc.

Biotope der Straße, Wege, Plätze (23), (24), (25), (26):
siehe (1) - (4) für gärtnerisch gepflegte Flächen (Grünstreifen, Autobahnböschungen, Kleeblattinnenfläche), Maßnahmen zum Schutz und Erhalt der Straßenbäume, Reduzierung der Versiegelung von Gehwegen und Parkplätzen, Förderung von Säumen an den Rändern von Gehölzbeständen, Steigerung des Werts linearer Biotope als Wanderwege für Flora und Fauna in die Stadt durch Beseitigung überflüssiger Unterbrechungen (Pflasterungen von Randstreifen, Stillegung überflüssiger Straßenabschnitte)

Biotope der in Betrieb befindlichen Müll- und Schuttdeponien sowie der Klärbecken (27):
keine Abdeckung von Deponien, Entgasung abgedeckter Flächen, Flächen nicht gärtnerisch gestalten oder aufforsten sondern sich selbst überlassen, als Einzelmaßnahmen Pflanzen von Hecken und Anlage von Teichen

Biotope der nicht rekultivierten Kies-, Sand- und Mergelgruben (28):
Schaffung und Erhalt ungestörter Teilbereiche, Erhalt vegetationsfreier Steilhänge, Flächen nicht gärtnerisch gestalten sondern sich selbst überlassen, als Einzelmaßnahmen Pflanzen von Hecken, Anlage von Teichen, Lenkung der Besucher; Maßnahmen zum Schutz und zur Förderung der gefährdeten, gebietstypischen Tierarten

Biotope der Grünanlagen (29), (30), (31), Biotope des Zoologischen Gartens (55)
siehe (1) - (4) sowie Abstufung der Nutzungsintensität durch unauffällige Besucherlenkung, Schaffung ungestörter Teilbereiche, Anpassung von Gestaltung und Pflege an herrschende Standortbedingungen, Erhalt alter Gehölzbestände, Zerfallenlassen alter und toter Bäume ohne baumchirurgische Maßnahmen in ungestörten Bereichen, Förderung von Säumen und Krautschicht auch durch Einbringung von Wildpflanzen, naturnahe Gestaltung der Gewässer und Rückbau technischer Uferbefestigungen (Bongossiholzfaschinen)

Biotope der Friedhöfe (32), (33), (34):
siehe (1) - (4) sowie Erhalt des alten Baumbestands, in Waldfriedhöfen Nachpflanzung von Gehölzen bodensaurer Eichenmischwälder, in Park- und Zierfriedhöfen von Gehölzen nährstoffliebender Laubwälder und Gebüschen, Erhalt und Neuausbringung standortgemäßer Waldstauden sowie Förderung von Krautschicht und Säumen an Gebüschen und Hecken, Erhalt alter Gräber mit Spontanbewuchs sowie von Flechten, Moosen und Farnen auf Grabsteinen und Mauern und ungestörter Teilflächen mit natürlicher Sukzession, Verhinderung von Bebauung und Zerschneidung durch Straßenneubauten

Gartenbrachen (36), Ackerbrachen (37), Grünlandbrachen (38):
Schutz von Brachflächen mit wertvollem Artenbestand (z.B. Ackerödland mit Trockenrasenarten und Gewässeruferhochstaudenfluren), Rückverwandlung von Brachen in Äcker und Wiesen, Erhöhung der Diversität von Brachflächen in gärtnerisch genutztem Gebiet (z.B. Kleingartengelände), Verbot von Herbizidanwendung, regelmäßige Müllentfernung

Biotope der Rieselfelder (39):
Weiterführung von landwirtschaftlicher Nutzung und Berieselung auch mit vorgereinigtem Abwasser, Erhalt der Spontanvegetation an Wegrändern, Böschungen und Rainen, Nachpflanzung von Hecken und Obstgehölzen, Mähen höchstens 2mal jährlich sowie Belassen toter Bäume, Reduzierung der Grabenpflege und Rückbau der Uferbefestigungen, Verbot von Kfz-Verkehr, Großveranstaltungen und umweltschädigenden Sportarten, Maßnahmen zu Schutz und Förderung der gebietstypischen Fauna

Äcker (40):
Schutz vor weiterer Bebauung, Zerschneidung, Aufforstung, Nutzungsaufgabe und Umwandlung in Grünanlagen, Erhöhung der Vielfalt durch Pflanzung von Hecken, Feldgehölzen und Schaffung von Feucht- und Naßstellen unter Berücksichtigung historischer und ökologischer Zusammenhänge, Wiederbewirtschaftung brachliegender und aufgeforsteter Äcker, Neuschaffung von Äckern, Biozidverzicht und sparsamer Düngereinsatz, Schaffung weiterer Feldflorareservate, Beschränkung der Erholung auf naturschonende Formen, Maßnahmen zum Schutz und Förderung gebietstypischer Tierarten

Weiden (41):
teilweise Umwandlung in Wiesen, Trockenrasen und Äcker, Beweidung unter Berücksichtigung ökologischer Kriterien

Frischwiesen (42):
Schutz vor weiterer Bebauung, Zerschneidung, Umwandlung in Weiden, Nutzungsaufgabe und Aufforstung, sparsame Düngung auf Parkwiesen keine Düngung, Anpassung von Schnitthöhe, Schnitttermin und Schnitthäufigkeit an den Artenbestand von Flora und Fauna, Herbizidverzicht, Wegegebot bei besonders wertvollen und landwirtschaftlich genutzten Wiesen, Maßnahmen zur Förderung und Schutz der gebietstypischen Fauna

Feucht- und Naßwiesen (43):
Schutz vor Bebauung, Zerschneidung, Nutzungsaufgabe, Umwandlung in Weiden und Entwässerung, Anhebung des Grundwasserstands, Erhalt von Gräben und Feuchtgebüschen, Erhalt besonders wertvoller Flächen durch weitere Bewirtschaftung, sparsame Düngung und Herbizidverzicht, kein Umbruch und Einsaat von Klee und Futtergräsern, Anpassung von Schnitthöhe, Schnitttermin und Schnitthäufigkeit an den Artenbestand von Flora und Fauna, Maßnahmen zur Förderung und Schutz gebietstypischer Tierarten

Magerrasen (44):
Schutz aller Flächen, Entkusselung, Offenhalten von Trockenrasenlichtungen in Wäldern, Verhinderung von Eutrophierung durch Abfallbeseitigung, Besucherlenkung und Verzicht auf Düngung, Schutz vor mechanischer Beanspruchung (Militärische Übungen, Motorsport), Umwandlung von wenig betretenen Zierrasen auf armen, trockenen Sandboden in Trockenrasen durch Pflegeextensivierung (einmal jährl. Mahd, Entfernung des Mähguts, Verzicht auf Düngung, Wässerung und Herbizide) und Einbringung von Trockenrasenarten

Feucht-, Naß- und Bruchwälder, grundwasserbeeinflußte Forsten (46):
siehe (46) "Kiefern-Eichenwälder" sowie Wiederanhebung des Grundwasserspiegels, zum Schutz der Auenbereiche siehe unter Havel (52)

Buchenwälder (46):
siehe (46) "Kiefern-Eichenwälder" sowie Schutz aller Buchenwälder vor Umwandlung in Forsten

Kiefern-Eichen-Wälder (46):
Reduzierung des Holzeinschlags, Erhalt von Altbaumbeständen, Verjüngung im Plenterbetrieb, Nachpflanzung standortgerechter, einheimischer Baumarten, Erhalt von Lichtungen, Waldmänteln und Säumen, Zerfallenlassen von absterbenden und toten Bäumen, Schaffung von Ruhezonen durch Besucherlenkung und Unterlassung militärischer Übungen, kritische Überprüfung der Schalenwilddichte, Bekämpfung der Traubenkirsche, Fahrverbot auf Straßen in den Forsten, Maßnahmen zum Schutz und Förderung gebietstypischer, gefährdeter Tierarten

Sonstige Wälder und Forsten (46):
siehe (46) "Kiefern-Eichenwälder" sowie Schutz seltener Waldgesellschaften (Eichen-Hainbuchenwälder), Umwandlung von Forsten in Wälder mit standortgemäßer Baumartenzusammensetzung

Offene Moore (47):
Wiedervernässung entwässerter Moore durch Grundwasseranreicherung mit nährstoffarmem Wasser, Erweiterung offener Moorflächen durch Entkusselung und Entfernung von Randgehölzen, Anlage kleiner Torfstiche in stark ausgetrockneten Mooren als Sofortmaßnahme, Wegegebot, Maßnahmen zum Schutz und Förderung gefährdeter, gebietstypischer Tierarten

Pfuhle, Weiher und andere Kleingewässer (48):
siehe (50) sowie Erhalt aller Kleingewässer einschließlich ihres hydrologischen und biologischen Einzugsbereichs, Unterschutzstellung naturnaher Gewässer, Erhaltung charakteristischer Wasserstandsschwankungen mit gelegentlichem Austrocknen, Schutz der Ufer vor Vertritt durch geeignete Wegeführung und Gebüschstreifen, Reduzierung der Zerschneidung des Einzugsbereichs durch Straßen, Terrassenstufen etc., Beseitigung des Besatzes mit Nutzfischen oder faunenfremden Fischarten (Graskarpfen)

Fließgewässer mit verbauten Ufern (49):
Soweit als möglich Rückbau von senkrechten Uferbefestigungen (Spundwände, Mauern etc.), soweit als möglich Ausbildung schräger Uferböschungen mit ingenieurbiologischen Methoden oder bepflanzbaren Steinschüttungen, Duldung spontaner Vegetation, Berankung senkrechter Uferbefestigungen und Anlage von Ausstiegen, Verringerung der Abwasserbelastung, Schutz und Erhalt von Altarmen und nicht mehr benutzten Häfen etc.

Fließgewässer ohne verbaute Ufer (50):
Verbesserung der Wasserqualität, keine Einleitung stark verschmutzten Oberflächenwassers, Vorreinigung kleiner Zuflüsse und Einleiter durch Sumpfklärbeete, keine Uferbefestigungen (Bongossiholzfaschinen) und Sohlenversiegelungen (Betonplatten, Rasengittersteine), gegebenenfalls Rückbau, Erhalt oder Wiederherstellung naturnaher Uferbereiche, Extensivierung der Pflege der umgebenden Flächen, Wiederherstellung von Feucht- und Naßwiesen, Verzicht auf Biozide und Dünger, Anpflanzung standortgerechter Gehölze, Schutz naturnaher Ufervegetation, auf den Stock setzen überalterter Weiden und Erlen, Müllentfernung, Maßnahmen zum Schutz und Förderung gefährdeter, gebietstypischer Tierarten; Erhalt des Tegeler Fließes als letztes, weitgehend unverbautes Fließgewässer in einer Umgebung mit landwirtschaftlicher Nutzung

Gräben (51):
siehe (50) sowie Untersagung weiterer Verrohrungen, Grabenreinigung nur abschnittsweise in 3-jährigem Turnus, dabei Verzicht auf Herbizide, Mahd der Böschungen 2mal jährlich bei Erhaltung von Hochstaudenfluren und Gehölzbeständen in Teilbereichen, Einschränkung von Düngung im Einzugsbereich, Vermeidung einer übermäßigen Entwässerung der Umgebung

Havel und Havelufer (52):
Drastische Verbesserung der Wasserqualität, Herabsetzung der Geschwindigkeit von Motorschiffen, Wasser- und landseitige Sicherung von Schwimmblatt- und Röhrichtbeständen vor Zerstörung, Schaffung von wellenberuhigten Zonen durch ingenieurbiologische Maßnahmen zum Schutz der Ufer und Vegetation, an zerstörten Ufern Renaturierung durch ingenieurbiologische Maßnahmen und Wiederanpflanzung von Röhricht, Fütterungsverbot für Wasservögel, Versagung von Baugenehmigung für Erholungseinrichtungen etc. im Uferbereich, Rückbau von technischen Ufersicherungen (auf den Stock setzen überalterter Weiden und Erlen), Lenkung des Erholungsbetriebs, Konzentration auf bestimmte Badestellen, Wegegebot im Uferbereich, Einrichtung von Schutzgebieten, Wiederanhebung des Grundwasserspiegels im Auebereich, Maßnahmen zum Schutz und zur Förderung gefährdeter, gebietstypischer Tierarten

Seen (53):
drastische Verbesserung der Wasserqualität, Entschlammung bei Schonung von Pflanzen- und Tierbeständen, Einhaltung von Wasserstandsschwankungen auf geringer Jahresamplitude, Rückbau technischer Ufersicherungen, Wiederansiedlung von Röhricht, Sicherung von Röhricht- und Schwimmblattpflanzen gegen Vertritt und Befahren, Lenkung des Erholungsbetriebs, Wegegebot, Wiederanhebung des Grundwasserspiegels im Auebereich, auf den Stock setzen überalterter Weiden und Erlen, Maßnahmen zum Schutz und Förderung gefährdeter, gebietstypischer Tierarten

Quellen und Quellhänge (54):
Erweiterung des Schutzgebiets nach Süden (Pufferzone zum Schutz vor Bioziden und Mineraldünger), auf einem Teil der Fläche Ablauf der natürlichen Sukzession, auf der übrigen Fläche Entkusselung und 2mal jährliche Mahd der Wiesen, 1mal jährliche Mahd der Riede und Röhrichte, Abtransport des Mähguts, Einstellung der Grabenräumungen, Schutz vor Vertritt, Maßnahmen zum Schutz und zur Förderung gefährdeter, gebietstypischer Tierarten

Biotope der Großbaustellen (56), Biotope der militärischen Anlagen, nicht untersuchbar (57):
Weitestgehender Schutz der wertvollen Artenbestände

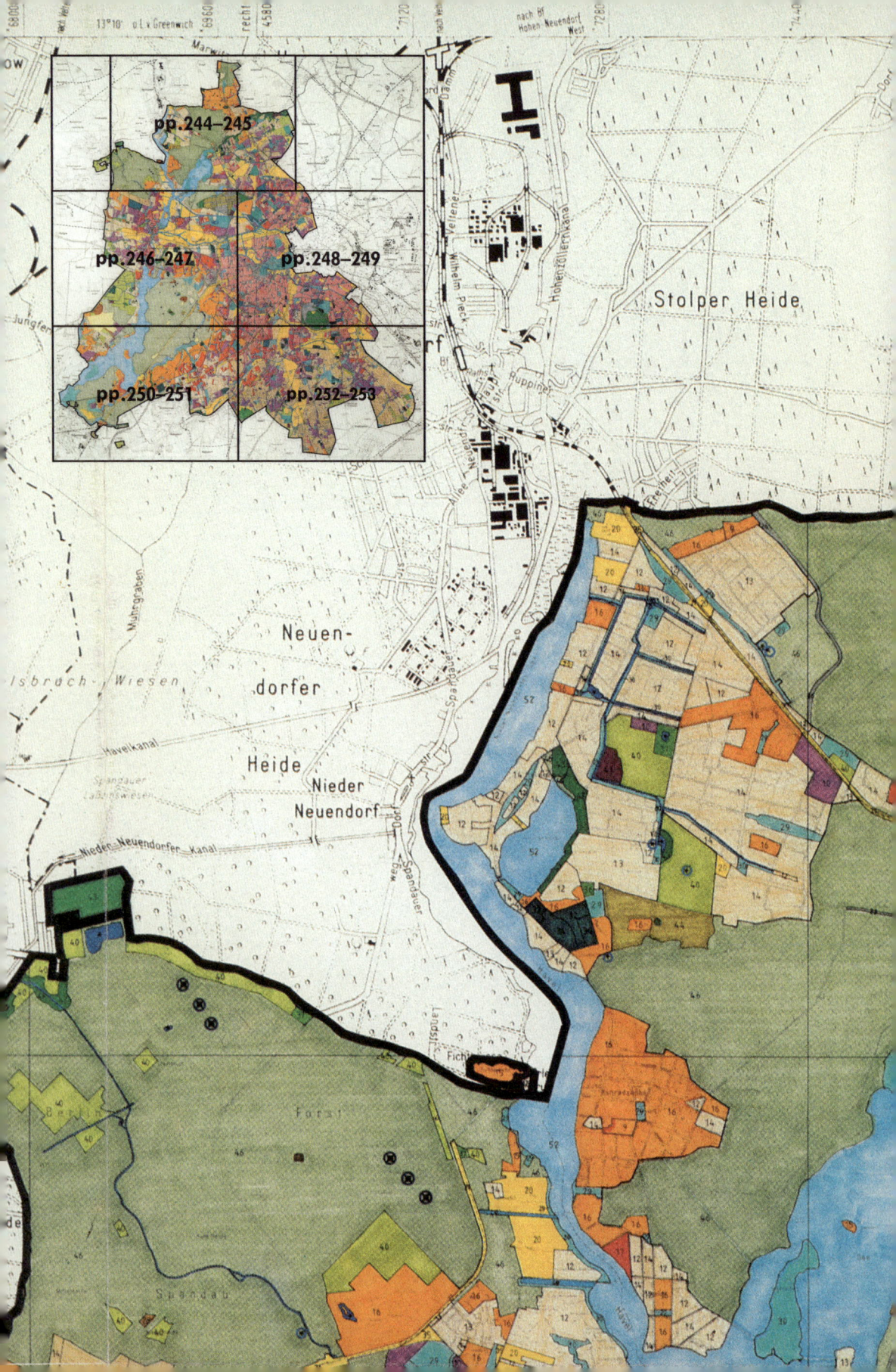

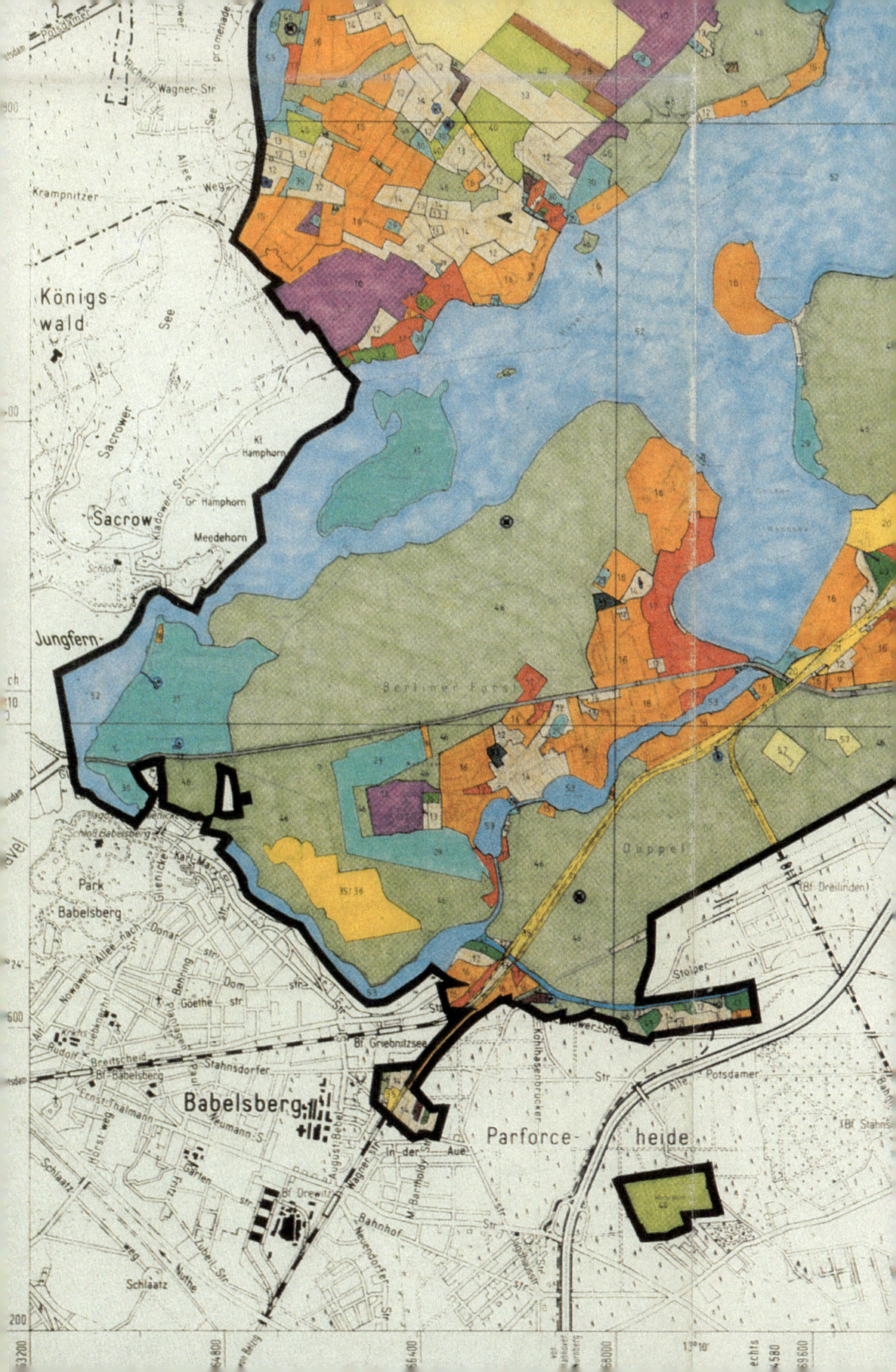

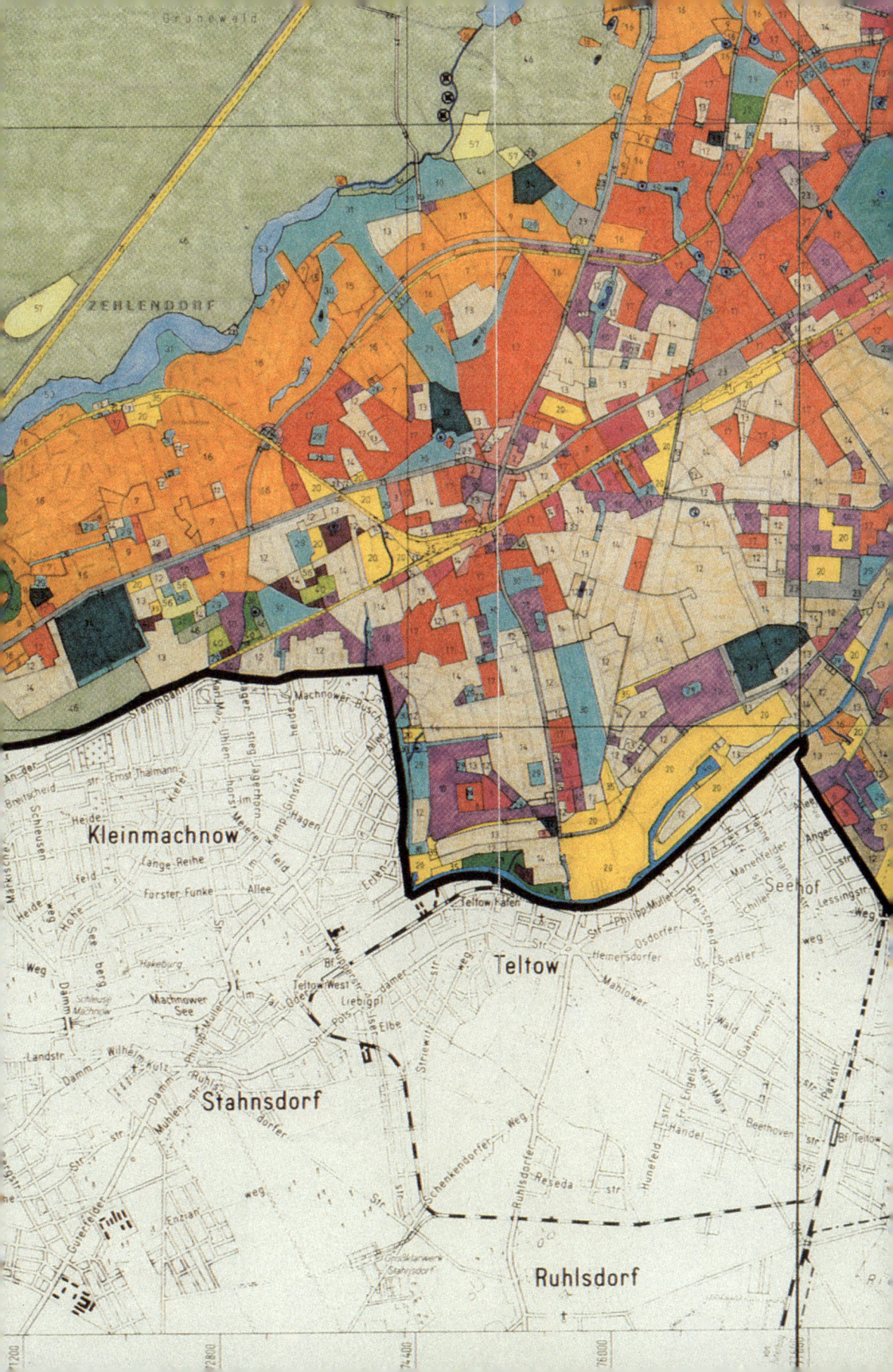

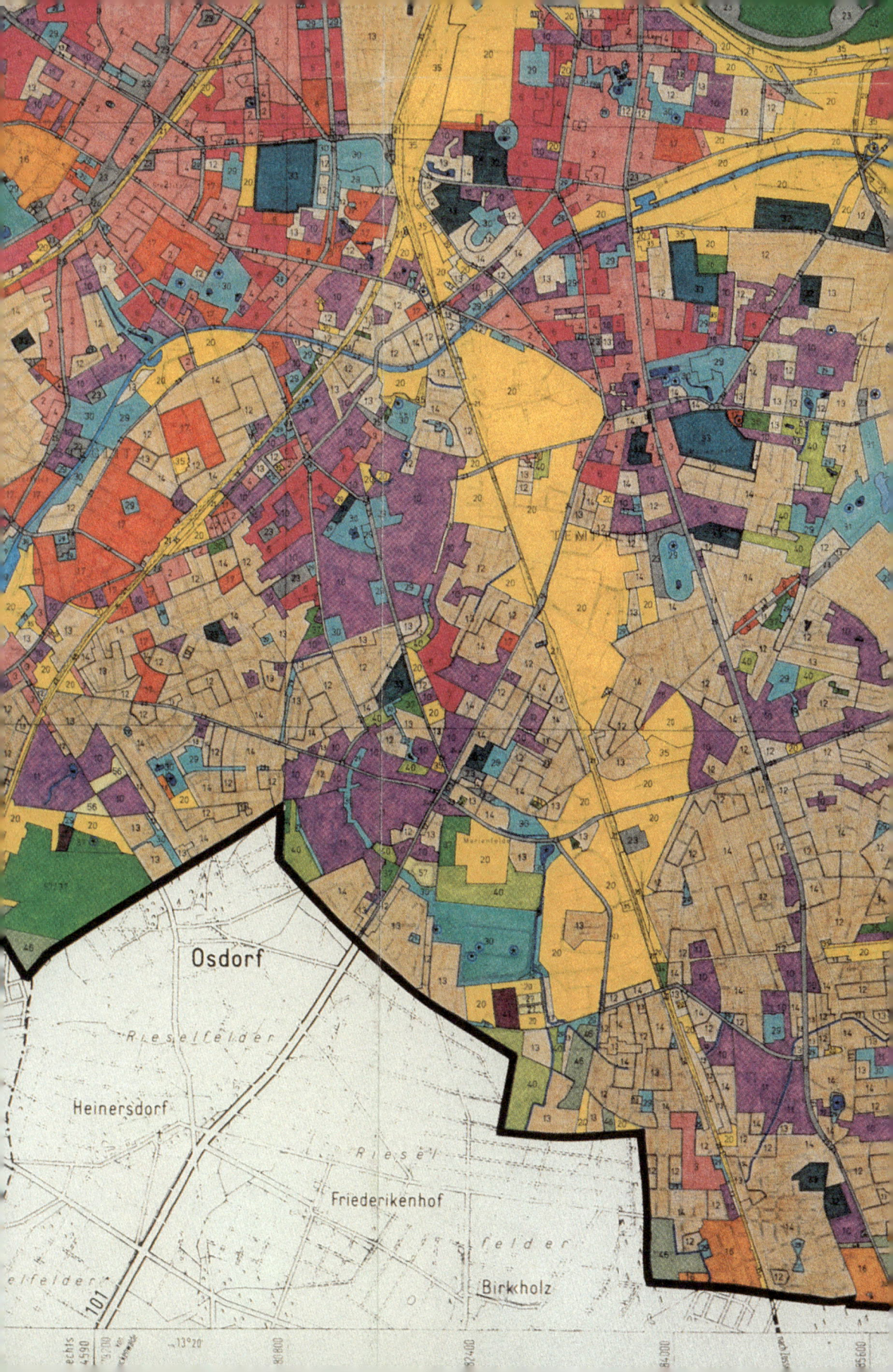

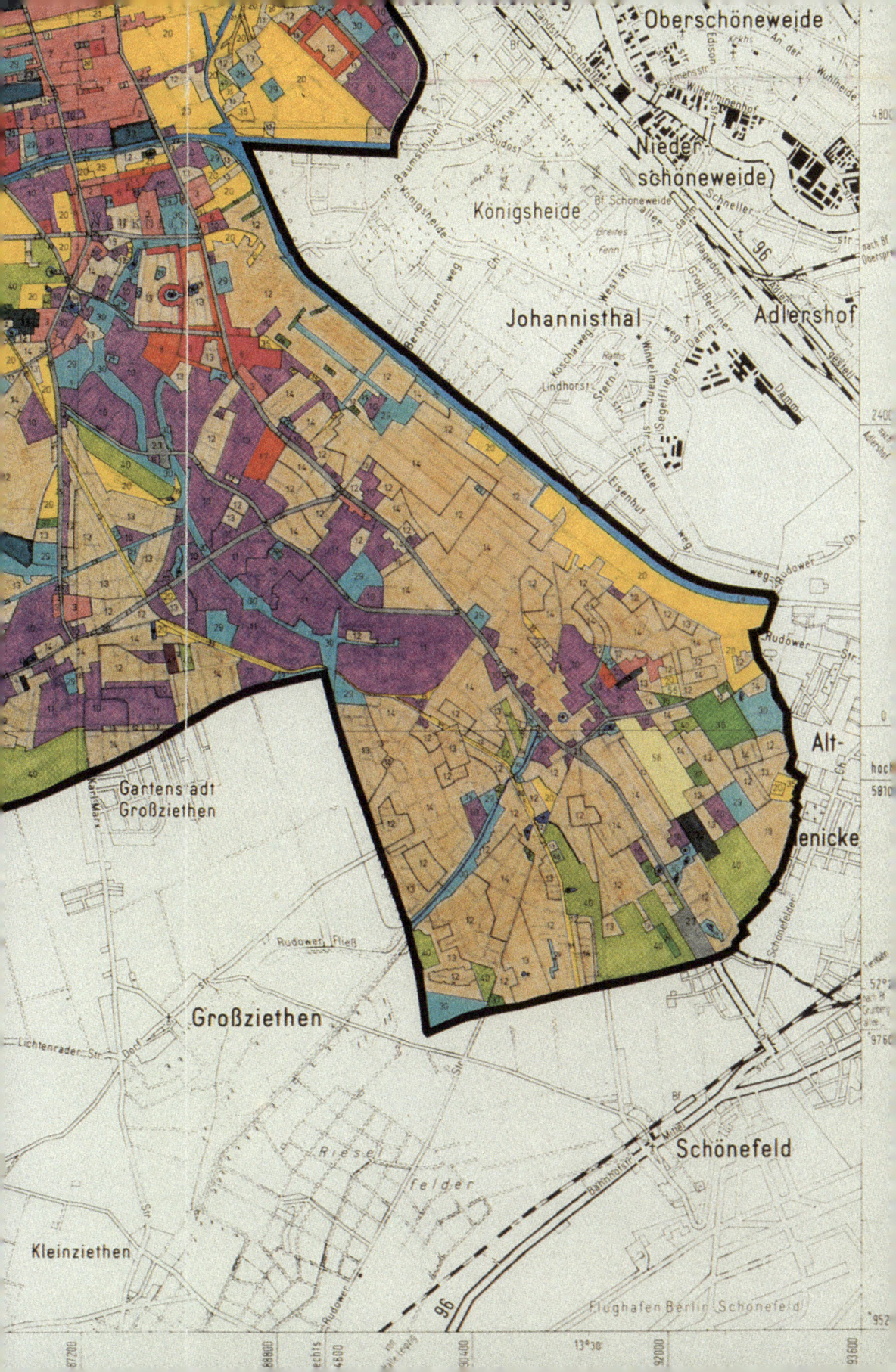

IMAGE INDEX

TRANSGRESSING HERITAGE

- p. 16 Tiergarten's underforest, 2014. Photograph: Sandra Bartoli.
- p. 17 Hein Gorny, Tiergarten (1946). Courtesy Collection Regard, Berlin.
- p. 18 A plan of Tiergarten where the Großer Stern is first shown, 1698. Anonymous author. Courtesy Landesarchiv Berlin.
- p. 19 Tiergarten near the Death Strip, 1984. Courtesy Landesarchiv Berlin.
- p. 20 Farming in Tiergarten, 1946–48. Anonymous author. *Garten und Landschaft*, September 1952.
- p. 21 *Verbascum thapsus* in a replanted Tiergarten, 1954. Author anonymous. *Garten und Landschaft*, February 1955.
- p. 22 Johann Heinrich Gustav Meyer, *Lehrbuch der schönen Gartenkunst* (1860). Courtesy Digitale Sammlungen der Universitätsbibliothek der Bauhaus-Universität, Weimar.
- p. 23 *Robinia pseudoacacia* in Pfaueninsel, 2015. Photograph: Sandra Bartoli.
- p. 24 Tiergarten's Command Tower turning into an island, 1947. Anonymous author. *Garten und Landschaft*, September 1952.
- p. 25 Bird sanctuary island in Tiergarten, 2016. Photograph: Sandra Bartoli.
- p. 26 Venus Basin, Tiergarten, 2013. Photograph: Silvan Linden.
- p. 27 Plan of Tiergarten with mulberry plantings on Bellevue, 1765. Anonymous author. Courtesy Landesarchiv Berlin.

ALESSANDRA PONTE
- Fig. 1 A map of the zoo in Hamburg. Jakob von Uexküll and Georg Kriszat, *Streifzüge durch Umwelten von Tiere und Menschen (A Foray into the Worlds of Animals and Humans)* (Berlin: Springer, 1934); drawing by Kriszat.
- Fig. 2 Gabriel Thouin, "Jardin Parcs ou Carrières,„ *Plans raisonnés de toutes les espèces de jardins* (Paris: Madame Huzard, 1828), plate no. 25. © Bibliothèque des lettres et sciences humaines, Université de Montréal.
- Fig. 3 Gabriel Thouin, "Projet d'agrandissement du Jardin des Plantes de Paris," *Plans raisonnés de toutes les espèces de jardins* (Paris: Madame Huzard, 1828), plate no. 13. © Bibliothèque des lettres et sciences humaines, Université de Montréal.
- Fig. 4 Gabriel Thouin, "Jardin du Roi," *Plans raisonnés de toutes les espèces de jardins* (Paris: Madame Huzard, 1828), plate no. 97. © Bibliothèque des lettres et sciences humaines, Université de Montréal.
- Fig. 5 Gabriel Thouin, "Ile et Batimens de la Ferme expérimentale," *Plans raisonnés de toutes les espèces de jardins*, (Paris: Madame Huzard, 1828), plate no. 51. © Bibliothèque des Lettres et sciences humaines, Université de Montréal.
- Fig. 6 Gabriel Thouin, "Projet d'une ferme expérimentale de la zone torride," *Plans raisonnés de toutes les espèces de jardins* (Paris: Madame Huzard, 1828), plate no. 52. © Bibliothèque des lettres et sciences humaines, Université de Montréal.
- Fig. 7 André Thouin, "Greffes," *Monographie des greffes, ou, description technique des diverses sortes de greffes employées pour la multiplication des végétaux* (Paris: Librairie encyclopédique de Roret, 1851), first section, plate no. 3. © Bibliothèque des lettres et sciences humaines, Université de Montréal.
- Fig. 8 André Thouin, "Greffes," *Monographie des greffes, ou, description technique des diverses sortes de greffes employées pour la multiplication des végétaux* (Paris: Librairie encyclopédique de Roret, 1851), first section, plate no. 4. © Bibliothèque des lettres et sciences humaines, Université de Montréal.
- Fig. 9 Jakob von Uexküll and Georg Kriszat, *Streifzüge durch Umwelten von Tiere und Menschen (A Foray into the Worlds of Animals and Humans)* (Berlin: Springer, 1934); drawing by Kriszat.

GUNNAR KLACK
- Fig. 1 A plan for green areas (part of the Kollektivplan) by Reinhold Lingner, 1946. Johann Friedrich Geist and Klaus Kürvers, *Das Berliner Mietshaus: 1945–1989*, vol. 3 (Munich: Prestel, 1989).

Fig. 2 A design for Tiergarten by Reinhold Lingner, 1947; drawing by A. Waschneck. Folkwin Wendland, *Der Große Tiergarten in Berlin: Seine Geschichte und Entwicklung in fünf Jahrhunderten* (Berlin: Mann Verlag, 1993).

Fig. 3 A design for Tiergarten by Willy Alverdes, 1952; drawing by A. Waschneck. Folkwin Wendland, *Der Große Tiergarten in Berlin: Seine Geschichte und Entwicklung in fünf Jahrhunderten* (Berlin: Mann Verlag, 1993).

Fig. 4 A section of the Kollektivplan showing the Berlin city center, 1946. Johann Friedrich Geist and Klaus Kürvers, *Das Berliner Mietshaus: 1945–1989*, vol. 3 (Munich: Prestel, 1989).

Fig. 5 Three-dimensional model of the Kollektivplan, 1946. Johann Friedrich Geist and Klaus Kürvers, *Das Berliner Mietshaus: 1945–1989*, vol. 3 (Munich: Prestel, 1989).

Fig. 6 An illustration of the Kollektivplan by Selman Selmanagić showing the view from a residential building onto the rebuilt city, 1946. Jörn Düwel, „Berlin: Planen im Kalten Krieg," in *1945: Krieg – Zerstörung – Aufbau. Architektur und Stadtplanung 1940–1960*, ed. Akademie der Künste Berlin. (Berlin: Henschel, 1995).

Fig. 7 A design proposal for Tiergarten with a university campus by Georg Béla Pniower, 1947. Folkwin Wendland, *Der Große Tiergarten in Berlin: Seine Geschichte und Entwicklung in fünf Jahrhunderten* (Berlin: Mann Verlag, 1993).

Fig. 8 Aerial view of the replanned city of Chicago by Ludwig Hilberseimer, 1944. Ludwig Hilberseimer, *The New City: Principles of Planning* (Chicago: Theobald, 1944).

LUISE RELLENSMANN

Fig. 1 Goldfish Pond in the eastern section of Tiergarten, 1984. Courtesy Landesarchiv Berlin.

Fig. 2 Venus Basin (former Goldfish Pond) in the eastern section of Tiergarten, 2016. Courtesy Aerowest.

ELIZABETH FELICELLA

pp. 66–95 All photographs Elizabeth Felicella (2016).

TRANSGRESSING URBANISM

p. 98 Homeless campsite, Tiergarten, 2013. Photograph: Sandra Bartoli.

p. 99 Fanmeile World Championship, Tiergarten, 2014. Photograph: Sandra Bartoli.

p. 100 Rhododendron grove, Tiergarten, 2015. Photograph: Sandra Bartoli.

p. 101 Daniel Nikolaus Chodowiecki, *Gesellschaft im Tiergarten* (1760). Courtesy Museum der bildenden Künste, Leipzig.

p. 102 Plan of Tiergarten with a description of areas and use (1793). Anonymous author. Courtesy Landesarchiv Berlin.

p. 103 Picnic in Tiergarten, 2013. Photograph: Sandra Bartoli.

JÖRG STOLLMANN

Fig. 1 Film still from *Mamma Roma*, Pier Paolo Pasolini (1962) with a view of the neighborhood of Tuscolano / Cecafumo.

Fig. 2 Dutch artist, after Claude Lorrain, with figures by Andries Booth, *The Campo Vaccino, Rome*, (ca. 1635-41), oil on canvas, 78.1 × 106.1 cm, DPG174. Courtesy Dulwich Picture Gallery, London.

Fig. 3 "In Campo Aperto: The Open Field," reenactment series of Pier Paolo Pasolini's *Mamma Roma* (1962) with Susanne Heinrich, 2011. All photographs: Jörg Stollmann.

Fig. 4 Campo abusivo La Barbuta, Rome, an informal Roma camp, 2011. Photograph: Jörg Stollmann.

Fig. 5 Campo ufficiale La Barbuta, Rome, the official camp planned for the relocation of most of the inhabitants of La Barbuta, 2011. Photograph: Jörg Stollmann.

Fig. 6 Campo abusivo, Rome, an illicit camp of Romanian migrants, 2011. Photograph: Jörg Stollmann.

TRANSGRESSING ECOLOGY

p. 148   Johann Heinrich Gustav Meyer, illustration from *Lehrbuch der Schönen Gartenkunst* (1860). Courtesy Digitale Sammlungen der Universitätsbibliothek der Bauhaus-Universität, Weimar.
p. 149   Map showing the most valuable biotopes in West Berlin, 1984. Senator für Stadtentwicklung und Umweltschutz Berlin, eds., "Entwicklung- und Maßnahmen der Artenschutzprogramm," Fachbereich Landschaftsentwicklung, Technische Universität Berlin (1984).
p. 150   Beech stump, Tiergarten, 2017. Photograph: Sandra Bartoli.
p. 151   Windstorm aftermath, Tiergarten, 2017. Photograph: Sandra Bartoli.

KARIN REISINGER
Fig. 1   Film stills INTO the Losiny Ostrov park in Moscow, 2014. Film: Karin Reisinger.
Fig. 2   Film stills INTO the Gorongosa park, Mozambique, 2011. Film: Karin Reisinger.

EVA HAYWARD
Fig. 1   Charley Harper, *Serengeti Spaghetti* (1979), 24 × 18 in., acrylic on canvas. Courtesy Charley Harper Art Studio.
Fig. 2   Charley Harper, *Last Sunflower Seed* (1973), 19 × 13 in., acrylic on canvas. Courtesy Charley Harper Art Studio.
Fig. 3   Charley Harper, *Jesus Bugs* (1969), 19 × 45 in., acrylic on canvas. Courtesy Charley Harper Art Studio.
Fig. 4   Charley Harper, *Skipping School* (1977), 17 × 18 in., acrylic on canvas. Courtesy Charley Harper Art Studio.
Fig. 5   Charley Harper, *Bark Eyes* (1986), 18 × 18 in., acrylic on canvas. Courtesy Charley Harper Art Studio.

ELIZABETH FELICELLA
pp. 178–91   All photographs Elizabeth Felicella (2016).

TRANSGRESSING HUMANISM

p. 194   Bobby the gorilla, Zoo Berlin icon, 1930. Lutz Heck, *Tiere: Mein Abenteuer. Erlebnisse in Wildnis und Zoo* (Ullstein, 1952).
p. 195   Bird thing, Tiergarten, 2013. Photograph: Sandra Bartoli.
p. 196   *Fagus sylvatica*, Tiergarten, 2015. Photograph: Sandra Bartoli.
p. 197   Mining bee nest, Tiergarten, 2017. Photograph: Sandra Bartoli.
p. 198   Poplar tree stump, yew bush, and human couple, 2018. Photograph: Sandra Bartoli.
p. 199   Windstorm aftermath, Tiergarten, 2017. Photograph: Sandra Bartoli.
p. 200   Kulturforum, Berlin, 2014. Photograph: Sandra Bartoli.
p. 201   Ancient beech tree, Tiergarten, 2015. Photograph: Sandra Bartoli.

STEFANO MANCUSO
Fig. 1   Film stills of an exploring bean plant, International Laboratory of Plant Neurobiology, Firenze, 2010. Courtesy ILPN Firenze.

SANDRA BARTOLI
Fig. 1   A grove of beech trees with underforest in Tiergarten, 2017. Photograph: Sandra Bartoli.
Fig. 2   Spontaneous trees (*Ailanthus altissima*) in a courtyard used as a parking lot, Berlin. 2018. Photograph: Silvan Linden.
Fig. 3   The banks of the Landwehrkanal, treated with low maintenance and ecologically sound principles by the district of Kreuzberg, Berlin, 2018. Photograph: Sandra Bartoli.
Fig. 4   Poplar grove, Potsdamer Platz, 2018. Photograph: Sandra Bartoli.
Fig. 5   Park auf dem Anhalter Bahnhof, 2018. Photograph: Sandra Bartoli.
Fig. 6   Park auf dem Anhalter Bahnhof, with visible old tracks, 2018. Photograph: Sandra Bartoli.
Fig. 7   Park auf dem Anhalter Bahnhof, 2018. Photograph: Sandra Bartoli.
Fig. 8   An island grown wild to effect on the Neuer See in Tiergarten, 2017. Photograph: Sandra Bartoli.
pp. 241–53   Map of care and development of the biotopes in West Berlin, Artenschutzprogramm Berlin, 1984. Sukopp et al.

CHRISTOPHER ROTH
pp. 255–70   All photographs Christopher Roth (2018).

BIOGRAPHIES

FAHIM AMIR is a philosopher and artist based in Vienna. He works at the intersections of naturecultures and colonial historicities, transcultural agency and urbanism. Amir was curator of Live Art Festival 2013: "Zoo3ooo: Occupy Species" at Kampnagel Hamburg; *Salon Klimbim: Feeding Vegetarian Tigers – Entertaining Utopian Sensibilities*, Vienna Secession, 2014; and "Excess. Forum for Philosophy and Art," Darmstadt International Summer Courses for New Music, 2016. Amir coedited *Transcultural Modernisms* (Sternberg Press, 2013), provided the afterword to the German translation of Donna J. Haraway's *Companion Species Manifesto* (Merve, 2016), and recently published *Schwein und Zeit. Tiere, Politik, Revolte* (Nautilus, 2018).

MICHAEL BAERS is an American artist, writer, and researcher based in Berlin since 2005. In 2014, he received his PhD from the praxis-based program of the Academy of Fine Arts Vienna. Baers has contributed essays and graphic works to many journals, including *A Prior*, *e-flux journal*, and *Modern Painters*, as well as to print initiatives such as *Art Workers: Material Conditions and Labour Struggles in Contemporary Art Practice* and *Reform*. In 2012, Haus der Kulturen der Welt commissioned him to make a graphic novel based on his research on the 2011 project *Picasso in Palestine*. The resulting work, *An Oral History of Picasso in Palestine*, is among the most comprehensive account of the *Picasso in Palestine* project to date. Since 2013, he has researched the relationship between photographic representations and intractable conflict through a long-term study on an "informal collective" and their dialogical work with photographs belonging to Moroccans collected by Western Saharan soldiers during its war with Morocco. In addition, Baers has published essays on many topics including artistic research, memory studies, and drawing practice. He also remains active as an artist, contributing a commissioned work to the 2017/18 Haus der Kulturen der Welt exhibition, *Parapolitics: Cultural Freedom and the Cold War*. Baers is currently at work on a project about the regional elections of 1933 in Innsbruck, which saw the first significant showing by the NSDAP party in Austrian politics.

SANDRA BARTOLI is a cofounder, with Silvan Linden, of the Büros für Konstruktivismus in Berlin. In her practice of architecture and research, an attention for high resolution and raw context, both found and constructed, is exercised. An example is the ongoing publishing series *AG Architektur in Gebrauch* (Architecture in use), started by the office in 2014, in which "use" is explored as an aesthetic category that informs the development and transformation of architectural space. She has taught at Technische Universität Berlin and Akademie der Bildenden Künste Nürnberg. During 2017 and 2018, Bartoli worked on her research theme The City's Future Natural History as an Endowed Professor for Visionary Forms of Cities at the Institute for Art and Architecture, Academy of Fine Arts Vienna, and is now full professor at the Munich University of Applied Sciences.

ELIZABETH FELICELLA is an artist and architectural photographer living in New York. Her long-term projects include *Reading Room: A Catalog of New York City's Branch Libraries (2008–2016)* which was exhibited in its entirety at the Center for Architecture New York in 2016; *Sea Level: Five Boroughs at Water's Edge*, which was commissioned by the AIA for the South Street Cultural district in 2016 ; and *Idlewild: An Atlas of the Periphery of Kennedy Airport (1999– 2006)*. In 2013, she was the first artist-in-residence at Brooklyn Public Library, where she worked closely with the collection's archive and photographic holdings. Her projects have received support from the Graham Foundation and the New York State Council for the Arts. She was a fellow at the Design Trust for Public Space in 2000–3 and a Fulbright Scholar in Germany in 1994–96.

EVA HAYWARD is assistant professor in Gender & Women's Studies at the University of Arizona, Tucson. Her research focuses on aesthetics, environmental and science studies, and trans and sexuality studies. She has published articles in *Transgender Studies Quarterly*, *differences*, *Cultural Anthropology*, *Parallax*, and *Women's Studies Quarterly*. Her book *SymbioSeas: Captivity, Sexuality, and Marine Science* is forthcoming.

GUNNAR KLACK, PhD, studied architecture at the Universität der Künste Berlin and the Glasgow School of Art. He completed a doctoral dissertation on the work of architects Fehling + Gogel at Technische Universität Berlin. Klack was a trainee at Berlinische Galerie, and a teaching and academic assistant at the Chair for Historic Preservation at the Institute for Urban and Regional Planning, TU Berlin. Currently, he is assistant curator at the Historical Technical Museum Peenemünde.

STEFANO MANCUSO is professor of Plant, Soil & Environmental Science at the University of Florence and cofounder of the International Laboratory of Plant Neurobiology. Mancuso is a founder of the study of plant neurobiology, which explores signaling and communication at all levels of biological organization, from genetics to molecules, cells, and ecological communities. He is coauthor (with Alessandra Viola) of *Brilliant Green: The Surprising History and Science of Plant Intelligence* (Island Press, 2015) and the author of *The Revolutionary Genius of Plants: A New Understanding of Plant Intelligence and Behavior* (Atria Books, 2018).

SANDRA PARVU is an architect and faculty member of ENS d'Architecture Paris-Val de Seine; a research fellow at the LAA-LAVUE (UMR 7218 CNRS);

and holds a PhD from EHESS, Paris. Parvu's research focuses on large-scale planning, housing policy, and the politics of landscape in France. Parvu is the author of *Grands ensembles en situation. Journal de bord de quatre chantiers* (Metispresses, 2011), and more specifically the question of time and landscape is dealt with in two chapters of the book: "The Gestures of Drawing in Landscape Participatory Design" (2015), and with Alice Sotgia, "Le temps requalifié. Quelques réflexions sur les cycles de construction et de rénovation à la cité des 4000, La Courneuve" (2018). Forthcoming is an article with Piero Zanini, "L'entretien du présent" (2019).

ALESSANDRA PONTE is a full professor at the École d'architecture, Université de Montréal. She has taught history and theory of architecture and landscape at Pratt Institute New York, Princeton University, Cornell University, Istituto Universitario di Architettura di Venezia, and ETH Zurich. Ponte organized the exhibition *Total Environment: Montreal 1965–1975* at the Canadian Centre for Architecture, Montreal, in 2009, and collaborated on the exhibition and catalog *God & Co: François Dallegret Beyond the Bubble* (with Laurent Stalder and Thomas Weaver, Architectural Association Publications, 2011). She has also published *The House of Light and Entropy* (Architectural Association, 2014) and contributed to *Arctic Adaptations* (2014) and *Extraction* (2016), both at the Canadian Pavilion for the Venice Architecture Biennale.

KARIN REISINGER is an architect, researcher, and lecturer. She is currently a 2018–19 fellow at ArkDes in Stockholm. Her PhD about parks and conflicts, *Grass Without Roots. Towards Nature Becoming Spatial Practice* (Visual Culture Unit, Vienna University of Technology, 2014), contains research conducted at the Universidade Católica de Moçambique and was followed by a postdoc fellowship at KTH Stockholm, School of Architecture. Following the coorganization of the 13th Architectural Humanities Research Association (AHRA) conference *Architecture and Feminisms*, Reisinger edited, together with Meike Schalk, *field* 7, no. 1 and *Architecture and Culture* 5, no. 3, both 2017. Forthcoming texts include "Insomnia: Viewing Ecologies of Spatial Becoming-With," on mining, in *After Effects* (Actar), and "Connective Oscillations: Architectures Between the Devil and the Deep Blue Sea," about feminist ecologies, in *More* (Didapress).

LUISE RELLENSMANN is an architectural critic and researcher based in Berlin. She holds a BA in European Studies and an MSc in Building and Conservation. She has taught at the department of architectural conservation at Brandenburg University of Technology BTU Cottbus and at the department of architecture theory and design at Kassel University. From 2012 to 2013 she was a graduate intern at the Getty Conservation Institute in Los Angeles. Since 2015, Rellensmann has been a board member of the national committee of the International Council on Monuments and Sites (ICOMOS), Germany. She is currently a PhD candidate at the DFG Research Training Group 1913 "Cultural and technical values of historic buildings" at BTU Cottbus-Senftenberg.

CHRISTOPHER ROTH is a film director and artist, and lectures at ETH Zurich. *Legislating Architecture*, *The Property Drama*, and *Architecting after Politics* (all with Brandlhuber+) have been shown, among other venues, at the Venice Architecture Biennale and the Chicago Architecture Biennial. In 2002, Roth's feature film *Baader* won the Alfred Bauer Prize in Berlin. He has also produced *Hyperstition*, a film with Armen Avanessian, and *80*81 What Happened?*, a research project with Georg Diez that led to thirteen books and thirty theater pieces worldwide. In 2018, he launched three web TV channels: *Realty-v* (with Tirdad Zolghadr), *S+* (with Brandlhuber's chair at ETH) and *42* (with Fahrbereitschaft): space-time.tv. Roth is represented by Esther Schipper.

JÖRG STOLLMANN is an architect and urban researcher based in Zurich and Berlin. He is professor for urban design at the Institute for Architecture, Technische Universität Berlin. The chair focuses on collaborative and cooperative design processes, mediatization of planning, and inclusive urban development. Stollmann graduated from the Universität der Künste Berlin and Princeton University. He has worked in collaboration with the artist Ines Schaber, was principal of INSTANT Architects, and was part of the curatorial team of the International Architecture Biennale Rotterdam in 2009. He has taught at Universität der Künste Berlin and ETH Zurich.

CHRIS WILBERT was, until recently, a senior lecturer at Anglia Ruskin University, England. He was coeditor (with Christopher Philo) of the book *Animal Spaces, Beastly Places: New Geographies of Human-Animal Interactions* (Routledge, 2000). He also coedited the books *Technonatures* (with Damian White, 2009) and *Killing Animals* (with the Animal Studies Group, 2005). He has published articles and chapters on environment politics and cultures of tourism. He is a member of the editorial collective of the journal *Radical Philosophy*, an editor (with Samantha Hurn) of the Multispecies Encounters book series for Routledge, and continues to research human-animal entanglements.

PIERO ZANINI is research fellow at the Laboratoire Architecture Anthropologie (UMR-Lavue CNRS) and associate lecturer in Urban Anthropology at the École Nationale Supérieure d'Architecture de Paris-la-Villette. Through an anthropological approach, Zanini's research explores the ways and forms that structure the changing relationship between people and the places they inhabit, in urban and alpine contexts, and with a particular attention to the temporal dimensions of this phenomenon. He has published essays and articles on borders as a social construction, the metaphorical landscape of sea straits, and morality as a "practice" at work in everyday life. Forthcoming publications include *Exploration chronotopique d'un territoire parisien*, edited with A. Guez, A. de Biase, and F. Gatta (Èditions du LAA, Recherche, 2018).

ACKNOWLEDGMENTS

We wish to thank the experts who from 2013 to 2015 led us to excursions in Tiergarten and provided valuable documents and information for the book: first of all, Christoph Schaaf, who in his role of Fachbereichsleiter and chief gardener of the Park Department worked for more than twenty years with such an understanding and care of Tiergarten up until the early 1990s; Derk Ehlert in his view of Berlin as a seamless habitat for wild animals; Maria Sofie Rohner and Angela von Lührte, landscape planners and botanists who see the value of the city in making room for wild plants and ancient trees; ornithologist Jens Scharon; Jan Uhlig, passionate Fachbereichsleiter at the Pfauneinsel; Gabriele Holst, Steffi Kieback, and the fierce AK Steppengarten; current Fachbereichsleiter Jürgen Götte and all the people at the Grünflächenamt Mitte, Stefanie Schwetje of Büro des Landesbeauftragten für Naturschutz und Landschaftspflege; Reiner Haase of the Umwelt und Naturschutzamt Bezirksamt Mitte; Achim Appel of the admirable Bäume am Landwehrkanal (BaL); Wolfram Kunick and Herbert Sukopp for their work leading to the understanding of the extended ecology that makes the city of Berlin.

Furthermore, we wish to thank 60pages, Estelle Blaschke, Samuel Bürgler, Martin Conrads, Mathias Heyden, Antje Jakupi of the Stiftung Naturschutz Berlin, Andreas Lechner, Franziska Morlok, NABU, Kito Nedo, Inge Schaaf, Ines Schaber, Katrin Schulze, Anna-Sophie Springer, Videodrom Berlin; the Tiergarten seminar students of TU Berlin: Paul Achter, Anne Marie Arera, Tobias Birkefeld, Nora Brinkmann, Frederik Eilers, Tabea Hilse, Georg Hubmann, Kristina Illieva, Joke Leon Klein, Kathrin Krell, Leon Jank, Jessica McInally, David Leinen, Björn Lotter, Sören Mackel, Debora Mendler, Tim Nebert, Stephanie Nick, Ortal Gazit, Anna Papageorgiou, Camilla Parrella, Ruiqi Shan, Franziska Wilch, Mei Zhang, particularly the student tutors Dorothee Hahn and Daniela Mehlich who also took part in the seminars with excellent field research; the entire chair for Urban Design and Urbanization at TU Berlin; Haus der Kulturen der Welt, Bernd Scherer, Olga Sievers, Kirsten Einfeldt; we would also like to thank Eva Guttmann of Park Books for her unrelenting support, Mark Soo for his accuracy and deep knowledge, and Silvan Linden, who asked the first important questions and has followed this project closely with substantial criticism both requested and unrequested. Finally we wish to thank the extended family of animals and plants.

Editors: Sandra Bartoli and Jörg Stollmann
Copy editing and proofreading: Mark Soo
Transcription (Alessandra Ponte and Stefano Mancuso): Amy Leonard
Design: Studio Yukiko
Printing and binding: DZA Druckerei zu Altenburg GmbH, Thuringia

© 2019 the editors and Park Books AG, Zurich
© for the texts: the authors
© for the images: the artists

Park Books AG
Niederdorfstrasse 54
8001 Zurich
Switzerland
www.park-books.com

Park Books is being supported by the Federal Office of Culture with a general subsidy for the years 2016–2020.

This book originates from the symposium "Tiergarten, Landscape of Transgression (This Obscure Object of Desire)," held July 4, 2015 at Haus der Kulturen der Welt, Berlin.

This book was made possible with the generous support of Technische Universität Berlin, Institute for Architecture, Chair for Urban Design and Urbanization.

All rights reserved; no part of this publication may be reproduced, stored in a retrieval system or transmitted in any form or by any means, electronic, mechanical, photocopying, recording, or otherwise, without the prior written consent of the publisher.

The authors and publisher gratefully acknowledge the permission granted to reproduce the copyrighted material in this book. Every effort has been made to identify copyright holders and to obtain permissions for their use. Copyright holders not mentioned in the credits are asked to substantiate their claims, and recompense will be made according to standard practice.

Bibliographic information published by the Deutsche Nationalbibliothek: The Deutsche Nationalbibliothek lists this publication in the Deutsche Nationalbibliografie; detailed bibliographic data are available online at http://dnb.d-nb.de.

ISBN: 978-3-03860-033-6